1 MONTH OF
FREE
READING

at

www.ForgottenBooks.com

By purchasing this book you are eligible for one month membership to ForgottenBooks.com, giving you unlimited access to our entire collection of over 1,000,000 titles via our web site and mobile apps.

To claim your free month visit:

www.forgottenbooks.com/free1247210

ISBN 978-0-428-59417-6
PIBN 11247210

HP-73

WORLD HOG AND PORK PROSPECTS

Summary

Increased feed crop production in the United States in 1935 is now
being reflected in heavier weights of hogs slaughtered compared with last
year. A considerable increase is also likely in the number of pigs produced in late 1935 and 1936 as a result of the more plentiful supplies
and lower prices of feed grains in this country. This increase in the
number of pigs produced, however, will probably not be reflected in
increased hog slaughter until next summer.

The British quota for imports of bacon and hams from non-Empire
countries for the first 6 weeks of 1936 will be at the same weekly rate
as in the last 3 months of 1935, according to a recent announcement.
Under this rate imports of cured pork from non-Empire countries in the
first 6 weeks of 1936 will be about 16 percent smaller than in the
corresponding period of 1935. The allocation to the United States
continues to be 8.1 percent of the total quota. British imports of
bacon continued to decline in October. As a result of the quota system
for non-Empire countries, imports of bacon into Great Britain from
Canada and the Irish Free State have increased materially in the last
2 years relative to imports from other countries.

There has been little change in the livestock and meat situation
during the last month in continental Europe. The present shortage of
fats is resulting in some reductions in trade barriers. Marked decreases
in the import duty on lard have been made in Germany, Czechoslovakia,

and Austria. Because of the lack of foreign exchange however, trade in lard is still largely on a barter basis. Germany has recently negotiated or renewed trade agreements with Poland, Denmark, and Hungary providing for the exchange of German industrial goods for hogs, lard, and other animal products of the other countries.

United States

The increase in feed crop production in 1935 is now being reflected in heavier weights of hogs slaughtered than in 1934. Although the increase in supplies of feed grains is also resulting in a marked increase in the number of pigs produced, the chief effect of the greater feed supplies upon supplies of pork and lard in the next 3 months will be to increase the average weight of hogs marketed. In October the average weight of hogs slaughtered was about 14 pounds heavier than a year earlier and a similar increase occurred in November. The increase in average weights, however, will offset only a part of the decrease in the number of hogs slaughtered during the current winter season compared with last year.

Hog prices advanced somewhat during November after having declined sharply from late September through October. The rise in prices was brought about largely by seasonal improvement in the demand for hog products although the low level of slaughter supplies and the very small storage holdings of hog products probably were contributing factors of some importance. From late September to early November the price of hogs declined about $2.00 per 100 pounds. The Chicago average price for the week ended November 9 was $9.08 but by the first week of December this average had advanced to $9.75. The average price of hogs at Chicago for the month of November was $9.31 compared with $9.83 in October and $5.66 in the corresponding month of 1934. The spread between prices of the different classes and weights of hogs in November was very small and was much less than usual for this time of year.

Slaughter supplies of hogs in November were larger than in October but the increase was less than average for this period. Inspected hog slaughter in November, totaling about 2,422,000 head, was about 13 percent greater than in the preceding month but it was the smallest for November since 1907. As compared with November last year the decrease in inspected slaughter was about 44 percent or about the same as the rate of decrease in other recent months.

Market prices of corn shifted to a new crop basis in early November. The average price of No. 3 Yellow corn at Chicago for November was 62.1 cents per bushel compared with 82 cents in October and 83 cents in November 1934. Farm prices of corn also declined sharply in November. The United States average farm price on November 15 was 56.4 cents per bushel compared with 71.8 cents on October 15 and 88.1 cents on November 15 last year. The decline in farm prices of corn in recent weeks reflects not only the shift to a new crop basis, but it is also partly the result

of the low average quality of the 1935 corn crop. The hog-corn price
ratio in the North Central States on November 15 was 16.6, the highest
since early 1933. This higher ratio is largely responsible for the
heavier weight of hogs marketed in the last month compared with a year
earlier. It is reported that hogs are now being finished in a much more
desirable condition than for some time and this is doubtless due to the
more plentiful supplies and lower prices of corn.

According to the November crop report the indicated corn crop in
1935 for the United States is 2,211,268,000 bushels which is 61 percent
greater than the small 1934 crop but it is about 14 percent below the
5-year 1928 to 1932 average. The following table shows the estimates of
corn production for the entire country for specified regions for 1934 and
1935 and the 1928 to 1932 average production. It will be observed from
this table that the largest increase in the corn crop compared with last
year occurred in the West North Central States which was the area most
severely affected by the 1934 drought. Production in these States in 1935,
however, is 32 percent below the 1928 to 1932 average. Corn production
in the East North Central States in 1935 is only 2 percent below the 5-year
average and in all States outside the Corn Belt production is about 7
percent above average.

Corn production in the United States, by specified regions,
average 1928-1932, 1934 and 1935

Region	Average 1928-32	1934	1935 1/	1935 as a percentage of Average 1928 - 32	1934
	1,000 bushels	1,000 bushels	1,000 bushels	Percent	Percent
North Central States-					
East	713,659	442,570	697,929	97.8	157.7
West	1,195,966	348,561	813,722	68.0	233.5
Total	1,909,625	791,131	1,511,651	79.2	191.1
Other states	652,522	585,995	699,617	107.2	119.4
United States	2,562,147	1,377,126	2,211,268	86.3	160.6

Division of Statistical and Historical Research. Compiled from report of
the Division of Crop and Livestock Estimates, Bureau of Agricultural
Economics.
1/ November 1935 preliminary estimates.

Wholesale prices of fresh pork tended to advanc
but prices of most cuts of cured pork were steady to l
declined during the month. The composite wholesale pr
at New York was $23.71 per 100 pounds in November comp
in October and $15.90 in the corresponding month of 19

Exports of pork and lard in October continued a
than a year earlier. Exports of pork in October were
in September but they were only about one half as larg
last year. Lard exports in October although larger th
were equal to only about 10 percent of the export move
Shipments of pork and lard in the principal United Sta
November continued much below those of a year earlier.

Exports of hams and shoulders, the principal po
about the same in October as in September but the tota
pounds was about 1,300,000 pounds smaller than in the
of 1934. The United Kingdom continued to be the chief
for these cuts. Bacon exports in October totaled only
compared with about 903,000 in October last year. In
years prior to 1931 bacon was an important item in the
pork with the monthly export movement usually varying l
and 10,000,000 pounds.

Exports of lard in October amounted to 2,769,00
with 27,096,000 in October last year. Shipments of la
Britain during the month totaled 2,017,000 pounds whil
they were more than 20,000,000 pounds. Lard exports t
reduced considerably in the last 2 months. In October
time in several months it was reported that a small vo
exported to Germany. The decrease in domestic lard pr
early 1935 has been even greater than the decline in h
the shortage of lard is primarily responsible for the
exports in 1935.

The trade agreement recently adopted by the Uni
Canada, which will become effective January 1, 1936, l
the Canadian duties on imports of hogs and hog product
States. The Canadian duty on live hogs from the Unite
reduced from 3 cents to 1-1/4 cents per pound. The du
was reduced from 5 to 2-1/2 cents, that on lard from 2
and that on bacon, hams, and shoulders from 5 cents to
pound. Prior to 1931 when Canadian import duties were
a considerable volume of ham and shoulders were shippe
1930 for example exports of hams and shoulders to that
to about 10,000,000 pounds. A fairly large quantity o
also were exported to Canada prior to the duty increas
duties on hogs and hog products in the United States w
by the Canadian agreement.

New Adjustment Program for Corn and Hogs in the United States

A 2-year adjustment program for corn and hogs was recently announced by the Secretary of Agriculture following a conference of farmers, representatives of various state agricultural colleges, and officials of the Agricultural Adjustment Administration. According to recent announcements the major objectives of the new program are to maintain a balance between production and consumption of corn and hogs, to establish the income to the corn-hog producers at a fair level over a period of years, and to maintain the productive capacity of the land. Briefly the new program is designed to accomplish three things (1) prevention of an excessive production of corn in 1936 and 1937, (2) allowance of an increase in the 1936 pig crop that would be at least as great as it is estimated would take place if no adjustment program were in effect and, (3) prevention of an excessive 1937 pig crop.

The chief provisions of the program as related to 1936 are as follows:

(1) Producers signing contracts agree to adjust their corn acreage from 10 to 30 percent below their corn base. Planting of at least 25 percent of the base corn acreage is required.

(2) In order to receive the maximum adjustment payment producers shall raise for market a number of pigs not less than 50 percent and not more than 100 percent of their market hog base.

(3) Adjustment payments on corn will be at the rate of 35 cents per bushel on the appraised yield of the adjusted corn acreage. Adjustment payments on hogs will be at the rate of $1.25 per head for the number of hogs in the market hog base.

(4) The adjusted acreage must be used for soil improving or erosion preventing crops and the acreage of such crops must be in addition to the area normally devoted to such purposes.

(5) Bases on both corn and hogs are to be established by community committees with review by county allotment committees and state corn-hog boards to insure uniformity. It is contemplated that in any county or state the total of the corn and hog bases for contract signers who participated in the 1935 program will not exceed the 1932-33 aggregate average production of hogs and average corn acreage for all such contract signers. Bases for those persons who wish to participate in the 1936-37 program whether or not they participated in 1935 will be established by community committees largely on the basis of the number of hogs produced by them and the acreage of cultivated crops on their farms in recent years.

(6) Local administrative expenses for the corn-hog program in both 1936 and 1937 will be deducted from the adjustment payments on corn and hogs.

Unlike earlier corn-hog programs the contract which producers will sign in early 1936 will cover 2 years, 1936 and 1937. The provisions of the contract relating to 1936 were described in the foregoing paragraphs. The provisions relating to 1937 are as follows:

(1) In the case of corn, producers will not be required to adjust their planted acreage below 75 percent of their base nor will they be required to plant more than 25 percent of their base corn acreage. The rate of adjustment payment to be paid on the yield of their adjusted acreage will not be less than 30 cents per bushel. The definite rate of adjustment and the rate of payment for corn will be announced by November 30, 1936.

(2) In order to secure the maximum adjustment payment on hogs in 1937 producers will not be required to produce more than 60 percent of their market hog base nor will they be required to make a downward adjustment from their base of more than 25 percent. The 1937 adjustment payment on hogs will not be less than the 1936 rate which as already stated will be $1.25 per head on the market hog base. The adjustment required on hogs and the rate of payment on hogs for 1937 will also be announced by November 30, 1936.

(3) All contracts are to be in full force through November 30, 1937 unless the Secretary of Agriculture (a) terminates all corn-hog contracts with respect to 1937 by an announcement not later than November 30, 1936 or (b) approves application made by a contract signer not later than April 1, 1937 for a termination of his contracts, or (c) terminates a contract because of non-compliance.

Canada

The price of bacon hogs at Toronto fell off slightly in November partly as a result of a seasonal increase in supplies. The price, however, was still above the average November price a year ago by about 24 cents per 100 pounds. The Toronto price for the 4 weeks ended November 28 was $7.90 per 100 pounds United States currency, compared with $8.81 per 100 pounds in October and an average of $9.62 for the 5 months May to September. Last year the average price for the same 4 weeks of November was $7.66.

Although there has been a seasonal increase in supplies recently the gradings of live hogs at stockyards and packing plants for the 4 weeks ended November 28, this year amounted to only 237,000 head compared with 276,000 head a year ago. This year so far, i.e., up to November 28, gradings including carcasses graded, totaled 2,667,000 head compared with 2,722,000 a year ago.

Shipments of live hogs to the United States have increased in recent months. During the 3 months August, September, and October, the number exported to the United States exceeded 1,000 head each month with September shipments alone exceeding 4,000 head. Shipments to this country for the 10-month period ended October amounted to 8,039 head compared with only 1,008 during the same period a year ago and only 92 in the same period of 1933. Shipments of live hogs from Canada to this country have not been as large since 1928 when 20,661 head were sent to this country during the year. The spread between the Toronto and Buffalo markets was not such as to warrant as heavy shipments as took place in September but on November 25 twelve decks of Canadian hogs were reported sold at Buffalo at $10.10 to $10.15 per 100 pounds.

Bacon exports to the United Kingdom are still slightly larger than a year ago and almost twice as large as in the same period of 1933. The total for the 10 months ended October was 105,363,000 pounds compared with 100,509,000 pounds a year earlier. Lard shipments to the United Kingdom during the same period this year reached 10,168,000 pounds compared with only 1,009,000 pounds last year for the same period.

Hog numbers in Canada in June 1935 were officially estimated at 3,549,000, a decrease of 3 percent below 1934 and were the smallest they have been since 1920. The decrease was in the prairie provinces as hog numbers increased in the two most important eastern provinces, Ontario and Quebec, where the total reached 1,836,000 in June 1935, which was 6 percent above 1934. In the three prairie provinces, i.e., Manitoba, Saskatchewan, and Alberta, there was a further decline in 1935 to 1,507,000 which is 13 percent below the number reported in 1934. The number in the latter provinces has been declining each year since 1931 when it was the largest on record, or 2,391,000 head.

United Kingdom and Irish Free State

The total import quota for cured pork set by Great Britain for the first 6 weeks of 1936 is 64,853,000 pounds, according to cabled advices from Agricultural Attache' C. C. Taylor at London. This figure represents an extension of the rate of weekly quotas established for the last 3 months of 1935, and is a decrease of 16 percent from the quota for the first 6 weeks of 1935. The United States continues to receive an allotment of 8.1 percent of the total quota. On that basis, the United States quota for the first 6 weeks of 1936 will be approximately 5,253,000 pounds, or about 876,000 pounds per week.

The British cured-pork import quotas are fixed from time to time on the basis of contracts made by British producers to deliver domestic hogs to pork-curing establishments. Anticipated arrivals from Empire countries also influence the quotas set for other countries. Continuation of the rate of quota imports prevailing in the last 3 months of 1935 suggest that deliveries of bacon pigs are not expected to show a significant increase during the early weeks of 1936. Contracts for additional pigs are being made and the total contracts for 1936 are as yet indefinite.

In administering the quota system, the British authorities make initial allocations to cover any given quota period. These allocations, however, are subject to certain adjustments. In establishing the quota for the first 6 weeks of 1936, the original quota for the last 3 months of 1935 was used as a base. The adjusted quota for those 3 months, however, was considerably larger than the basic quota. See table, page 10. Taking this fact into consideration, it would seem that the total quota allotments for the first 6 weeks of 1936 are about 2,500,000 pounds smaller than the comparable adjusted quota for the last 6 weeks of 1935. In the case of the United States, the quantity involved in the 1936 quota is the same as the quota for the last 6 weeks of 1935.

Shipments of cured pork from quota countries do not always correspond to the quota allocations, with a result that many adjustments on account of overshipments and undershipments must be made in succeeding periods. Methods for stricter enforcement of the quotas are now being discussed. Consideration is also being given to the allocation of small quotas to Yugoslavia, Rumania, and Bulgaria, in addition to those granted the 11 original quota countries.

The easier tendency noticeable in all pork-product quotations in Liverpool during November was reflected in the average for the month of $18.66 per 100 pounds on Danish Wiltshire sides as compared with $20.00 in October and $19.17 in October a year earlier. The drop in Canadian green sides was even more pronounced, representing at $16.04 a decrease of 14 percent from the October average quotations and of 10 percent from the November 1934 average. Liverpool quotations on American green bellies were nominal.

Imports of bacon continued their downward movement, reaching a new monthly low for post-war years of 58,170,000 pounds. This figure is 11 percent below October 1934 imports and represents a decrease from the imports of October 1932 of 49 percent. This decline in imports is in line with the lower quotas in effect for the last quarter of 1935, which contemplate a 12.5 percent reduction in monthly imports from foreign sources from those of the third quarter of 1935 and a 14 percent reduction from imports of October-December 1934.

Bacon imports from Denmark during October fell to less than 34,500,000 pounds, the lowest monthly figure since last February, and with the exception of that month the lowest for any post-war month. The quota allotment to Denmark calls for importation of 31,400,000 pounds during each of the last 3 months of 1935 as against 35,751,000 pounds during the comparable 1934 months. October imports represented a decline of 9 percent and 55 percent from respective 1934 and 1932 figures. Danish imports for the month were equal to 59 percent of the total imports from all sources and 72 percent of the bacon received from non-Empire countries. In October 1932 Denmark sent 66 percent of the total bacon imports to the United Kingdom and 68 percent of those from all foreign countries.

The United States shipments of bacon to the United Kingdom for October continued the downward trend of the past two seasons. At 111,000 pounds, they were 55 percent below October 1934 figures and 84 percent below those of 1933.

Imports of bacon from Canada were maintained during October at the high levels of the past 2 years, though the slight decline in evidence since last May continued. The monthly figure of 5,193,000 pounds represented a decrease of 18 percent and 11 percent, respectively, from comparable 1933 and 1934 imports, but it was nearly 4 times as large as the October 1932 figure. Bacon imports from the Irish Free State, which have maintained a steady and almost unbroken monthly increase since the inauguration of the quota system 3 years ago, were up 10 percent from the September figures and, respectively, 155 percent, 70 percent, and 25 percent from October 1932, 1933, and 1934 imports. Together, Canada and the Irish Free State supplied 18 percent of the total imports of bacon into the United Kingdom during October as against 16 percent during September and 3 percent, 11 percent, and 16 percent for October 1932, 1933, and 1934, respectively.

Liverpool Quotations on American short cut green hams for the month of November averaged $20.13, a drop of $1.39 from the October average, but still $1.20 above the November 1934 figure. Imports of ham into the United Kingdom from all sources continue to decline, amounting in October to but 4,797,000 pounds as against an average for the season ended September 30 of 6,075,000 pounds. The October 1935 figure represented a decrease of 11 percent from the comparable 1934 amount, 31 percent from imports of October 1933, and 36 percent from those of 1932. Imports of ham from the United States showed a much greater percentage decline than did total ham imports. The United States supplied 48 percent of the total ham imports into the United Kingdom during October, whereas last season United States ham imports represented 63 percent of the total imported. In October 1934 United States imports were 64 percent and in 1933 70 percent of the total.

Poland, which in 1932 supplied about 14.6 percent of total ham imports, furnished during October only 5.5 percent. Argentina, which, like the United States, fills practically all of its cured-pork quota with ham, shipped during October 349,000 pounds. This is equivalent to 100 percent of the cured-pork quota allowance of 0.7 percent of the total quota as well as of the total non-Empire cured pork imported for the month. Canada, in pre-quota years an insignificant supplier of ham to United Kingdom markets, in October 1935 furnished 32.5 percent of the total ham imports. The Irish Free State also furnished a fair share with 288,000 pounds. The percentage of the total cured-pork imports furnished by Dominion countries for October was 20.

The fresh pork quota allotted to the United States for the first 3 months of 1936 is placed at 40,900 hundredweight (4,580,000 pounds), including 2,300 hundredweight (257,600 pounds) imported for curing. The figures are the same as those in force during the first quarter of 1935.

Supplies of British and Irish pork at London Central Markets for October reached 9,735,000 pounds, the largest figure for any month since December 1932. This total represents an increase of 23 percent over comparable 1934 supplies. Domestic supplies of fat pigs at English, Welsh, and Scotch markets for the period January 1-November 30, 1935, showed an increase of 9 percent over corresponding 1934 figures. Supplies of store pigs for the same markets and period, at about 622,000 head against 589,000 head for the comparable 1934 period, showed an increase of 6 percent. Pigs bought for curing in Northern Ireland and the Irish Free State during the first 46 weeks of 1935 exceeded similar purchases in 1934 by 12 percent. Exports of live hogs were also higher during 1935, especially from the Irish Free State, and represented an increase of 40 percent over 1934 exports.

United Kingdom: Cured-pork import quotas, October-Dece
1935

Country	Basic allocation	Percentage of total	Adjusted allocation	P
	Cwt.	Percent	Cwt.	
Denmark ....:	796,666	63.50	1/ 841,437	
Netherlands .....:	119,186	9.50	119,186	
Poland ....:	99,740	7.95	99,740	
Sweden ....:	58,966	4.70	58,966	
Lithuania ......:	37,011	2.95	37,011	
Estonia ....:	9,410	.75	2/ 9,979	
Finland ....:	5,018	.40	2/ 5,322	
Latvia ....:	8,782	.70	2/ 9,314	
U.S.S.R. ... ...:	10,664	.85	2/ 11,311	
Argentina ......:	8,782	.70	2/ 9,314	
United States ...:	100,367	8.00	3/ 101,622	
Total ....:	1,254,592	100.00	1,303,202	

Includes 5,303,760 pounds as an adjustment for deficiencies i
m Denmark in 1934, less 289,400 pounds transferred by special
regulated countries with less than 1 percent allocations.
Includes share of Danish quota adjustment.
Includes additional allowance of 0.1 percent of total quota be
orts from the United States consigned through Canada.

Central European Meat and Fat Situation

The shortage of pork in Central Europe noted in recent mor
tinued into December, according to Agricultural Commissioner k
t specialist at Berlin. The maldistribution of available supp
ting from trade barriers and other restrictions which affect s
ts also have been in evidence. The small hog surpluses which
st on the Continent have been drawn upon by the deficit countr
ent permitted by current trade balances, and the ability of su
itries to absorb the industrial goods of deficit countries is
reasing importance as a factor in determining hog prices.

Supplies of hogs on continental markets during the latter
ober and the month of November have been irregular, but hog pr
ied to advance. Surplus beef has been used to some extent to
shortage of pork, but a realization that supplies of beef wil
smaller has prompted negotiations with South American surplus
itries in an effort to obtain frozen beef supplies for the fut

Further reductions in trade barriers which affect fats occ
ember in connection with attempts of the deficit fat countries
inental Europe to increase their supplies of edible fats thro
eased imports. Marked reductions in the tariff on lard have
ermany, Czechoslovakia, and Austria, but the trade in lard is
ely confined to dealings with countries which have compensati

ments with the deficit countries. In some instances the inability of European surplus countries to fill the lard contingents granted by the deficit countries has necessitated the use of foreign exchange for American lard, which has been held in storage at continental ports. The reduction in the lard tariff and the use of foreign exchange in obtaining lard from European surplus countries should tend to divert supplies which otherwise would go to England and, if so, the smaller supplies available for the British market should have a favorable reaction on American lard prices.

Outstanding moves to increase fat supplies in deficit areas, particularly in Germany, have been the negotiation of new or extended trade agreements which should increase imports of hogs, lard, and butter, provided the supplying countries are able to absorb increased quantities of industrial goods from the deficit fat countries. Efforts have also been made to increase the production of margarine and other artificial fats, and the increased demand for raw materials for this purpose has resulted in a hardening tendency in world prices. This tendency would have been more pronounced had it been possible for all deficit fat countries to use foreign exchange in purchasing raw materials.

The present season's output of whale oil is reported to be practically sold and present prices are now more than twice last year's prices. The surplus of butter which exists in certain continental countries has been drawn upon for partially alleviating the fat shortage, and the butter situation in surplus producing countries, accordingly, has been greatly modified. It also appears that the movement to curtail the production and sale of artificial fats, which has been making progress in certain countries, has subsided somewhat as prices of all fats have advanced and the fat shortage has become more generally recognized.

Germany

The fat situation continues as the outstanding problem in Germany, according to Agricultural Commissioner H. E. Reed at Berlin. Trade agreements have permitted increased imports of all categories of edible fats, but the increase has not been sufficient to meet requirements. In late Octo·. a new order authorized the duty-free import of lard until December 3·, .. if and when the authorities deem such procedure advisable. The ·· .·. .n oleomargarine, premier jus, and tallow were reduced from RM 100 to RM 30 per 100 kilogram until December 31. It is unlikely, however, that the reduced import duties will have any effect upon business with the United States.

Lard imports into Germany for October, at 13,762,000 pounds, were the largest for any month since January 1934 and were more than 3 times larger than the October 1934 imports. Of the current figure, about half came from Hungary, with Yugoslavia and Denmark following in that order. The United States, France, Latvia, Norway, and Sweden are all credited with contributing to the October 1935 imports. The figure for the United States is placed at only 178,000 pounds.

Increased imports of raw materials for margarine production took place in October; and, in view of the improved margarine supply situation, production has likely been stepped up, although it is still conducted under contingents. Better grade margarine is reported to be in larger supply at the shops. Large sales of the new season's whale oil output have been reported as being made to Germany at $98.50 per ton, compared with last season' average of about $44.00.

Increased imports of butter have failed to offset entirely the reduction in domestic butter production, and the latter has assumed increased importance in the present and immediate future fat supply situation in Germany. A seasonal increase in domestic butter production is ordinarily to be expected by December, but the greatly reduced supplies of supplemental feeds this year seem to preclude any marked increase. In fact, the nitrogenous supplement situation is such that the cumulative effect of the last year's short supplies and the immediate effect of the present shortage may cause some decrease in milk and butter production during the first quarter of 1936.

The continued small marketings and slaughter of hogs in Germany brought October figures down to unusually small totals, Mr. Reed reports. Data on market receipts have lost a considerable amount of their significance owing to measures taken to avoid selling hogs at the fixed minimum prices. Some increase in market receipts occurred during November, however, following measures taken to secure a more equitable distribution of available supplies. Effective October 15, direct buying was prohibited. The markets on which slaughterers could operate were specified, and, since November 9, monthly slaughter at any establishment has been limited to 60 percent of the slaughter for the corresponding month of last year; a limit of 80 percent was set on October 1, and of 70 percent on October 15. These measures were designed to force slaughter hogs away from smaller markets to the larger ones.

In addition to the regulations mentioned, home slaughter also has been under control since November 5. The home slaughterer may kill only hogs in his possession for at least 3 months. A system of sales slips and slaughter permits also has been put into operation for commercial slaughterers. Slaughter of hogs under 180 pounds live weight has been prohibited in the larger cities. In the smaller cities, it is illegal to kill hogs under 190 pounds live weight. It is expected that the present scarcity of hogs will be eased somewhat by increased imports of live and dressed hogs as a result of recently negotiated trade agreements. Reports indicate receipts of 5,600 hogs weekly from Poland during November-December. Other countries, presumably Denmark and Hungary, are expected to supply 170,000 carcasses during the same period.

So far there have been no indications of an increase over recent months in total hog slaughter, Mr. Reed reports. The October 1935 slaughter at 36 points declined to 134,000 head against 156,000 in September and 426,000 head for October 1934. Current marketing regulations have not been in effect for a period sufficiently long to reflect their full effect. Failure of receipts to fulfill expectations, however, probably has been the result in large part of the abandonment of the fixed minimum prices which placed a premium on light, unfinished hogs. Restoration of price margins between hog classes has tended to encourage feeding to heavier weights, with consequent delays in marketing. Increased receipts and slaughter, however, are to be anticipated in the near future, if hog numbers on farms have been reflected accurately in the census figures.

Danube Basin

Exports of hogs and pork products from the Danube Basin during the first 10 months of 1935 reached unusually high levels, according to a report from the Belgrade office of the Foreign Agricultural Service. Hungary is the leading exporting country in the Basin. Factors favoring exports from Hungary include: (1) A reduction in hog numbers and in pork and lard production in Central Europe and the United States; (2) the development of barter and trade agreements; and (3) hog-feed price relationships which encourage fattening and breeding. While corn supplies in Hungary are short, current prices of hog products, notably lard, are stimulating imports of feed grains, including Argentine corn, especially since Hungary is now importing feed grains free of duty.

A small hog population is the outstanding limitation on continued expansion of pork products exports from Hungary. In March, the period of the usual annual hog census, there were only slightly over 3,000,000 hogs in Hungary, the Belgrade office reports, against about 2,500,000 head in 1934 and a 1929-1933 average of about 2,400,000 head. The Hungarian system of hog management admits of a fair amount of increased production of hog products without a corresponding increase in hog numbers. In addition, it is evident that an increase in hog numbers was under way in 1934 and the first half of 1935. The increase, however, appears to have been little more than enough to support current marketings.

The indicated increase in hog numbers in March 1935 over 1934 figures was about 26 percent. The unusually heavy marketings and exports, however, suggest that the number of marketable hogs must have been materially reduced during the last 6 months. Arrivals of hogs at Budapest account for more than one third of all of the Hungarian hogs entering commercial channels. In the period March-October 1935, arrivals at Budapest were about 22 percent larger than the comparable 1934 figures. It would seem, therefore, that present hog numbers in Hungary may be about the same as those of a year ago.

Lard exports.- Lard exports from the Danube Basin during the 10-month period January-October 1935, totaled approximately 52,587,000 pounds as compared with 21,856,000 pounds exported during the same period in 1934, with 32,203,000 pounds as the total of exports during the entire calendar year 1934, and with 13,941,000 pounds as the 5-year average calendar-year exports during 1929-1933. During the first 10 months of 1935, more lard was exported from the Danube Basin than during any calendar year since the World War. Of the 1935 total, Hungary supplied about 45,554,000 pounds, or nearly 87 percent, whereas practically all of the remainder originated in Yugoslavia. See table, page 15. In 1935 the most important country of destination was Germany, followed by England and Czechoslovakia. In previous years Czechoslovakia took most of the Hungarian lard surpluses, followed by Germany, Austria, and Italy, which latter two countries have received practically no Hungarian lard during 1935.

Exports during September showed a decline when compared with subsequent months as a result of a temporary standstill in Hungarian lard shipments to Germany. In October, Hungarian deliveries to Germany were resumed and approximately 5,482,000 pounds, almost double the September shipments, were exported from the Danube Basin. October exports were also promoted by considerable price increases in Czechoslovakia and England, combined with the decreasing of the Czechoslovakian lard import duty from 3.00 Czech crowns per kilogram (5.67 cents per pound) prior to August, to 2.00 crowns (3.76 cents) in August-September, 1.50 (2.82 cents) for October, and 1.20 (2.25 cents) for November 1, 1935, to January 31, 1936. Further large shipments were expected during November-December.

The short corn crop in Hungary is not now regarded as so serious an obstacle to continued lard exports as was thought earlier in the season, provided lard prices in importing countries continue at high levels. Hungary imported over 3,937,000 bushels of corn in the period April - September 1935, principally from Rumania and Yugoslavia, with Argentine corn also reaching Hungary in recent months. This is the first time since the War that Hungary has imported corn in such quantities. Imports may be expected to continue as long as prices for export pork products, especially lard, warrant such action. Argentine corn prices are relatively low this year as a result of the unusually large 1934-35 crop in that country. London prices of Hungarian lard have been well maintained during the last 2 months at around $15.43 per 100 pounds. The November average for American refined lard at Liverpool was $16.50. In view of the scarcity of the American product in the United Kingdom, it is probable that that market will continue to attract Hungarian lard until export supplies of the American product return to more usual levels.

Hog exports.- Exports of live hogs from the Danube Basin during the 10-month period January-October 1935, totaled approximately 418,000 head, as compared with 267,200 head exported during the same period in 1934, with 342,468 head as the total of exports during the calendar year 1934, and with 551,200 head as the 5-year average annual exports for 1929-1933. It is improbable that hog exports during 1935 will reach the 5-year average, although exports during August, September, and October were considerably in excess of any previous month's total for the year thus far. The increase in hog exports during the fall months was due to considerable price advances in Austria and Czechoslovakia, combined with the granting of extra quotas by both Governments to Hungary, Rumania, and Yugoslavia. 1/

1/ The reasons for the granting of extra quotas by the Austrian Government were the following, according to Hungarian trade sources: (1) Low point in the production cycle of meat hogs (the proportion of domestic hogs in total shipments to Vienna decreased from about 75 percent to 50 percent) (2) an attempt to reduce lard prices, which increased to 3-4 Austrian schillings per kilogram by the middle of October on account of the advance in lard prices on world markets combined with Austrian consumers' fear of further increases as a result of the Italo-Ethiopian conflict. In Czechoslovakia, the same situation prevailed, which explains the granting of extra quotas by that country.

Pork lard: Exports from Danube Basin countries,
January-October 1934 and 1935

Period	Hungary		Yugoslavia		Danube Basin	
	1934	1935	1934	1935	1934	1935
	1,000 pounds	1,000 pounds	1,000 pounds	1,000 pounds	1,000 pounds	1,000 pounds
Jan.	1	4,648	122	801	123	5,449
Feb.	342	5,142	2	1,066	344	6,238
Mar.	814	7,343	3	816	817	8,159
Jan.-Mar.:	1,157	17,140	127	2,683	1,284	1/19,846
Apr.	988	3,421	0	556	988	3,977
May	2,138	4,207	57	662	2,195	4,869
June	1,879	4,520	1	154	1,880	4,674
Apr.-June:	5,005	12,148	58	1,372	5,063	13,520
July	2,006	5,325	293	491	2,299	5,816
Aug.	4,064	3,568	320	973	4,384	4,541
Sept.	3,666	2,302	331	721	3,997	3,023
July-Sept:	9,736	11,195	944	2,185	10,680	13,380
Oct.	3,748	5,071	441	772	4,189	5,843
Total, 10 months:	19,646	45,554	1,570	7,012	21,216	1/32,589

Compiled by the Belgrade office of the Foreign Agricultural Service.
1/ Includes 22,000 pounds of lard exported from Bulgaria and 1,000 pounds from Rumania.

Carcass and pork exports.- According to trade sources. Hungary exported to Germany between September 15 and October 30, 1935, a total of 198 carloads of halved-hog carcasses, equivalent to about 18,370 hogs, or, approximately, 3,535,000 pounds, and 70 carloads of meat from Mangolica hogs slaughtered for lard. This export was made on the basis of an agreement concluded between the German and Hungarian Governments early in September.

Bacon exports to England from Bulgaria, Hungary, and Rumania continue on the usual basis of around 176,000 pounds monthly from each country. A total of 4,865,000 pounds was exported from these three countries between January 1 and September 30, 1935.

Live hogs: Exports from Danube Basin countries,
January-October 1934 and 1935

Month	Hungary		Yugoslavia		Rumania	
	1934	1935	1934	1935	1934	1935
	Number	Number	Number	Number	Number	Number
Jan.	11,884	13,814	18,310	14,635	4,356	7,816
Feb.	9,522	12,422	10,752	9,614	4,004	5,168
Mar.	6,914	15,531	9,482	13,305	5,172	4,683
Jan.-Mar.	28,320	41,767	38,544	37,554	13,532	17,6
Apr.	3,438	16,136	8,854	13,184	4,055	4,984
May	8,417	12,407	10,353	18,921	5,834	8,851
June	5,330	14,522	6,618	16,043	4,623	11,527
Apr.-June	17,185	43,065	25,825	48,148	14,512	25,362
July	11,739	15,246	7,997	16,675	4,396	9,513
Aug.	12,017	12,545	11,891	25,709	7,558	17,788
Sept.	14,790	16,409	10,791	20,134	7,995	15,788
July-Sept.	38,546	44,200	30,679	65,518	19,949	43,089
Oct.		3/		3/		3/
Oct.	15,365	16,000	14,786	20,000	9,6 3	15,000
Total, 10 months	99,416	145,032	109,834	171,220	57,636	101,118

Compiled by the Belgrade office of the Foreign Agricultural Serv:
1/ Includes 314 head exported from Bulgaria.
2/ Includes 531 head exported from Bulgaria.
3/ Estimated.

Hogs and pork products: Foreign and domestic average prices per 100 pounds
for the month indicated, and stocks at the end of each month

Item	1909-1913 average	1925-1929 average	Oct. 1934	Sept. 1935	Oct. 1935
	:Dollars	Dollars	Dollars	Dollars	Dollars
Prices					
Hogs, Chicago, basis packers' and shippers' quotations	7.93	10.67	5.60	10.95	9.83
Corn, Chicago, No. 3 Yellow	1.12	1.55	1.39	1.49	1.46
Hogs, heavy Berlin live weight .	12.27	16.82	17.74	18.80	18.78
Potatoes, Breslau feeding	.31	.49	.86		
Barley, Leipzig	1.70	2.20	2.98	3.08	3.12
Lard					
Chicago	11.20	15.51	10.88	16.97	16.00
Liverpool	12.50	14.95	9.24	16.23	16.94
Hamburg	25.37	15.52	19.06	19.11	17.07
Cured pork					
Liverpool					
American short cut green hams	14.30	25.19	19.09	22.96	21.52
American green bellies		22.81	Nominal	Nominal	Nominal
Danish Wiltshire sides	15.50	24.33	19.32	18.67	20.00
Canadian green sides	14.87	22.71	17.56	17.35	18.73
	1,000 pounds	1,000 pounds	1,000 pounds	1,000 pounds	1,000 pounds
Stocks					
United States					
Processed pork 2/		437,982	504,737	277,605	240,663
Lard in cold storage		73,010	105,519	45,350	40,702

/ One week. Other weeks nominal.
/ Dry salt cured and in process of cure; pickled, cured, and in preces of cure,
and frozen.

Hogs and pork products: Indices of foreign supplies and demand

Country and item	Unit	1909-10: to :1913-14: average	1924-25: to :1928-29: average	October 1932	1933	1934	1935
United Kingdom							
Production							
Supplies, domestic	:1,000 :						
..fresh pork, London .	:pounds:			6,747	9,130	7,540	7,907	9,735
Imports							
. Bacon							
Denmark	"	20,380	40,385	75,730	47,545	37,837	34,403
.. Irish Free State ..	"		6,261	2,164	3,251	4,401	5,511
United States	"	14,312	8,439	261	695	244	111
Canada ....'..	"	1,799	6,979	1,056	6,310	5,853	5,193
Others	"	4,914	12,237	35,099	25,470	17,203	12,953
.Total	"	41,405	74,301	114,310	83,272	65,537	58,170
Ham, total	"	6,322	7,979	7,497	6,992	5,419	4,797
Lard, total	"	26,821	18,836	19,799	25,407	26,932	12,161
Denmark							
Exports							
Bacon	"		39,596	74,261	48,461	36,186	34,341
Canada							
Slaughter							
Hogs, inspected	:1000's:	141	219	189	235	230	263
Germany							
Production							
Hog receipts 14 cities:	"		274	273	275	320	85
Hog slaughter, 36							
centers	"	379	335	363	376	426	134
Imports	:1,000 :						
Bacon, total	:pounds:	282	2,470	4,623	2,446	4,367	1,783
Lard, total	"	18,871	20,484	27,535	8,741	4,301	13,762
United States							
Slaughter							
Hogs, inspected	:1000's:	2,421	3,294	3,605	3,058	3,546	2,135
Exports							
Bacon	:1,000 :						
United Kingdom	:pounds:	9,453	4,726	269	325	183	69
Germany	"	132	1,491	23	54	0	0
Cuba	"	627	1,728	376	281	394	112
Total	"	14,175	11,750	1,492	2,304	903	233
Hams, shoulders							
United Kingdom	"	9,018	9,857	4,352	5,061	3,563	2,594
Total	"	10,986	11,962	5,064	5,745	4,346	3,071
Lard							
United Kingdom	"	9,689	15,757	21,064	22,463	20,111	1,997
Germany	"	11,515	12,942	19,590	13,695	360	190
Cuba	"	2,810	6,661	377	915	4,398	411
Netherlands	"	2,590	2,587	4,489	4,999	9	0
Total	"	33,825	52,553	53,573	49,812	26,870	2,731

HP-74   January 20, 1936

WORLD HOG AND PORK PROSPECTS

Summary

Larger domestic slaughter supplies of hogs in the summer of 1936 and
in the winter of 1936-37 are probable on the basis of the December 1935
Pig Crop Report rec·ntly released by the Bureau of Agricultural Economics.
The 1935 fall pig crop, which will be marketed mostly next summer was
estimated to be 31 percent greater than the small fall crop of 1934. An
increase in sows to farrow in spring of 1936 of 24 percent was also
indicated by the Pig Crop Report. An increase in the 1936 spring pig
crop will be reflected in larger slaughter supplies in the winter season
of 1936-37. It appears therefore, that the downward trend in hog production which began in late 1933 has been checked and that increasing
slaughter supplies of hogs are likely during the next 12 months at least.

The German hog census as of early December 1935 indicated that an
increase in slaughter supplies of hogs in Germany was probable during
1936. Although the total number of hogs in Germany in early December was
reported to be 2 percent smaller than a year earlier, the number of bred
sows on hand was 11 percent larger and the number of pigs under 2 months
old was 5 percent greater. The shortage of fats in Germany continues to
be a problem of outstanding importance. Imports of lard and hog fats
into Germany have increased considerably, but they are small in relation
to imports of such products prior to 1934. Imports of all meats and livestock also have increased in recent months.

Lard exports from the Danube Basin have been relatively large during the last year. Exports from that region in November of 6,800,000 pounds were nearly as large as the reduced exports from the United States in that month. Lard exports from the Danube Basin have come chiefly from Hungary and have been shipped mostly to Germany and Czechoslovakia, although a limited quantity has been exported to Great Britain. Exports of live hogs and hog carcasses from Hungary to Central European countries also have increased considerably in recent months.

United States

On the basis of the December 1935 Pig Crop Report recently released by the Bureau of Agricultural Economics it appears that supplies of hogs for slaughter in the summer of 1936 and in the winter of 1936-37 will be materially larger than in the same periods a year earlier. The increase in the 1935 fall pig crop compared with that of 1934 amounted to 31 percent for the entire country and 42 percent for the Corn Belt States. The fall pig crop is normally marketed in the summer months, roughly from May through September. The Pig Crop Report also indicated an increase of about 24 percent in the number of sows to farrow in the spring of 1936. An increase in the 1936 spring pig crop will be reflected in an increase in hog slaughter in the winter months of 1936-37. Thus, it appears that the downward trend of hog production which developed largely as a result of the droughts of 1933 and 1934 has been checked and that increasing slaughter supplies in the next 12 months at least are probable.

The estimates of pigs saved and sows farrowed given in the fall Pig Crop Report are shown in the table on page 5 for the United States and the major geographic divisions. For the country as a whole the number of pigs saved in the fall season of 1935 was estimated at 20,272,000 head, an increase of 4,750,000 head or 31 percent over the number saved in the fall of 1934, but a decrease of 27 percent from the average fall pig crop in the 5 years 1929 to 1933. Increases in the fall pig crop were reported in all areas but the largest increase occurred in the North Central States (Corn Belt). In the West North Central States the 1935 fall pig crop was 64 percent greater than that of 1934 and in the East North Central States it was 23 percent greater. A considerable part of the decrease in the number of pigs produced in 1934 occurred in the West North Central States because of the severity of the 1934 drought in that area.

The combined spring and fall pig crop of 1935 for the United States was estimated at 50,674,000 head, a decrease of 2,655,000 head or 5 percent from the combined crop of 1934. In the Corn Belt States the combined pig crop of 1935 of 37,566,000 head was 2,678,000 head or 6.7 percent smaller than that of 1934. Nearly all of the decrease in the Corn Belt was in the States west of the Mississippi River. In the North Atlantic and South Atlantic States the combined pig crop of 1935 was larger than that of 1934.

The number of sows to farrow in the spring season of 1936 for the United States is estimated at 6,220,000 head. This is an increase of about 24 percent over the very small number farrowed in the spring season of 1935 but is 4 percent smaller than the number farrowed in the spring of 1934 and 29 percent smaller than the average spring farrowings of 1932 and 1933. Although increases in spring farrowings are indicated in all States there was considerable variation in the rate of increase as among States. The largest increases estimated were for the Western Corn Belt States.

Hog prices advanced irregularly in December. A marked rise occurred just prior to the Christmas Holidays but most of this was lost in the 3 days December 27, 28, and 30. At the end of the month prices were about the same as at the beginning of the month. Prices tended to decline in the first few days in January but after January 6 following the decision of the United States Supreme Court holding processing taxes invalid, hog prices advanced sharply but unevenly at the several markets. With relatively large supplies at all markets during the week ended January 11, hog prices generally were about 50 cents higher at the end of the week than at the beginning. The average price of hogs at Chicago for the month of December was $9.57 compared with $9.31 in November and $5.89 in the corresponding month last year. In recent weeks light weight hogs (160 to 200 pounds) have been selling at slightly higher prices than medium weight hogs for the first time in nearly 2 years. This change in price relationship has been brought about chiefly by the increasing proportion of heavy weight hogs in the slaughter supplies in the last month.

Slaughter supplies of hogs increased from November to December but the increase was somewhat less than usual for this period of the year. With hog prices relatively high in relation to corn prices there has been a marked tendency to feed hogs to heavier weights thus delaying marketings. It seems therefore that the proportion which slaughter in the 3 months October to December will represent of the total slaughter for the 1936-37 winter marketing season (October to April) will be unusually small. Hog slaughter under Federal inspection in December amounting to 2,875,000 head was the smallest for the month since 1910 and was 32 percent less than the slaughter in December,1934. Average weights of hogs slaughtered in recent months have been relatively heavy. The average weight of hogs slaughtered under Federal inspection in November was the heaviest for the month in the last 16 years for which records have been available.

Corn prices were fairly steady for December after having declined in late November. The average price of No. 3 Yellow corn at Chicago was 59 cents per bushel compared with 62 cents in November and 93 cents in December 1934. On the basis of farm prices on the 15th of the month the hog-corn price ratio in the North Central States in December was 18.5 compared with 16.6 in November and 5.9 in December a year earlier. The average hog-corn price ratio in the 10-year period 1924 to 1933 was 12.8. The marked change in the ratio from a figure much below average to one materially above average in the last year is largely a result of the differences in feed crop production in 1934 and 1935. Greatly reduced production of corn and other feeds in 1934 brought about by the drought resulted in high prices of corn and a low hog-corn price ratio. The shortage of feed and the low ratio caused hog production to be reduced and hog slaughter has been small and hog prices high in 1935. With the return

of more normal weather conditions in 1935 feed crop production increased
and corn prices have declined materially in recent months while hog prices
have continued high. That the present high corn-hog price ratio is now
encouraging an increase in hog production is evidenced by the increase
in the 1935 fall pig crop, and the high ratio is also an important reason
for the heavier weights of hogs slaughtered in recent months compared
with a year earlier.

Wholesale prices of fresh pork declined in the first 3 weeks of
December but advanced somewhat in the last week of the month. Prices
of most cuts of cured pork tended to strengthen in December but lard
prices declined somewhat. The composite wholesale price of hog products
at New York was $23.28 per 100 pounds in December compared with $23.71
in November and $16.50 in December 1934.

Exports of both pork and lard increased materially in November
as compared with the preceding month but they continued at a level
much below that of a year earlier. Lard exports in November were larger
than in any month since last May and pork exports were the largest since
July. The increase in exports probably was caused in part by the seasonal
increase in hog slaughter in October to November and in part by the short
supplies and high prices of hog products in foreign countries. Shipments of pork and lard from the principal United States ports in
December were considerably smaller than in the same month of 1934 but
there was some tendency for pork exports to increase in December compared
with November.

Exports of hams and shoulders from the United States in November
totaling 4,723,000 pounds were about 50 percent larger than in October
but they were nearly 39 percent less than in November 1934. Of the total
exports of hams and shoulders in November about 4,154,000 pounds or
88 percent were confined to the United Kingdom. Bacon exports from the
United States in December amounted to only 207,000 pounds compared with
874,000 in December 1934.

Lard exports in November amounted to 7,988,000 pounds compared with
2,769,000 in October and nearly 20,000,000 pounds in November 1934.
Shipments of lard for the United Kingdom in November totaled 5,750,000
pounds which were nearly three times as large as the quantity shipped to
that country in October. Exports of lard to Cuba in November amounted to
1,572,000 pounds compared with 4,011,000 pounds in October. About
334,000 pounds of lard were shipped to Germany in November while in the
6 months prior to October practically no lard was exported to Germany.
November shipments to that country, however, represent only a small
fraction of the average monthly exports of lard to Germany in the post-war
years prior to 1934.

Imports of pork into the United States have increased considerably
in the last 6 months. In November 1935 such imports amounted to
1,265,000 pounds compared with about 200,000 pounds in November last year.
In the first 11 months of 1935 imports of pork totaled 9,263,000 pounds,
while only 1,464,000 pounds were imported in the same months of 1934.
Despite the recent increase, imports are still very small in relation to
exports or to domestic production. In the period from January to
November 1935 exports of pork amounted to 84,000,000 or about nine times

as much as imports during the period. In the first 11 months of 1935 the total dressed weight of hogs slaughtered under Federal inspection was 3,911,000,000 pounds.

United States: Fall pig crop, by geographic divisions, 1934 and 1935

Geographic division	Fall pigs saved (June 1 to Dec. 1)			Fall pigs saved per litter		Sows farrowed in fall (June 1 to Dec. 1)		Sows to be farrowed spring 1936 compared with spring 1935, (Dec.1 to June 1)		
		1935 1/							1936 2/	
	1934	Total	Per-centage of 1934	1934	1935	1934	1935	1935	Total	Per-centage of 1935
	Thou-sands	Thou-sands	Per cent	Num-ber	Num-ber	Thou-sands	Thou-sands	Thou-sands	Thou-sands	Per cent
North Atlantic	504	596	118.3	6.27	6.35	80	94	82	101	123.6
East North Central	5,170	6,354	122.9	6.27	6.43	824	988	1,345	1,643	122.2
West North Central	4,581	7,509	163.9	5.66	5.97	810	1,257	2,503	3,211	128.3
Total North Central	9,751	13,863	142.2	5.97	6.18	1,634	2,245	3,848	4,854	126.1
South Atlantic	1,795	1,895	105.6	5.65	5.78	318	328	370	395	106.9
South Central	2,758	2,981	108.1	5.49	5.72	502	521	552	651	117.9
Mountain and Pacific(West)	714	937	131.2	5.83	5.98	122	157	170	219	129.1
United States	15,522	20,272	130.6	5.84	6.06	2,657	3,344	5,021	6,220	123.9

Compiled from the United States 1935 Fall Pig Crop Report as of December 1, 1935, Bureau of Agricultural Economics, Division of Crop and Livestock Estimates.
1/ Preliminary.
2/ Number indicated to farrow from breeding intention reports.

Canada

The Canadian bacon hog market was characterized by short supplies and advancing prices in December. Price prospects were described in the Canadian Government Livestock Market Report as favorable with no immediate prospects of an increase in supplies. The average price of bacon hogs at Toronto for the 4-week period ended December 26 was $8.35 per 100 pounds American currency compared with $7.90 in November and $8.23 in December 1934.

Gradings of live hogs at all stockyards and packing plants during the 4 weeks of December numbered only 255,000 head, a decrease of 12 percent compared with December a year ago. The decrease in supplies for the year 1935 compared with 1934 was 6 percent. There was an increase of 12 percent in the number graded as selects in 1935 with a decrease of 7 percent in those graded as bacon hogs. There is a premium of $1.00 per hog paid for the select bacon type.

Exports of bacon to the United Kingdom increased in November, reachin 11,512,000 pounds, and were 20 percent above exports for the same month of 1934 and 77 percent above October exports. The quantity shipped to the United Kingdom for the 11 months ended November was 117,000,000 pounds, an increase of 6 percent above the same period of 1934 and 70 percent above the same period of 1933.

There has been a fairly large increase in shipments of live hogs to the United States in 1935. In November alone over 2,000 were exported to this country whereas in November 1934 there were no shipments at all. Total shipments to this country during the first 11 months of 1935 reached 10,217 head against 1,008 in the same period of 1934 and only 99 in the corresponding period of 1933 when they were very small.

United Kingdom and Irish Free State

Details of the British cured-pork import quotas for the first 6 weeks of 1936, preliminary figures for which were announced December 10, 193! by the British Board of Trade, have recently been received from Agricultural Attaché C. C. Taylor at London. Adjustments made in the original quotas make it possible for the quota countries to ship at the same rate as during the last quarter of 1935; that is, the adjustments as well as the basic quotas were continued at the rate prevailing from October to December 1935.

The discrepancy between the announced quota and the allowed imports is largely accounted for by the adjustments made in favor of Denmark because of deficiencies in shipments from that country during 1935. Thus, in addition to the Danish quota allotment of 41,182,000 pounds, Danish shippers may export 2,314,000 pounds during the first 6 weeks of this year. This brings the Danish share of 63.5 percent of the unadjusted quota up to 64.57 percent of the adjusted quota. The United States quota of 8 percent, 5,188,000 pounds, plus an adjustment of 0.1 percent, or a total of 5,253,000 pounds, is equal to 7.8 percent of the allowed imports for the January 1 - February 11 period. The countries allotted less than 1 percent of the total quota, which last quarter were granted a share of the Danish undershipments adjustment, are permitted to retain for the first 6 weeks of 1936 this increase in their share of the total quota. (See table, page 9).

The British Pigs Marketing Board is soliciting additional contracts from producers for deliveries of bacon hogs during 1936. The results of this action should be known in the near future, and the Board of Trade will then be in a position to announce quotas for a period beginning February 12.

The tendency of Liverpool bacon prices to decline somewhat during December from the unusually high levels maintained during the 1934-35 season was a continuation of the November price movement. Danish Wiltshire sides averaged $18.09 per hundred pounds for December, a drop of 57 cents per hundred pounds from the November average and of 73 cents from the December 1934 average. Canadian green sides, at $15.34 per hundred pounds, showed a decrease in the monthly average of 70 cents from the November average price and $1.36 from the comparable 1934 average.

Imports of bacon into the United Kingdom from all sources for the first 2 months (October - November) of the 1935-36 season continued fairly steady at the reduced level contemplated for the last quarter of 1935 by the import-control program. At a little over 119,000,000, they showed a 10 percent decrease from comparable 1934 imports. They represented only 52 percent of the imports of October - November 1932, the last 2 months of unrestricted cured-pork imports into the United Kingdom .

Imports from Denmark for October and November stood at approximately 65,000,000 pounds. This figure represents reductions of 12 percent, 29 percent, and 55 percent, respectively, from imports of comparable months of the 1934-35, 1933-34, and 1932-33 seasons. Danish imports this season were about 55 percent of the total imports into the United Kingdom from all sources, as against 56 percent a year ago and 67 percent the same months of the 1931-32 season. The Danish share of total bacon imports from non-Empire countries in the first 2 months of the 1931-32 season stood at 70 percent. In 1932-33 they represented 66 percent, and for the current season 69 percent. The Danish share of total cured pork imported into the United Kingdom from all sources during the first 2 months of the current season, however, was 64.68 percent. This percentage corresponds very closely to the adjusted quota allotted Denmark for the last quarter of 1935. In 1931-32 Denmark supplied 66 percent, and in 1932-33, before the application of the quota system, 62 percent.

Imports of bacon into the United Kingdom from the United States continue negligible. The 350,000 pounds imported during October - November represent a reduction of some 52 percent from the small imports of a year ago and of 99 percent from comparable average 1909-10 to 1913-14 imports. During the latter period, imports from the United States represented around 34 percent of the total imports of bacon into the United Kingdom, whereas, for the current season, United States imports were but 0.3 percent. The American share of total cured-pork imports, including ham, was 4 percent, and of the total non-Empire imports 5 percent, during the first 2 months of the current season.

Imports from Canada during November were the highest for any month since last June and almost 1,400,000 pounds higher than those of a year earlier. For the season to the end of November they stood 5 percent above those of a year ago. Imports for the first 2 months of the 1935-36 season were over nine times as great as imports of October - November 1932, the last 2 months before the inauguration of the quota system. Canada during October and November furnished 12 percent of total imports of bacon, against 1 percent in 1932.

Imports from the Irish Free State in November amounted to 5,400,000 pounds. For the October - November period, they show incresse of 21 percent over.comparable 1934 imports and of 105 p over those of 1932, the year of lowest imports of bacon from the Free State recorded since the War. Imports for the current sea still 30 percent below October - November 1928-29 shipments. Th Free State so far the current season has accounted for 9 percent total imports against 7, 4, and 2 percent, respectively, for the three seasons and 10 percent in October - November 1928-29.

American short cut green ham averaged $20.28 per hundred during December and was the only cured pork to show an increase average price over that of November 1935 and December a year ago Total ham imports for the 1935-36 season to November 30 amounted nearly 10,000,000 pounds, of which about 5,000,000 pounds were s by the United States. Total imports of hams were about 12 perc smaller than the imports in 1934-35 when the United States share 64 percent, and they were 34 percent less than those of 1933-34 the United States shipped 67 percent of the total. In 1929-30, imports of ham into the United Kingdom stood at over 13,000,000 for the months October - November, the United States share being 81 percent of the total.

The price of refined lard on the Liverpool market continue decline slightly from the record level attained during the last months of the 1934-35 season. The December average stood at $1 $1.44 below the November average but $3.88 higher than the compa 1934 average. Lard imports into the United Kingdom continue at greatly reduced levels. At around 25,000,000 pounds for the fir 2 months of the season, they were 50 percent smaller than receipt a year before. The United States furnished only 21 percent of t current season's total, whereas last year American lard represent 89 percent of the total imported. Canada this season supplied nearly 16 percent of the imports, whereas for the calendar years and 1934 that country shipped but 1.5 and 0.45 percent respective About 37 percent of the lard imported into the United Kingdom du October and November came from sources not usually shipping to th market.

United Kingdom: Cured-pork import quotas, January 1 -
February 11, 1936

Country	Basic allocation		Percent- age of total	Adjusted allot- ments	Percent- age of total
	Original unit	Conversion			
	Hundred weight	1,000 pounds	Per- cent	1,000 pounds	Per- cent
Denmark ....:	367,692	41,182	63.50	1/ 43,496	64.57
Netherlands ....:	55,009	6,161	9.50	6,161	9.15
Poland ....:	46,034	5,156	7.95	5,156	7.65
Sweden ....:	27,215	3,048	4.70	3,048	4.52
Lithuania ... .:	17,082	1,913	2.95	1,913	2.84
Estonia . ...:	4,343	487	0.75	2/ 516	0.77
Finland . ...:	2,316	259	0.40	2/ 275	0.41
Latvia .. ..:	4,053	454	0.70	2/ 431	0.71
U.S.S.R. ....:	4,922	551	0.85	2/ 585	0.87
Argentina ....:	4,053	454	0.70	2/ 481	0.71
United States......:	46,323	5,188	8.00	3/ 5,253	7.80
Total.........:	579,042	64,853	100.00	67,365	100.00

Foreign Agricultural Service.
1/ Denmark will be permitted to ship 2,314,000 pounds because of
deficiencies in imports from that country in 1935.
2/ All countries whose quotas are less than 1 percent of the total are
permitted to ship at the rate of 106 percent of their original allotments.
3/ The United States is granted an additional 0.1 percent because of
adjustments made in connection with imports consigned through Canada.

Germany

The official control of German livestock and meat markets in
evidence during the last half of 1935 is being continued and, to some
extent, intensified in 1936. Hog prices at principal markets have not
been permitted to advance beyond fixed maximum levels. The December
average price of heavy hogs at Berlin remained at or near $17.70 per
hundred pounds. Monthly hog slaughter at commercial centers is being
limited to 60 percent of the comparable figures of a year ago. These
and other restrictive measures are being taken to assist in building
up the number of hogs in Germany.

Returns from the hog census as of December 3, 1935, point toward increased market supplies of hogs later this year. Total hog numbers as of that date were still 2 percent below the comparable 1934 total and smaller than in any December in the 5 years, 1930 to 1934. An increase of 28 percent, however, sppeared in the number of bred sows 6 months to 1 year old, while bred sows 1 year old and over showed an increase of 6 percent over the December 1934 figures. The current figure for pigs under 8 weeks showed an increase of 5 percent above the comparable 1934 figures. Young pigs from 8 weeks to 6 months old showed a decline of 5 percent, with all slaughter hogs over 6 months old down 5 percent from the December 1934 figure.

Germany: Number of hogs on December 3, 1935, with comparisons

Year	Farrows under 8 weeks	Pigs 8 weeks to 6 months	6 months to 1 year			Over 1 year			Grand total
			Total	Brood sows		Total	Brood sows		
				Total	In farrow		Total	In farrow	
	Thou-sands	Thou-sands	Thou-sands	Thou-sands	Thou-sands	Thou-sands	Thou-sands	Thou-sands	Thou-sands
1930	5,469	10,035	5,484	674	369	2,455	1,503	942	23,442
1931	5,128	10,484	5,782	494	241	2,414	1,458	870	23,808
1932	4,834	9,884	5,812	485	259	2,329	1,384	851	22,859
1933	5,126	10,353	5,984	549	306	2,427	1,465	923	23,890
1934	4,506	10,030	6,319	451	244	2,270	1,328	832	23,125
1935	4,747	9,542	5,591	541	313	2,850	1,405	880	22,730

Division of Statistical and Historical Research. Compiled from cable from Agricultural Commissioner H. E. Reed and original official sources.

The current reduction in domestic meat supplies, principally pork has stimulated measures to increase the volume of imported livestock and meat. Barter arrangements with other European countries, notably Denmark, Netherlands, and Hungary, provide for a movement into Germany of live hogs and pork, principally fatbacks. The volume of meat represented by these arrangements, however, continues relatively small when compared with the usual amount of pork secured from domestic production.

The general scarcity of all fats in Germany would suggest the necessity of imports on a scale considerably larger than those reflected by current figures. German trade policy with respect to fats, however, continues to limit imports to a restricted volume. Imports of lard in the last few months of 1935 were considerably larger than those of a year earlier, but the United States has scarcely been represented in the trade. Barter agreements with Hungary, Denmark, and Yugoslavia continue to provide most of the imported lard. German lard imports for the first 2 months (October - November) of the 1935-36 season exceeded 21,000,000 pounds against about 10,000,000 pounds a year earlier, and nearly 25,000,000 pounds in the corresponding months of 1933.

Danube Basin

Lard exports during November from the Danube Basin are estimated at about 6,834,260 pounds, which is the second largest monthly lard export made during 1935, according to the Belgrade, Yugoslavia, office of the Foreign Agricultural Service. Of the quantity indicated, about 5,732,000 pounds were supplied by Hungary, mostly to Czechoslovakia and Germany, with a small amount going to England, and 1,102,000 pounds by Yugoslavia, primarily to Germany. The continued small American exports, combined with the seasonal effects of cold weather and the approach of the Christmas holidays, were largely responsible for the further increase in Danubian lard exports. With still larger December exports anticipated, shipments abroad during the calendar year 1935 were expected to mark a post-war record.

According to Hungarian trade sources, import quotas for 70 carloads (about 2,315,000 pounds) of Hungarian melted lard and 30 carloads (about 992,000 pounds) of unrendered fat sides were granted by Germany for December. Continued exports of relatively large quantities to Czechoslovakia also appeared probable, and light Hungarian lard stocks as of December 31, 1935, were in prospect. Extra quotas were granted for December by Czechoslovakia, which facilitated the marketing of both Hungarian and Yugoslav lard and fat sides during that month.

The Danube Basin office of the Bureau of Agricultural Economics estimates that exports of live hogs in December probably were larger than the estimated November exports of 61,500 head. This movement has been stimulated by the granting of additional import quotas by Central European countries, notably Germany and Czechoslovakia. The movement of hog carcasses also has tended to increase in connection with the pork shortages which developed in Germany and Czechoslovakia. Limited quantities of Hungarian hog carcasses also have moved to Belgium in recent weeks. It is reported also that Germany has been buying hog carcasses in Yugoslavia and Rumania.

Hogs and pork products: Indices of foreign supplies and demand

Country and item	Unit	1909-10 to 1913-14 average	1924-25 to 1928-29 average	Oct. - Nov. 1932-33	1933-34	1934-35	1935-36
UNITED KINGDOM-							
Supplies,							
domestic fresh: 1000							
pork,London...:pounds:			13,120	18,527	15,232	15,805	18,751
Imports - :							
Bacon - :							
Denmark.......:	"	39,476	80,800	146,175	92,133	73,995	65,201
Irish F.State:	"		12,380	5,327	6,233	8,981	10,907
United States:	"	27,769	14,857	687	1,353	722	350
Canada ......:	"	5,490	13,845	1,492	13,015	13,028	13,732
Others ......:	"	8,022	24,843	75,086	51,655	35,136	29,128
Total. ....:	"	80,757	146,725	228,768	164,389	131,862	119,317
Ham, total.. .:	"	13,407	17,945	15,495	14,924	11,306	9,871
Lard, total...:	"	40,098	38,144	41,104	48,708	49,514	24,861
DENMARK - :							
Exports - :							
Bacon ....:	"		80,142	138,043	94,330	72,572	69,081
CANADA- :							
Slaughter - :							
Hogs,inspected:1000's:		301	471	439	512	488	519
GERMANY - :							
Production - :							
Hog receipts :							
14 cities....:	"		545	544	522	604	208
Hog slaughter :							
36 centers...:	"	747	671	726	702	800	296
Imports - : 1000							
Bacon, total..:pounds:		537	4,242	7,049	5,011	8,900	4,746
Lard, total...:	"	36,421	35,487	47,817	24,936	9,996	21,048
UNITED STATES - :							
Slaughter - :							
Hogs,inspected:1000's:		5,437	7,302	7,383	7,559	7,569	4,557
Exports - :							
Bacon - : 1000							
United Kingdom pounds:		20,282	8,991	474	530	426	152
Germany .....:		362	2,103	208	878	0	0
Cuba ....:	"	1,257	3,481	645	749	816	167
Total......:	"	28,506	21,421	3,002	4,894	1,777	440
Hams,shoulders-:							
United Kingdom:	"	19,438	20,287	9,595	11,585	8,919	6,748
Total.... .:	"	23,093	24,712	11,266	13,371	10,994	7,794
Lard - :							
United Kingdom:	"	22,125	30,752	38,080	44,495	34,921	7,747
Germany ......:	"	21,980	23,920	29,106	24,835	872	524
Cuba ....:	"	5,791	13,003	11,099	1,951	7,135	1,983
Netherlands...:	"	5,165	5,216	6,200	8,770	9	0
Total......:	"	69,073	102,541	89,470	97,375	46,609	10,663

Hogs and pork products: Foreign and domestic average prices per 100
pounds for the month indicated, and stocks at the end
of each month

Item	1909–1913 average	1925–1929 average	Nov. 1934	Oct. 1935	Nov. 1935
	Dollars	Dollars	Dollars	Dollars	Dollars
PRICES –					
Hogs, Chicago, basis packers' and shippers' quotations.....:	7.48	9.98	5.66	9.83	9.31
Corn, Chicago, No. 3 Yellow...:	1.07	1.50	1.48	1.46	1.11
Hogs, heavy Berlin live weight ....:	12.05	16.47	17.91	18.78	17.70
Barley, Leipzig ....:	1.68	2.21	2.99	3.12	3.15
Lard –					
Chicago ....:	10.92	14.74	11.75	16.00	14.38
Liverpool . ...:	12.50	14.17	10.44	16.94	16.50
Hamburg ....:	14.46	14.97	19.75	17.07	16.09
Cured pork –					
Liverpool –					
American short cut green hams ....:	14.70	24.89	18.93	21.52	20.13
American green bellies....:		21.90	Nominal	Nominal	Nominal
Danish Wiltshire sides....:	14.80	23.47	19.17	20.00	18.66
Canadian green sides......:	14.02	21.76	17.91	18.73	16.04
	1,000 pounds	1,000 pounds	1,000 pounds	1,000 pounds	1,000 pounds
STOCKS –					
United States –					
Processed pork 1/..... ...:			428,894	569,664	240,663	252,927
Lard in cold storage ......:			52,476	103,988	40,702	37,530

1/ Dry salt-cured, and in process of cure; pickled, cured, and in process
of cure; and frozen.

- - 0 - -

Annual Pig Crop

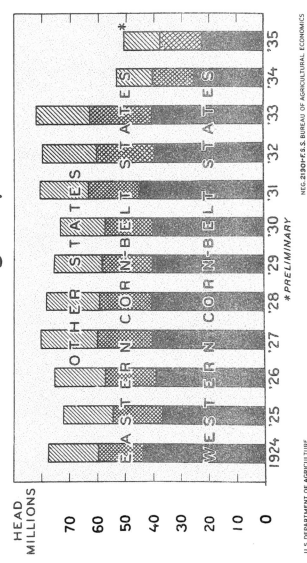

HOG SITUATION

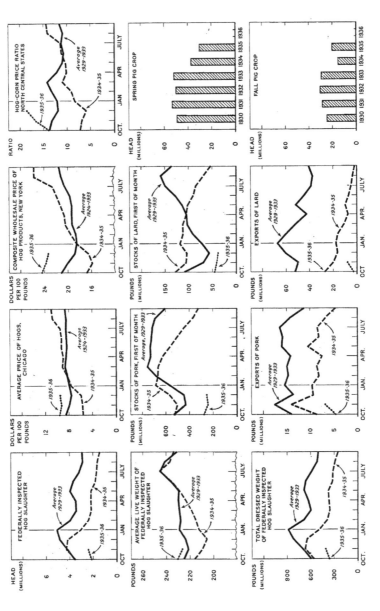

U.S. DEPARTMENT OF AGRICULTURE   NEG. 29720   BUREAU OF AGRICULTURAL ECONOMICS

HP-75

February 29, 1936.

WORLD HOG AND PORK PROSPECTS

Quarterly Summary

Hog production is now beginning to increase in Denmark and the United States, the two leading surplus hog producing countries, after declining in both countries during the last 2 years. In Germany and the Netherlands, also, some increase in production apparently is in prospect, but in most other Continental European countries hog numbers are not likely to increase during the first half of 1936. Substantial increases in hog numbers in the first half of 1935 were reported in the Danube Basin and in Great Britain. Decreases were reported during this period in Poland and Czechoslovakia.

Larger numbers of pigs are now being produced in the United States, and a material increase in hog slaughter in 1936 is probable. In Denmark and the Netherlands the increase in hog production and hog slaughter may be limited by production control measures, and in Germany the shortage of feed supplies may prevent a large increase in hog production. In the Danube Basin larger supplies of hogs for slaughter and export are probable in the first half of the present year.

The shortage of fats continues to be an important feature in the German hog situation. Although import duties on fats were reduced and imports of lard and butter were increased in the last half of 1935, such imports have not been sufficient to offset the decline in domestic production of fats. Despite the increased imports in the last half of the year, total imports of lard into Germany in 1935 were much below average. Most of the German lard imports in 1935 came from the Danube Basin and Denmark and were made possible by compensation or clearing agreements. The foreign exchange

situation, together with the decreased production of hogs in the United
States due to the drought, prevented large imports of American lard into
Germany. In 1935 a considerable part of the German imports of fats and oils
consisted of whale oil, but imports of this oil in 1936 will be reduced,
since world supplies of whale oil have been sharply curtailed. In 1936 an
increase in supplies of both domestic and imported lard in Germany seems
likely, as do a decrease in domestic supplies of butter and an increase in
butter imports.

According to official announcement, the permitted imports of bacon
and hams into Great Britain from non-Empire sources in March and April will
be at a rate slightly higher than the rate prevailing in January and February.
It now seems probable that the British quota system for cured pork will be
continued during the present year, after which it is proposed that, as a
substitute for the quota, a tariff be levied on bacon and hams for the purpose
of assisting British pig producers. Under this proposal a preferential rate
of duty would be granted to Empire countries. Imported supplies of bacon
and hams in Great Britain have been reduced about 35 percent in the 3 years
since 1932 in which the quota system has been in effect.

United States exports of both pork and lard were greatly reduced
in 1935, the total exports for the year being the smallest in several decades.
This marked reduction in exports resulted chiefly from the large decrease
in hog slaughter which was brought about by the severe drought in 1934.
However, domestic slaughter supplies of hogs in January increased considerably
and continued increases during the remainder of 1936 and in 1937 are probable.
It is expected, therefore, that exports of both pork and lard will increase
materially in the next 2 years.

Hog Numbers

The greatly increased interest in hog breeding and the present favorable hog-feed ratio in several important hog producing countries indicates an increase in hog numbers by midsummer of 1936 as compared with the low level reached in the summer of 1935. Although the actual number of hogs on hand in Germany and the Netherlands at the beginning of 1936 was somewhat smaller than at the same time a year ago, an increase of 12 percent in bred sows in Germany has been reported. In Denmark, the number of hogs on hand at the beginning of 1936 (December 28, 1935) was 3,216,000, an increase of 6 percent above a year earlier. There was an increase of 17 percent in bred sows, indicating a still further increase in numbers this year. The Netherlands also showed an increase of 3 percent in bred sows in November 1935 compared with a year earlier. In midsummer of 1935 hog numbers were the smallest in years in the United States, Canada, Denmark, and Netherlands, which countries furnished approximately 90 percent of the world exports of pork and pork products during the 5-year period 1925-1929.

The number of hogs in Germany 1/, the principal continental deficit country at the end of 1935, was only 22,699,000, a decrease of 2 percent below the same date of 1934. A large increase of 28 percent in bred sows of 6 months and over and a 7 percent increase in those above 1 year indicates an increase in market supplies in 1936. Czechoslovakia, another important deficit country, showed some decrease in 1935 from the high level reached in 1934. However, there has been a sharp increase in numbers in the United Kingdom since 1933, in accordance with the British policy of the last few years of encouraging home production by limiting imports. The number in the United Kingdom by midsummer 1935 had reached 4,526,000, an increase of 29 percent above 2 years earlier.

Hog numbers in 14 deficit and surplus producing countries in midsummer 1935 are estimated at 49,522,000, a reduction of 5 percent as compared with 1934. In 8 surplus European countries there was an increase of 1 percent, due chiefly to the increases in the Irish Free State and Hungary. The United States is not included in these totals owing to the lack of a midsummer estimate. The number of pigs saved from December 1 to June 1 in 1934 and 1935, however, was only about 73 percent and 58 percent respectively of the number saved in the same period of 1933.

The 6 deficit European countries reporting showed a reduction in hog numbers to 27,994,000 in midsummer 1935, a decrease of 9 percent compared with the same date of 1934, the reductions being chiefly in Germany and Czechoslovakia. (See the table on page 4 for details by countries.)

1/ These figures exclude the Saar, as comparable estimates are not given for earlier years for bred sows. See the table on page 24 for estimates including and excluding the Saar for other classes.

Hogs: Numbers in specified surplus and deficit countries
in midsummer 1935, with comparisons

Country	Date of estimate	1931	1932	1933	1934	1935
		Thousands	Thousands	Thousands	Thousands	Thousands
SURPLUS COUNTRIES						
Non-European						
United States 1/..	June 1	53,622	50,342	52,089	37,807	30,402
Canada	"	4,717	3,639	3,801	3,654	3,549
European						
Irish Free State...	"	1,227	1,108	931	968	1,088
Denmark, in rural communities	July 15	5,453	4,886	2/ 4,407	3,061	3,034
Netherlands	May-June	2,434	2,244	(2,100)	3/2,022	4/ 1,629
Poland	June	7,321	5,844	5,753	7,053	6,703
Hungary	July	2,715	2,361	1,899	2,502	3,176
Latvia	June	712	582	586	686	802
Estonia	Summer	323	303	277	282	289
Lithuania	June 30	1,569	1,390	1,306	1,288	1,258
Total 8 surplus European countries reporting to 1935		21,754	18,718	17,259	17,862	17,979
DEFICIT COUNTRIES						
England and Wales ...	June 1	2,783	3,185	3,069	3,320	3,812
Scotland ....,....	"	162	165	167	206	256
Northern Ireland	"	236	220	271	380	458
Total United Kingdom	"	3,181	3,570	3,507	3,906	4,526
Germany	"	22,529	21,289	21,174	22,368	20,042
Czechoslovakia	July 1	5/ 3,088	3,082	3,314	3,888	3,016
Norway	June	317	304	319	550	410
Total 6 deficit European countries reporting to 1935		29,115	28,245	28,314	30,712	27,994
Total 14 surplus and deficit countries reporting to 1935, including Canada		55,586	50,602	49,374	52,230	49,522

Division of Statistical and Historical Research. Compiled from reports of United
States Department of Agriculture officials abroad, official sources and the
International Institute of Agriculture. Figures in parentheses interpolated.

1/ Spring pig crop, i.e., number of pigs saved December 1 - June 1.
2/ June 20.
3/ By August 1934 the number had fallen to 1,875,000.
4/ August.
5/ Census May 1930.

Summary of International Trade in Live Hogs and Hog Products

The international trade in live hogs and hog products fell to a new low level in 1935 and was 22 percent smaller than in 1934. There was an increase in exports of live hogs but a further large decrease in exports of hog products. The combined export of hog products and live hogs, converted to a meat basis, from the principal European surplus producing countries and the United States and Canada is estimated at approximately 1,306,000,000 pounds compared with 1,676,000,000 pounds in 1934 and 2,047,000,000 pounds in 1933.

Exports of hog products, as such, from the six most important European surplus producing countries in 1935 totaled 834,000,000 pounds, a reduction of 2 percent compared with 1934. This decrease was small compared with the reduction of 24 percent between 1933 and 1934 and 22 percent between 1932 and 1933. The quantity exported from these countries in 1935 was only 55 percent of that exported in 1931. There was an increase, however, in exports of live hogs from European surplus producing countries. In 1935 the number amounted to 873,000 head, an increase of 28 percent above 1934. The combined export from eight European countries of hog products and live hogs converted to a meat basis is estimated at 974,000,000 pounds, or about 1 percent above 1934.

The quantity of hog products exported from Denmark declined 6 percent between 1934 and 1935 and those from the Netherlands, 11 percent. Exports from these two important surplus countries, combined, last year constituted only 51 percent of exports in 1931. On the other hand, exports increased 18 percent from the Irish Free State and 66 percent from Hungary between 1934 and 1935, the latter mostly lard and fat backs. The greatest increase in live hog exports in 1935 was from the Danube basin countries, going principally to Germany and Italy.

There was a further marked decline in exports of hog products from the United States, which fell to the very low level of 186,000,000 pounds in 1935 compared with 585,000,000 pounds in 1934 and an average of 1,121,000,000 pounds for the 5-year period 1925-1929. On the other hand, exports from Canada increased 18 percent in 1935 to reach 146,000,000 pounds. This increase was due principally to the fact that the United Kingdom has not restricted imports of pork from the British Dominions.

In 1935, the United Kingdom and Germany imported only 1,311,000,000 pounds of hog products, as such, a decrease of 17 percent compared with 1934. In 1932 the imports into these two countries reached 2,045,000,000 pounds. Pork production in these two countries has increased substantially in the past 2 years. Production in the United Kingdom and Irish Free State has increased from 964,000,000 pounds in 1931-32 to 1,045,000,000 pounds in 1934-35, or 8 percent, whereas production in Germany has increased from 4,364,000,000 pounds in 1932 to approximately 5,000,000,000 pounds in 1935, or 15 percent. (See tables for details by countries.)

orts from principal European surplus producing
countries, 1928-1935

Nether-: lands 1/	Irish : Free :State 1/	Sweden 1/	Poland 1/ 2/	Hungary 3/	Total 4/
Million pounds	Million pounds	Million pounds	Million pounds	Million pounds	Million pounds
274	116	51	49	11	1,151
203	96	45	52	14	1,006
210	78	64	78	22	1,100
286	85	68	161	12	1,510
258	61	50	138	8	1,438
194	55	48	101	14	1,123
126	71	44	59	32	853
112	84	31	6/ 62	53	834

l and Historical Research. Compiled from official
ts submitted by United States Department of Agricult
annual figures include: Pork, fresh, canned, pickl
and sides, Wiltshire sides, hams and shoulders, lard
l lard, hog casings, lard in heads and feet.
ish market.   2/ Corrected figures for Poland.
ria, Czechoslovakia, and Italy now. Previous to 192
market for fresh pork.   4/ Including corrected
   5/ Preliminary.   6/ Estimate for year based on
onths of 1935 compared with same period of 1934.

ports into principal deficit European countries,
1928-1935

many:	France:	Czecho- slo- vakia	Austria	Belgium	Italy	Total
Million pounds	Million pounds	Million pounds	Million pounds	Million pounds	Million pounds	Millio pound
241	102	72	31	20	30	1,92
276	58	79	39	36	29	1,92
238	78	60	23	35	11	1,94
266	72	60	21	47	3	2,17
325	30	45	20	39	16	2,19
229	35	34	13	34	12	1,92
152	12	30	6	14	9	1,66
/132						

and Historical Research. Compiled from official
exports for items included.
Estimate for year based on exports for first 11
with same period of 1934.

Commercial Hog Slaughter

Commercial hog slaughter in 20 important surplus and deficit countries for 1935 is estimated at 68,000,000 head, a decrease of 23 percent or 20,000,000 fewer hogs slaughtered than in 1934. The reduction as compared with 1933 was 24 percent. Hog slaughter was smaller in both surplus and deficit countries in 1935 than in 1934.

The reduction in slaughter in the 12 surplus countries was 30 percent, representing about 18,000,000 hogs. There was a reduction of 37 percent in non-European surplus producing countries to 31,000,000 head, owing chiefly to a 41 percent reduction in Federally inspected slaughter in the United States. Australia and New Zealand were the only countries in this group to show increases. Seven European surplus hog producing countries showed a reduction of only 3 percent in hog slaughter to 11,400,000 head in 1935 compared with the preceding year, but a reduction of 14 percent as compared with 1933.

The reduction in slaughter in 8 deficit European countries in 1935 is estimated at approximately 5 percent, representing about 2,000,000 fewer hogs killed than in 1934. The estimated number slaughtered in the 8 countries was about 26,000,000 head. All of the deficit countries, including Germany, showed decreases except the United Kingdom where slaughter increased 13 percent. The decrease in Germany for the year is estimated at 6 percent or about 1,165,000 head.

United States

With the ratio of hog prices to corn prices continuing much above average it seems probable that the increase in the number of sows to farrow in the spring of 1936 will be at least as large as the 24 percent increase over 1935 indicated by the December 1935 Pig Crop Report, and perhaps larger. Thus, a large increase in hog slaughter in 1936-37 is likely. During the summer of 1936 commercial hog slaughters supplies probably will be much larger, possibly 35 to 40 percent, than a year earlier. This increase in summer slaughter will reflect not only the increase in the 1935 fall pig crop but also an increase in the marketings of packing sows which will farrow in the spring of 1936. Average weights of hogs slaughtered in the remainder of the 1935-36 marketing year probably will continue much heavier than a year earlier.

Hog prices advanced materially after early January, when the hog processing tax was invalidated. Although slaughter supplies increased substantially in the second and third weeks of the month, the rise in prices was well maintained in this period. As supplies were reduced in late January and early February prices again advanced, and in the second week of February the top price at Chicago reached $11.15, the highest price paid at that market since last October. The average price of hogs at Chicago for the month of January was $9.85 compared with $9.57 in December and $7.70 in January last year. The rise in prices from early January to early February was greater on heavy hogs and packing sows than on light hogs, prices of packing sows and heavy butcher hogs rising from $1.00 to $1.25 per 100 pounds and those of light hogs from 60 to 80 cents.

Hog slaughter under Federal inspection in January
head, was about 19 percent larger than in December, the
period being much greater than usual.   In January, for
October 1934, inspected hog slaughter exceeded that of t
month a year earlier. A large part of the increase in s
January was due to the unusual price advance in that per
probable that marketings had been delayed somewhat in Nc
because of the favorable feeding situation and that some
slaughter in January would have occurred even without th
advance. The unusually large increase, however, probabl
shift to January of hogs that under more normal conditio
marketed in February. Average weights of hogs marketed
only slightly heavier than in December, but they were co
than in January 1935. The average weight at the seven l
232 pounds, which was 19 pounds heavier than a year earl

Corn prices advanced slightly in January. The Un
farm price of corn on January 15 was 53.5 cents per bush
53 cents on December 15 and 85.3 cents on the correspond
Based on farm prices in the North Central States, the ho
in January was 18.9, the highest ratio for the month on
January last year this ratio was 8.4.   It should be rec
that the present corn supply is much below average in qu
lower farm price of corn this year than last is partly d
quality of corn.

The large increase in slaughter supplies of hogs
of January resulted in a marked decline in the prices of
The decline in prices of cured pork continued into Febru
fresh pork advanced somewhat in late January and early F
the decline in the first half of January. The composite
of hog products at New York in January was $21.92 per 10
with $23.28 in December and $18.54 for the corresponding
The wholesale price of lard declined considerably in Jan
price of refined lard at Chicago dropped from $13.25 per
last week of December to $12.25 in the last week of Janu

Total exports of pork in December showed a materi
those in November, while lard exports showed only a slig
period. Exports of both pork and lard in December, howe
smaller than those of a year earlier. Shipments of lard
ports increased in January compared with those of a mont
pork shipments were reduced. Shipments of both pork and
continued small in relation to those of the correspondin

Exports of hams and shoulders in December, amount
pounds, were 24 percent smaller than in November, but th
percent greater than the exports of December 1934. The
November to December was due chiefly to the smaller ship
Kingdom, the chief foreign market for these products. E
December amounted to 278,000 pounds. Although this figu
that of a month earlier, it is much smaller than that of
of any other December on record.

Pork and lard: Exports from the United States, 1900-1935

Year	Pork 1/	Lard 2/	Year	Pork 1/	Lard 2/
	1,000 pounds	1,000 pounds		1,000 pounds	1,000 pounds
1900 ....:	849,305	609,473	:1918 ...:	1,695,908	555,125
1901 ....:	860,005	607,266	:1919 ...:	1,854,863	783,859
1902 ....:	640,600	504,161	:1920 ...:	901,406	635,488
1903 ....:	560,283	535,376	:1921 ...:	738,345	892,892
1904 ....:	575,221	563,521	:1922 ...:	700,195	787,447
1905 ....:	669,060	701,679	:1923 ...:	928,959	1,059,510
1906 ....:	715,698	678,232	:1924 ...:	702,812	971,460
1907 ....:	597,487	589,268	:1925 ...:	519,435	707,683
1908 ....:	611,233	581,934	:1926 ...:	402,665	717,077
1909 ....:	464,472	458,261	:1927 ...:	282,500	701,699
1910 ....:	306,204	379,108	:1928 ...:	301,247	783,472
1911 ....:	447,931	604,979	:1929 ...:	343,684	847,868
1912 ....:	431,470	552,649	:1930 ...:	277,352	656,018
1913 ....:	446,163	575,492	:1931 ...:	159,876	578,296
1914 ....:	368,476	459,813	:1932 ...:	116,280	552,154
1915 ....:	884,424	486,676	:1933 ...:	142,035	584,238
1916 ....:	1,000,041	453,924	:1934 ...:	150,542	434,892
1917 ....:	917,611	382,145	:1935 ...:	88,630	97,359

Division of Statistical and Historical Research, Bureau of Agricultural Economics. Compiled from Monthly Summary of Foreign Commerce of the United States, December issues, and Foreign Commerce and Navigation of the United States.
1/ Includes bacon, hams and shoulders, and pork (canned, fresh, and pickled.) Lard oil included from 1900 to 1924.
2/ Includes neutral lard from 1910 to 1935.

' Exports of lard in December, totaling 7,900,000 pounds, slightly less than in November, but much smaller than in Decemł Most of the lard exported in December was consigned to the Unił Cuba. In January the sale of about 4,0'0,000 pounds of America Germany was unofficiall reported. This quantity is in excess States exports of lard to that country for the entire year of 1 the German import duty on lard was lowered several months ago, on foreign exchange had previously made impossible any large in American lard into Germany.

Exports of pork for the calendar year 1935 totaled about pounds compared with about 151,000,000 pounds in 1934. A large decrease was accounted for by the marked reduction in shipments frozen pork. Lard exports in 1935 amounted to 97,000,000 pound with about 435,000,000 pounds in 1934. Exports of both pork an 1935 were the smallest in many years, perhaps the smallest on r decrease in exports of hog products in 1935 was largely a resul drop in hog slaughter following the severe drought of 1934. A the annual exports of pork and lard from 1900 to 1935 is given Figure 2 which appears at the end of this publication, shows th graphically for the entire 36-year period.

Canada

The average price of bacon hogs at Toronto for January 19 $8.62 per 100 pounds American currency compared with $8.58 in Ja $8.07 in January 1934 and only $3.29 in January 1933. Supplies, by the number graded at stock yards and packing plants during th period ended January 30 amounted to 261,000 head and was 6,000 l during the similar 4-week period of December. According to the Government's Monthly Livestock and Meat Trade Review, it is expe increased marketings will materialize from Ontario in the early 1936 while Quebec will maintain its present level of marketings. recovery in the movement of supplies from the Prairie Provinces in the latter half of the year.

Gradings of live hogs for the year 1935 at all stockyards packing plants numbered 2,854,000, a decrease of 6 percent compa 1934 and the smallest number graded since 1931. The total numbe in Canada has decreased in each of the past 4 years from 4,717,C 1931 to only 3,549,000 in June 1935.

There has been a fairly large increase in the number of ł as selects, which produce the quality of bacon preferred in the market. In 1935 the number graded into the principal classifica with the percentage of 1934 given in parentheses was as follows: bacon hogs, 654,019 (113); bacon hogs, 1,201,036 (93); butcher (81); lights and feeders, 238,581 (87). Despite a decrease of in the total number graded there was an increase of 13 percent i number graded as selects.

As the price of hogs in Canada is dependent to such a large extent on the quantity and quality of bacon exported to the British market, two of the major problems of Canadian hog raisers are to improve the type of hog produced and to maintain the favorable position on the British market provided for in the Ottawa Agreement which went into effect in January 1933. Since that date the price of bacon hogs has risen over $5.00 per 100 pounds. By the terms of the Ottawa Agreement Canada was permitted entry into Great Britain of 280,000,000 pounds of bacon annually, which represents about 2,500,000 hogs. This agreement expires in December 1937. Exports of bacon from Canada to the United Kingdom in 1935 reached 124,000,000 pounds, an increase of 4 percent above 1934 and 72 percent above 1933. In 1932, before the Ottawa Agreement went into effect and before British bacon imports from non-Empire sources were restricted, only 31,000,000 pounds of bacon were sent to the British market. The bulk of bacon shipments from Canada has always gone to the United Kingdom, the largest exports being 241,000,000 pounds in 1919. Lard exports to the United Kingdom from Canada also increased greatly in 1935 reaching 13,772,000 pounds compared with only 911,000 pounds in 1934 and about 5,000,000 pounds in 1932.

There was a considerable increase in exports of live hogs to the United States in 1935, the number being 14,999 compared with about 1,000 in 1934. The bulk of these were sent in the last half of the year, the number in December alone being 4,783. In 1927 however, Canada exported 195,000 hogs to this country and in 1914 the number reached 215,000. Exports of pork to the United States in 1935 amounted to 3,866,000 pounds compared with only 156,000 pounds in 1934. The largest exports of pork to this country occurred in 1927 when they reached 16,000,000 pounds. Bacon and lard exports to the United States were negligible in 1935.

United Kingdom and Irish Free State

The British cured-pork import allotment to all quota countries has been placed at 922,282 hundredweight (103,296,000 pounds) for the period February 26 to April 30, according to cabled advices from Agricultural Attache' C. C. Taylor at London. The new figure represents a weekly allotment of nearly 11,500,000 pounds against the adjusted rate of approximately 11,200,000 pounds in effect since January 1. The new United States quota is placed at 74,705 hundredweight (8,367,000 pounds). The new rate represents a 6 percent increase over the former one of 875,000 pounds, and continues to represent 8.1 percent of the quota.

The current quota follows an extension over the first 8 weeks of 1936 of the quota rates in effect during the last 3 months of 1935. This second short quota period suggests incomplete returns from the 1936 campaign to place more hogs under contract to bacon factories, and continued uncertainty as to the future supply of domestic bacon hogs. While the current quota rate is slightly higher than that of the January 1 - February 25 period, it still represents a decline of about 9 percent from the rate prevailing at this time last year.

So far, the quota system has not brought the desired results, according to the London and Berlin representatives of the Foreign Agricultural Service. It is apparent that quotas on cured and frozen pork will be continued during 1936, but a policy of more liberal allowances is under consideration to follow the termination of trade agreements which now prevent the imposition of a tariff on non-Empire bacon. Such a duty, for which 10s. per hundredweight (2.2 cents per pound) is tentatively suggested, with preferential rates to Empire countries, would be known as a levy, and would be used to subsidize domestic hog producers. Meanwhile, the total foreign bacon and ham quota continues to be determined by deducting estimated Empire supplies and the contracted domestic production from the annual "normal consumption" figure of 10,670,000 hundredweight (1,195,000,000 pounds). The present world hog situation is regarded as more favorable for a modification of the quota restrictions than in other recent years.

The decline in world hog production during 1934 and 1935 was not reflected in prices paid to British producers. Continuing the downward trend which started in April 1934, when bacon prices were incorporated in the formula for determining contract hog prices, the contract hog prices reached a low of 10/2 per 20 pounds (12.66 cents per pound) dead weight in October, recovered to 11/2 (13.9 cents) in November, the month in which new contracts are made, and again dropped to 10/2 (12.66 cen s) in December. In January 1936 a new low of 9/11 (12.35 cents) was paid for contract hogs. Advancing bacon prices in January, however, should result in an increased contract price in February.

Producers have contracted about 2,000,000 hogs for delivery to curers in 1936. The 1935 figure was 1,854,249, an increase of 15.5 percent over 1934. It is reported that an additional 750,000 hogs must be put under contract to guarantee curers 72 percent of their stated requirements for 1936. In view of the difficulty entailed in securing sufficient numbers of contract hogs, it is suggested that the Pigs Marketing Board will contract with the curers for the required numbers and then default. That procedure would allow curers to buy in the open market, as was done in 1935 to secure 140,000 head, and again in the first 6 weeks of 1936.

The stronger British market for imported bacon in January resulted in Danish Wiltshire sides making an average of $19.43 per hundred pounds. That average was on advance of $1.34 over the December figure, but still 24 cents below the comparable figure of a year ago and 57 cents under the October average. Canadian green sides reached $16.45 per hundred pounds for the January average, over $1.00 higher than the average for the previous month. The december 1934 comparable figure was $17.46. American green bellies were quoted in January at $15.19 per hundred pounds. This was the first quotation on this product since last July. The January 1935 average was $15.55.

Imports of bacon from Denmark during December, at nearly 35,000,000 pounds, brought the total imports from that country for the first quarter of the 1935-36 season to over 100,000,000 pounds. During the comparable 1931-32 period, imports of Danish bacon stood at over 221,000,000 pounds, or 120 percent above the 1935-36 figure. Danish imports for the current season to December 31 represented 55 percent of the total as against 68 percent in the first quarter of 1931-32. Imports from the Netherlands have been almost as sharply reduced during the last few years as have those from Denmark. At a little less than 13,000,000 pounds for the current season to the end of December 31, 1935, they represented a reduction from comparable imports of 1932-33, the high point for Dutch imports into the United Kingdom, of 70 percent. Imports of bacon from other foreign sources amounted to a little over 45,000,000 pounds for the first quarter of the 1935-36 season. This represents a reduction of 57 percent from comparable imports of the 1932-33 season.

Bacon imports from Canada for the first quarter of the current season were about 1,200,000 pounds less than those for the first quarter of 1934-35, but were still over 2,650,000 pounds above the 1933-34 imports. Imports from the Irish Free State this season are well above those of last season, representing for the period October-December 1935 an increase of 13 percent over the imports for the first quarter of 1934-35. Imports of bacon from the United States remain unimportant, amounting for the first 3 months of the current season to 600,000 pounds as against 1,225,000 pounds for the first 3 months of the 1934-35 season and an average for comparable months of 1909-10 to 1913-14 of 44,343,000 pounds.

Total bacon imports into the United Kingdom from all sources reached only 183,700,000 pounds for the period October-December 1935, as against over 200,000,000 pounds the first quarter of last season and over 324,000,000 pounds during the comparable 1931-32 period. The 1935-36 figures represent a reduction of 43 percent from the high point reached in 1931-32.

The quota system has now been in operation for a full 3 years. A review of bacon imports during this time shows a progressive decline from the 1933 calendar-year high of 1,017,448,000 pounds. Imports from all sources for the calendar year 1934 amounted to but 851,005,000 pounds, representing a reduction of 16 percent. The reduction in allowed imports from non-Empire countries amounted to 24 percent. Empire countries, however, not only were not required to cut down their shipments, but were allowed to increase them, the result being an advance of 18 percent over shipments of the previous year.

Quota reductions, and consequent import reductions, in 1935 were less drastic than they had been during 1934. Imports from all sources reached 775,673,000 pounds for the year, amounting to 91 percent of the comparable figures for 1934. British Empire countries continued to increase their share in the total, but at a less rapid rate. In 1935 such imports amounted to 154,318,000 pounds, 20 percent of the total, against 141,461,000 pounds, 17 percent of the total in 1934, and only 79,673,000 pounds, 8 percent in 1933.

The January average price of American short cut green hams stood at $19.23 per 100 pounds, which represented a continuation of the decline in evidence since July 1935 and was over $1.00 below the January 1935 average.

Ham imports from the United States for the first quarter of the current season reached 9,422,000 pounds. This amount was equal to but 90 percent of the United States imports for the first quarter of the 1933-34 period and but 45 percent of the comparable 1929-30 imports. Total ham imports for the October-December period were about 9,000 pounds above comparable imports of the 1934-35 season, though they represented a 26-percent decline from imports of the same period in 1931-32. Sharply increased imports from the Empire countries, especially from Canada, account for the slight increase in ham imports during the first quarter of the season over those of the same period a year earlier.

Ham imports into the United Kingdom from all sources have declined at about the same rate as have bacon imports since the inauguration of the quota system. The 1935 ham imports amounted to 75,799,000 pounds or 93 percent of the 1934 total. During this period the Empire countries not only increased their share in the total imports but also in the actual amount imported; therefore, the reduction in ham imports from foreign sources was 13 percent. The 1934 total of 81,567,000 pounds from all sources represented a decline of 16 percent from the 1933 figures. The share of total ham imports furnished by Empire countries, however, was not reduced correspondingly. The reduction in imports from foreign sources caused by the enforced limitation of imports under the quota system was nearly 21 percent.

Refined lard quotations on the British market for the month of January averaged only $13.48 per 100 pounds. This figure is $1.58 below the December average and the lowest since last May. The January price, however, was 50 cents higher than the January 1935 price.

Imports of lard from the United States for the current season to December 31 amounted to only 9,000,000 pounds, a reduction from comparable 1934-35 figures of 84 percent. Total imports for the first quarter, of the current season at a little less than 35,000,000 pounds were 48 percent less than the October-December 1934 imports. Lard imports into the United Kingdom for the calendar year 1935 at less than 172,000,000 pounds were the smallest in many years, monthly imports throughout the entire year being about one-half the size of average imports during comparable months of the 5 previous years. The unusually small monthly receipts of lard were due almost entirely to the shortage of American supplies available for export.

Supplies of British and Irish fresh pork at London Central Markets during December were over 1,200,000 pounds above comparable 1934 figures. The total for the first quarter of the 1935-36 season at 28,300,000 pounds stood 17 percent above those for the first quarter of the 1934-35 season. The requirements of the fresh pork market continue to hinder the program for placing hogs under contract to bacon curers. The frozen pork quota for the United States during the first quarter of 1936 has been set at 4,584,000 pounds, of which about 258,000 pounds may be used for curing in the United Kingdom.

United Kingdom: Arrivals of Wiltshire sides in Great Britain
from continental countries, by weeks, 1934-35 and
1935-36 1/

Week ended	Danish at all ports	At London					Canadian at all ports
		Danish	Swedish	Dutch	Polish	Lithu-anian	
	Bales	Bales	Bales	Bales	Bales	Bales	Bales
Season 1934-35							
Oct.-June :	1,371,057	715,747	57,881	94,384	101,352	54,453	282,203
July 5 ....:	35,610	18,553	940	2,390	3,140	1,772	6,815
12 ....:	38,408	21,423	1,402	2,310	2,728	1,955	6,031
19 ....:	39,027	21,906	1,391	2,335	2,809	2,000	5,803
26 ....:	39,658	21,997	1,429	2,566	2,679	2,030	5,556
Aug. 2 ....:	40,007	21,745	1,476	2,757	3,346	2,017	6,107
9 ....:	39,986	21,484	1,815	2,785	2,583	2,041	5,950
16 ....:	39,483	21,249	1,526	2,879	3,802	2,000	4,603
23 ....:	39,295	20,553	1,504	2,818	3,011	1,979	4,054
30 ....:	39,076	20,996	1,420	2,929	3,816	1,973	5,150
Sept. 6 ...:	35,336	19,092	1,261	3,043	2,943	1,600	4,773
13 ...:	35,920	19,020	1,239	2,871	3,938	1,471	4,291
20 ...:	36,037	18,285	1,285	2,606	3,670	1,420	3,656
27 ...:	37,675	19,084	1,312	2,435	3,416	1,456	2,985
Totals for 1934-35 season ....:	1,966,575	981,134	75,881	129,108	143,233	78,167	347,977
1933-34 ...:	2,104,022	1,130,173	88,633	134,731	176,164	150,296	335,299
Season 1935-36							
Oct. 4.....:	38,389	19,814	1,348	2,326	3,635	1,394	2,754
11 ....:	32,332	16,271	1,223	2,014	3,225	1,509	2,694
18 ....:	32,306	16,493	1,309	1,180	3,539	1,450	3,622
25 ....:	32,759	17,028	1,154	1,806	2,791	1,795	4,006
Nov. 1 ....:	33,482	17,423	1,262	1,857	3,076	2,089	5,175
8 ....:	31,766	16,504	1,200	2,231	2,327	1,926	6,658
15 ....:	32,221	17,368	1,328	2,276	2,639	1,568	6,414
22 ....:	31,285	16,327	1,371	2,229	2,024	1,673	6,580
29 ....:	31,095	15,927	1,445	3,116	2,529	1,803	6,609
Dec. 6 ....:	31,321	16,187	1,441	3,024	2,167	1,975	5,202
13 ....:	33,283	17,505	1,430	2,660	2,740	1,688	5,296
20 ....:	37,590	19,096	1,465	3,320	2,628	1,840	6,586
27 ....:	26,543	13,189	710	1,784	2,308	2,382	4,335
Jan. 3 ....:	29,554	14,916	1,386	1,599	2,216	---	6,024
10 ....:	30,174	15,650	1,153	1,745	2,866	2,565	6,938
17 ....:	31,790	15,929	1,429	1,929	2,210	2,075	7,234
24 ....:	31,944	16,022	1,288	1,754	2,582	2,450	6,730
Totals to date:							
1935-36 :	547,834	281,649	21,942	35,850	45,502	30,182	92,857
1934-35 ..:	591,806	310,848	28,280	40,899	44,778	24,174	115,101

Transmitted by the London, England, office of the Foreign Agricultural Service.
1/ London Provision Exchange. Sides are packed 4 or 6 to the bale, according
to weight of sides. The most popular bale is that carrying 4 sides with the
total weight ranging 220-260 pounds.

United Kingdom: Total bacon imports, by months, 1928-29 to 1935-36

Month	1928-29	1929-30	1930-31	1931-32	1932-33	1933-34	1934-35	1935-36
	1,000 pounds	1,000 pounds	1,000 pounds	1,000 pounds	1,000 pounds	1,000 pounds	1,000 pounds	1,000 pounds
Oct.	82,378	72,402	95,809	109,051	114,310	83,272	65,537	58,170
Nov.	79,297	74,868	86,316	105,372	114,458	81,117	66,325	61,147
Dec.	76,771	85,603	112,267	109,857	92,817	66,612	68,370	64,374
Jan.	88,092	74,801	95,273	101,159	96,602	72,309	70,773	
Feb.	68,612	73,721	99,645	112,538	78,231	68,345	60,415	
Mar.	68,923	84,631	93,406	125,818	95,152	72,271	62,878	
Apr.	73,126	75,096	99,464	108,150	85,173	75,675	66,651	
May	87,845	84,615	108,136	89,052	92,804	79,089	67,156	
June	71,894	83,277	109,080	111,194	91,029	70,351	62,070	
July	80,360	85,457	105,607	102,004	87,203	76,298	68,519	
Aug.	82,290	84,758	106,367	104,395	83,361	70,528	69,308	
Sept.	73,505	88,206	105,978	101,571	83,069	64,943	64,237	
Total	933,093	967,435	1,217,548	1,260,161	1,114,209	880,810	792,239	

Foreign Agricultural Service Division. Compiled from Trade and Navigation of the United Kingdom.

United Kingdom: Total ham imports, by months, 1928-29 to 1935-36

Month	1928-29	1929-30	1930-31	1931-32	1932-33	1933-34	1934-35	1935-36
	1,000 pounds	1,000 pounds	1,000 pounds	1,000 pounds	1,000 pounds	1,000 pounds	1,000 pounds	1,000 pounds
Oct.	6,484	8,105	5,792	7,217	7,497	6,992	5,419	4,797
Nov.	6,782	8,125	5,755	7,550	7,998	7,932	5,887	5,074
Dec.	7,339	9,347	10,111	8,596	6,578	6,155	5,951	7,395
Jan.	8,788	7,920	7,101	4,602	7,100	4,743	5,012	
Feb.	8,232	7,989	6,507	5,146	5,556	4,233	5,223	
Mar.	6,828	8,601	5,337	6,530	5,981	7,288	5,623	
Apr.	8,981	9,539	7,597	5,764	7,874	7,542	7,119	
May	14,136	12,298	9,204	9,664	10,737	7,234	7,378	
June	10,499	10,983	9,773	8,466	9,207	7,021	8,408	
July	12,042	14,391	11,165	11,661	13,568	11,984	8,586	
Aug.	12,073	12,024	7,429	9,091	8,489	9,357	6,072	
Sept.	8,073	7,236	5,613	6,978	9,267	4,962	5,219	
Total	110,257	116,558	91,384	91,265	99,852	85,443	75,897	

Foreign Agricultural Service Division. Compiled from Trade and Navigation of the United Kingdom.

United Kingdom: Total lard imports, by months, 1928-29 to 1935-36

Month	1928-29	1929-30	1930-31	1931-32	1932-33	1933-34	1934-35	1935-36
	1,000 pounds	1,000 pounds	1,000 pounds	1,000 pounds	1,000 pounds	1,000 pounds	1,000 pounds	1,000 pounds
Oct.	18,079	21,844	22,897	17,329	19,799	25,407	26,932	12,161
Nov.	21,551	24,004	27,751	19,234	21,305	23,301	22,582	12,700
Dec.	17,480	27,160	27,270	21,276	17,658	25,855	17,365	10,096
Jan.	35,923	27,559	21,459	28,188	24,381	34,945	15,651	
Feb.	29,752	25,187	32,576	37,323	31,490	26,975	16,921	
Mar.	22,234	24,810	26,608	31,248	31,269	23,568	19,725	
Apr.	21,612	18,218	25,276	11,805	22,788	22,984	14,508	
May	26,479	20,772	23,771	20,565	24,305	34,335	16,009	
June	20,498	21,078	27,586	25,890	25,026	39,695	13,628	
July	25,977	31,801	28,538	22,221	26,673	22,564	16,374	
Aug.	21,204	20,438	25,001	16,477	31,403	24,151	15,526	
Sept.	16,899	12,976	17,022	18,556	29,484	19,200	9,063	
Total	277,688	275,847	305,755	270,112	307,581	322,980	204,264	

Foreign Agricultural Service Division. Compiled from Trade and Navigation of the United Kingdom.

United Kingdom: Bacon imports from Denmark, by months, 1928-29 to 1935-36

Month	1928-29	1929-30	1930-31	1931-32	1932-33	1933-34	1934-35	1935-36
	1,000 pounds	1,000 pounds	1,000 pounds	1,000 pounds	1,000 pounds	1,000 pounds	1,000 pounds	1,000 pounds
Oct.	50,703	47,486	70,906	71,154	75,730	47,545	37,837	34,403
Nov.	48,063	48,525	61,433	72,521	70,445	44,588	36,158	30,798
Dec.	45,580	53,490	81,294	77,467	59,332	37,159	37,776	34,912
Jan.	48,717	48,406	66,819	73,317	57,307	40,106	36,866	
Feb.	41,508	44,439	67,246	75,213	50,495	34,684	31,842	
Mar.	41,985	51,870	65,505	86,046	59,092	40,128	35,824	
Apr.	44,031	46,204	63,224	76,032	51,023	41,534	35,931	
May	46,758	56,206	67,190	48,717	59,195	43,595	36,996	
June	41,886	54,456	66,161	82,653	55,517	41,006	34,020	
July	46,570	55,213	68,704	72,174	53,125	45,676	38,482	
Aug.	48,121	55,066	68,094	70,019	53,152	43,503	40,379	
Sept.	48,350	59,751	67,893	67,587	48,558	37,384	38,130	
Total	552,272	621,112	814,469	874,900	692,971	496,908	440,241	

Foreign Agricultural Service Division. Compiled from Trade and Navigation of the United Kingdom.

Countries Important in British Market Supplies

Denmark.-The continued increase in hog production indicated for Denmark by the November 1935 census was checked in later weeks, according to the December figures reported by Mr. Reed. Numbers of bred sows in December were considerably in excess of the comparable 1934 figures, but the percentage increase over October figures was smaller in 1935 than in 1934. Most of the increase in total numbers found in the December 1935 returns occurred among slaughter hogs as a result of the increased breeding operations in evidence throughout 1935.

Numbers of hogs weighing 77 pounds or more on November 16 and December 28, 1935, were smaller than on December 1, 1934, but numbers of hogs under 77 pounds were about 15 percent larger, suggesting materially increased marketings after February 1936. The increased number of bred sows, which was the highest for any census date since August 1933, indicates that the heavy marketings will continue unless the hogs are taken out through control measures. Marketings, which ran 70,000 to 80,000 weekly in December, are expected to approximate 90,000 weekly for February. The increase was to be expected in view of the very favorable price ratio prevailing for "card" hogs (those intended for the British bacon market) and the very small losses experienced on hogs without cards.

Authorities have moved to prevent further marked increases in hogs by manipulating the prices paid for non-card hogs. From mid-November to January 1, 1936, the price of non-card hogs (those not intended for the British bacon market) was raised from 70 ore (7.16 cents) to 95 ore per kilo (9.72 cents per pound), dressed weight, a price which brought the pork-feed ratio for non-card hogs almost to a remunerative level. It was hoped that hog producers would take advantage of that price and liquidate. Early in December, producers were warned that the non-card hog price would be reduced on January 1. Since that date, the non-card price has been 79 ore per kilo (8.08 cents per pound), which represents a pork-feed ratio of 1:6.5. A ratio of 1:8 is needed on bacon-weight hogs to break even. Further decreases in the non-card price, and other measures, may be expected if future censuses indicate that production will exceed the requirements of remunerative outlets.

Hogs for export to Germany were included in the card issues for January and February. The card issues for the 2 months cover about 75,000 hogs weekly. Of those, 62,000 will be sent to Great Britain as bacon; 5,000 will go to Germany, largely as live hogs; and 8,000 will be used for home consumption. Originally, the card issues covered only those hogs going to Great Britain. Increased exports to Germany developed shortly after the British quota was reduced late in 1935. The new business proved helpful in marketing the increased receipts of Danish hogs. About 44,500 hogs were sent to Germany in 1935, more than 40,000 of which were exported in November and December. Hogs destined for Germany have been fed to much heavier weights than those marketed as bacon hogs.

Total exports of hogs in 1935 reached 54,000 head against 57,000 exported in 1934. Tne 1935 total for bacon, at 440,200,000 pounds, was 11 percent below the 1934 total, largely as a result of the British import restriction policy. Exports of lard in 1935 were about 15 percent larger than the 1934 figures and reached 27,000,000 pounds. Most of the increase in recent months represented trade with Germany. Denmark, however, has been unable to fill completely the lard quotas granted by Germany under the compensation agreement.

Denmark: Number of hogs from July 15, 1933 to date

Date	:Boars : 4 :months: :& over:	Brood sows In : farrow:	Not : in : farrow:	Total:	Other hogs (new classification) 132 : lbs.& : over :	77 to: 132 : lbs.:	Under : 77 : lbs. :	Suck- : ling : pigs :	Total
July 15, 1933 :	25	280	164	444	827	997	1,068	1,029	4,390
Oct. 14, 1933 :	24	244	161	405	825	951	1,075	916	4,169
Dec. 15, 1933 :	23	212	150	362	740	892	974	733	3,724
Jan. 16, 1934 :	21	210	141	351	669	817	890	726	3,474
Mar. 1, 1934 :	22	237	110	347	649	743	792	631	3,184
Apr. 14, 1934 :	22	238	110	348	639	694	719	659	3,081
June 1, 1934 :	22	284	115	363	595	664	672	711	3,027
July 15, 1934 :	21	231	124	355	523	647	737	774	3,057
Oct. 15, 1934 :	20	216	117	333	590	711	734	720	3,108
Dec. 1, 1934 :	20	238	106	344	621	646	745	653	3,029
Jan. 15, 1935 :	19	253	105	358	451	667	762	668	2,925
Mar. 1, 1935 :	20	255	114	369	508	637	738	695	2,967
Apr. 13, 1935 :	20	241	132	373	463	629	740	813	3,038.
May 25, 1935 :	20	255	125	380	500	635	797	724	3,056
June 20, 1935 :									3,056
July 16, 1935 :	20	275	114	389	456	729	761	760	3,025
Aug. 24, 1935 :	21	259	124	383	545	693	742	782	3,166
Oct. 5, 1935 :	21	264	141	405	534	683	792	860	3,295
Nov. 16, 1935 :	21	278	132	410	565	674	882	766	3,318
Dec. 28, 1935 :	21	278	127	405	450	723	885	732	3,216

Division of Statistical and Historical Research. Compiled from Statistiske Efterretninger published by the Statistical Department of Denmark, and reports from Agricultural Commissioner, H. E. Reed, United States Department of Agriculture.

Netherlands.- Further indications of an upturn in Netherlands hog numbers appeared in the November 1935 census returns. The 1935 upward trend was the reverse of the 1934 movement. Numbers in November 1935, at 1,669,000 head, were still slightly under the figures for a year earlier. The 1935 distribution by classes, however, was favorable for additional increases, there being more brood sows and young pigs on hand than a year earlier. There is little likelihood of hog numbers rising beyond the level desired by the control authorities. The earmarking of hogs to be matured is still in practice, as are also price-control measures. So far, the Dutch control plan has not resulted in the most desirable distribution of supplies on a seasonal basis, but the system appears to include machinery for improving that situation.

The shortage of hogs experienced in the summer of 1935 appears to have been overcome. The purchase of earmarks by producers increased in the last quarter of the year as increased breeding operations became evident. By December 28, 1,993,000 earmarks of the total of 2,321,000 allotted for 1935 had been taken up. The remaining 1934 marks were available in 1936 up to February 1. The issue for 1936 has been set at 2,250,000 against 2,321,000 in 1935, 2,520,000 in 1934, and 3,600,000 in the period October 1932 to December 31, 1933.

The indicated increased production has resulted in increased marketings. Weekly offers to the hog Centrale now average about 45,000, compared with the very low offers of around 10,000 weekly in late September 1935. Some increase in export slaughter appears to have developed in the last half of 1935, but the total for the year will be smaller than that of 1934. Bacon exports were well maintained in 1935, considering the hog shortage and the reductions in the British import quotas. Exports of other processed pork and of live hogs have been of little importance.

Netherlands hog and pork prices in October stood at the highest level reached for several years. October was the month in which the hog shortage was the most acute. The control agency has the power to fix prices for export bacon hogs, without regard to the open market price level. Since September 1935, however, the control authorities have been following open market prices in fixing export-hog prices.

Cattle supplies and the output of dairy products continue to present a problem to the Netherlands authorities. Government slaughter of cattle during recent winters apparently has not reduced numbers to a satisfactory level. The June 1935 census showed that cattle numbers still were 11.5 percent larger than in 1930. Plans to reduce milk allowances to dairymen have appeared unworkable, and proposals have been considered for the removal of another 100,000 head of dairy cows through government slaughter. No decision had been reached by mid-January.

Netherlands: Official estimates of number of hogs, by classes, specified dates

Date	Sows in farrow	Pigs under 6 weeks	Hogs up to 132 pounds	Hogs 132 to 200 pounds	Hogs over 220 pounds	Total hogs incl. boars
	Thousands	Thousands	Thousands	Thousands	Thousands	Thousands
Censuses						
May - June 1910	130	279	---	980	---	1,260
May - June 1921	147	371	---	1,148	---	1,519
May - June 1930	242	472	940	263	101	2,018
Estimates 1/						
Dec. 1, 1930	254	420	1,072	337	115	2,198
Mar. 1, 1931	232	571	1,053	430		2,286
June 1, 1931	210	557	1,250	321	96	2,434
Sept. 1, 1931	196	571	1,278	358	109	2,512
Dec. 1, 1931	213	434	1,241	355	139	2,382
Mar. 1, 1932	196	562	1,109	331	145	2,343
June 1, 1932	179	458	1,213	266	128	2,244
Sept.-Oct. 1932 2/	265	535	1,012	624	290	2,736
Apr. 18, 1933	235	544	769	367	189	2,112
Nov. 1933	239	434	982	399	406	2,468
May 1, 1934	157	453	707	366	380	2,070
May 15, 1934	153	321	817	391	334	2,022
Aug. 1934	146	296	572	470	385	1,875
Nov. 1934	142	329	448	355	470	1,750
Feb. 1935	145	271	445	310	217	1,393
June 1935	146	306	635	188	184	1,464
Aug. 1935	153	397	544	335	195	1,629
Nov. 1935	146	331	574	272	341	1,669

Division of Statistical and Historical Research. Compiled from Verslag oven den Landbouw in Nederland 1928 - Commercial Attache' J. F. Van Wickel, January 16, 1931, and International Institute of Agriculture Bulletin March, 1933. Later estimates from Agricultural Commissioner H. E. Reed of the Foreign Agricultural Service.

1/ Unofficial estimates based on percentage change from June 1930 numbers as furnished by Berlin office of Foreign Agricultural Service and Commercial Attache Van Wickel.

2/ Estimates of Varkenscentrale - not strictly comparable with any other estimate. The number for September 1, 1932 adjusted from these figures is officially estimated at 2,600,000 compared with 2,622,000 on the same date of 1930.

Poland.-Supplying the increased German import requirements late in 1935 was the outstanding development in the Polish hog situation, Mr. Reed reports. From mid-November to December 31, weekly exports of about 5,600 hogs or carcasses went to Germany under the recently negotiated compensation agreement. This expanded trade, however, had little if any stimulating effect on Polish hog prices as a whole, and total hog exports for 1935 were little, if any, greater than in 1934 despite the heavier movement late in the year. The official measures taken to aid the marketing of hogs from eastern Poland assisted that region materially. In western Poland, where little or no aid was given, there were indications of a surplus of hogs at the year-end. Despite these inequalities, however, hog prices at leading markets late in 1935 were at least 50 percent above comparable 1934 prices. The high point of the year was reached in October, but some decline resulted from lower British bacon prices and a weak domestic market.

Slaughter at the principal municipal abattoirs was much larger in the first 9 months of 1935 than in the same period of 1934. Indications are, however, that killings during the last quarter of the year were considerably reduced. Such a development was anticipated owing to the decline in hog numbers during 1935, the increase in exports, and the unfavorable economic position of Polish consumers. Further declines in the low Polish per capita consumption of pork are expected. The 1935 increase in exports resulted in a January-November advance over 1934 of 56 percent in exports of fresh pork to 4,630,000 pounds and of 240 percent in ham to 10,800,000 pounds. Exports of bacon were 12 percent smaller than in the 1934 period, totaling about 42,000,000 pounds. The increased exports of pork, ham, and lard, however, were not large enough to offset the decline for the period indicated in exports of hogs and in exports of bacon to Great Britain. A large part of the ham exports was tinned ham destined for the United States.

Sweden and Norway.- Reduced hog slaughter, smaller exports of bacon and lard, and increased imports of fat sides were the features of Sweden's pork trade in 1935. Swedish hog numbers have declined in response to the British restrictions on imports of cured pork. In the October 1935 hog census, total numbers were 11.6 percent under comparable 1934 figures. Declines were especially marked in young animals, indicating reduced marketings and slaughter in the first half of 1936. Smaller numbers of sows suggest a reduced slaughter in the last half of the current year. Slaughter in the first 11 months of 1935 reached 856,000 head against 921,000 in the comparable 1934 period. Swedish butter production also is now smaller than a year ago. Exports declined in 1935. Improved butter prices have resulted in cuts of 33.3 percent and 22.2 percent, respectively, in the excise tax and import duty on margarine for the first half of 1936.

In Norway, the October 1935 hog census indicated total numbers well below those of a year earlier. The seasonal tendency to increase hog numbers in the last half of the year, however, apparently was stronger in 1935 than in 1934. The October 1935 total for eight important hog-producing provinces reached 460,000 head against 560,000 head a year earlier, a decline of 13.1 percent. There was only a slight decline among young pigs, and bred sows were only 5.3 percent under 1935 figures. The more marked cut in slaughter hogs, however, indicates a further reduction in marketings for early 1936.

Baltic States.- Reductions in the British import quotas and loss of German trade have reacted unfavorably upon the Lithuanian hog industry, Mr. Reed reports. The census returns, however, show that country has not had to make as relatively drastic reductions in hog numbers as have more important producing countries, such as Denmark and Netherlands. June hog numbers for 1935 stood at 1,258,000 head against 1,288,000 head a year earlier. Bacon exports in 1935 were reduced by about 35 percent, but exports of lard and live hogs increased. Hog exports were more than double the 1934 figures, with Russia as the leading buyer. Most of the additional lard exports went to Great Britain, especially during the second half of the year, rather than to Germany, the usual chief outlet. Some additional pork also moved to Belgium.

In Latvia, where less than 1,000,000 hogs are reported annually, the 1935 figure of 802,000 head was an increase of more than 14 percent over 1934 figures. Exports to Germany of hogs and fatbacks also increased.

Central European Importing Countries

Germany.- The fixed price of heavy hogs at Berlin continued during January at the equivalent of $17.70 per 100 pounds, Mr. Reed reports. That figure represented an advance of $1.13 over the January 1935 average. By the end of 1935, the reestablishment of price differentials for hogs of varying weights and the setting of 180 pounds as a minimum slaughter weight was being reflected in an increased average slaughter weight. The percentage of hogs falling into the heavier weight classes at 12 markets also has shown a marked increase. Those groups were larger in November than at any time since July and August 1934, when premiums were being paid for excessively fat and heavy hogs in connection with the neutral lard production scheme.

The upturn in German hog slaughter from the low level reached in October 1935 resulted in a December figure for 36 centers of 253,000 head. That figure, while still well under the usual numbers for that month, represented a gain of 88 percent over October levels. Slaughter at 36 centers for the last 4 months of 1935, at 705,000 head, was lower than any comparable figure since 1926.

Increased imports of live hogs and somewhat larger supplies of domestic hogs both helped to improve the supply situation. Price and marketing regulations have been reflected in a better distribution of the continued relatively small supplies. A marked scarcity of the cheaper cuts of meat has developed, however, as a result of the price-fixing policy, since there has been a tendency to divert meat and fats into products having free prices. New regulations have been adopted in an effort to offset this tendency, and additional types of pork and its preparations have been put into the fixed-price group. For some of the higher-priced cuts, the salable quantity has been limited.

German hog numbers usually decline in the September-December period. In 1935, however, total numbers increased during that period, the December figure being only 1.93 percent under the 1934 total. Additional increases

were indicated by a 12 percent increase over December 1934 in bred so
of 5.17 percent in young pigs. The groups from which most of the sl
hogs will come in the next few months, however, were 5 percent under
1934 level. Farmers are being urged to feed the smaller numbers to
weights during the early months of 1936. home slaughter has been li
by the order in November requiring official permission to kill any h
not held by the owner for at least 3 months. The March 1936 census
expected to show an increase in total numbers over the March 1935 ce

The apparent future increase in hog numbers is focusing attent
on available supplies of feed. The larger numbers and the feeding to
weights in excess of 180 pounds suggest the possibility of feed potat
supplies being insufficient to meet requirements prior to the coming
the new crop. Hog feeding already has become unprofitable in some re
despite the high fixed hog prices, and measures have been taken to m
available grain held in government stocks.

Germany: Number of hogs, by classes, excluding and including
the Saar, on December 1, 1931-1935

Dec. 1	Young pigs		6 months to 1 year			1 year and ove		
	Under 8 weeks	:8 weeks: to 6 :months	Sows In :farrow : (bred):	Total	:Total :excl. :sows & :boars	Sows In :farrow :Total (bred):		:Total :excl. :sows :boars
	Thou- sands	Thou- sands	Thou- sands	Thou- sands	Thou- sands	Thou- sands	Thou- sands	Thou- sands
Excluding: the Saar:								
1931 ...:	5,128	10,484	251	494	5,238	870	1,458	893
1932 ...:	4,834	9,884	259	485	5,278	851	1,384	884
1933 ...:	5,126	10,353	306	549	5,386	923	1,465	899
1934 ...:	4,512	10,052	244	452	5,836	823	1,329	883
1935 1/.:	4,741	9,518	313	542	5,550	881	1,407	802
Including: the Saar:								
1931 ...:	5,146	10,539	----	496	5,261	----	1,464	896
1932 ...:	4,852	9,936	---	488	5,298	----	1,390	887
1933 ...:	5,153	10,413	----	552	5,406	---	1,474	902
1934 ...:	4,539	10,117	----	454	5,858	----	1,337	886
1935 ...:	4,762	9,562	314	544	5,575	884	1,413	805

Division of Statistical and Historical Research. Compiled from Deutsche
anzeiger, January 15, 1936.
1/ Estimate obtained by excluding Saarland.

Compensation and clearing agreements with Denmark, Poland, Hungary, Yugoslavia, Estonia, and Latvia have permitted the supplementing of short domestic pork supplies with imported hogs. Fairly large imports have been arranged for the early months of 1936. Later in the year the dependence on imports should decline if German feed supplies prove sufficient to fatten the prospective increased numbers of slaughter hogs. Some attention is being given, however, to the political and economic advantages of accepting agricultural products from Poland and Hungary in exchange for German manufactures. In fact, more Polish hogs would now be reaching Germany if Poland were in a better position to absorb consumers' goods.

In fats, the present German position is somewhat improved over that of late 1935. The fat supply situation, however, continues much more acute, than the pork situation and no permanent correction of the difficulties is in prospect. Reduced domestic hog production, depleted storage stocks of lard, greatly reduced lard imports, reduced domestic butter production arising from short protein feed supplies, and curtailed margarine production combined at the beginning of the fourth quarter of 1935 to create a serious fat problem.

Efforts to increase the supplies of fat have included larger imports of butter, lard, and other fats through compensation agreements, lowered tariffs, reduced equalization fees, increased margarine production, and, where possible, forcing milk supplies to the creameries where butter output is more efficient than on the farms. Wholesale distribution of all fat supplies has been controlled so as to place them where they are most needed. The retail trade has been rationing customers.

Imports of lard and butter have shown marked increases in recent months, but there has been little if any increase in the imports of American lard. Imports from the United States in December amounted to only 503,000 pounds, from Hungary 3,415,000 pounds, and from Denmark 1,817,000 pounds. Total imports for the month reached 6,685,000 pounds. In December 1934 the United States supplied 812,000 pounds, Hungary 2,817,000 pounds, Denmark 1,965,000 pounds. The total was 6,639,000 pounds. Despite the larger imports late in 1935, however, the total for the year, 91,190,000 pounds, was still 24,324,000 pounds under the 1934 total.

Compensation agreements with Netherlands, Hungary, Denmark, Austria, Yugoslavia, Latvia, and Estonia have made possible the large imports of lard and butter which have been received in exchange for German goods. The imports, however, have not been sufficient to offset the decline in domestic production and lard imports are still far below the monthly imports of 3 or 4 years ago. The larger imports of recent months, however, are expected to continue during 1936. Plans are under consideration for securing more lard from overseas countries in view of the relatively small European supplies. The reduced German tariffs on fats have been extended to June 30, 1936.

It appears that little improvement in the fat situation can be expected from domestic butter production. The domestic cattle industry, already handicapped by the shortage of protein feeds, appears to be entering a period of reduced numbers. About 3 years will be required to restore cattle numbers to the level prevailing prior to the 1934 drought.

The German Institute of Business Cycle Research has published estimates indicating that fat consumption in Germany in 1935 reached unusually low levels for the post-war period. Total per capita fat consumption for 1935 was placed by the Institute at 20.6 kilograms (12.8 pounds). That figure was 12 percent less than that for 1932, though not materially lower than in 1934. As compared with the average for the years 1909-1913, however, the 1935 figure indicates an increase of 27 percent. The reduction in fat consumption during the past 2 years has been largely the result of import restrictions on lard, butter, and fatbacks.

Germany: Consumption of fats as food,
average 1928-1929, annual 1932-1935

Commodity	Average 1928-1929	1932	1933	1934	1935 1/
	1,000 pounds	1,000 pounds	1,000 pounds	1,000 pounds	1,000 pounds
Domestic:					
Fatbacks and lard	666	653	679	714	684
Edible tallow	37	44	66	66	77
Total	703	697	745	780	761
	Pounds	Pounds	Pounds	Pounds	Pounds
Per capita consumption	11.0	10.8	11.5	11.9	11.5
	1,000 pounds	1,000 pounds	1,000 pounds	1,000 pounds	1,000 pounds
Imported:					
Fatbacks	9	38	24	29	24
Lard	194	229	157	88	66
Total	203	267	181	117	90
	Pounds	Pounds	Pounds	Pounds	Pounds
Per capita consumption	3.1	4.0	2.6	1.8	1.3
	1,000 pounds	1,000 pounds	1,000 pounds	1,000 pounds	1,000 pounds
Total fats:					
Total consumption	906	964	926	897	851
	Pounds	Pounds	Pounds	Pounds	Pounds
Per capita consumption	14.1	14.8	14.1	13.7	12.8

Institute of Business Cycle Research, Berlin.
1/ Estimated.

Austria.- The decline in Austrian hog production in 1935 has made Vienna, the leading market, more dependent upon imported pork production, Mr. Reed reports. Total supplies, however, have been below those of 1934. Marketings of hogs at the two leading Vienna markets for the first 11 months of 1935 reached 949,000 head, of which 395,000 head were imported. The comparable 1934 figures were 1,085,000 and 316,000 head, respectively. Despite the fact that Austria has a considerable cattle surplus, total meat consumption has declined since there has been no material increase in the use of beef.

The September 1935 production tendency census indicated a drop of 26.3 percent in total hog numbers below the comparable 1934 figures. The September 1935 figures, however, showed an increase of 6.7 percent when compared with the returns of last June. In 1934 the June-September gain amounted to only 5 percent. Most of the September 1935 decline resulted from smaller numbers of farrows, young pigs and slaughter hogs. A tendency toward increased production appears in the 10.5-percent increase in the number of young bred sows, and in the fact that older sows declined relatively less than did total numbers. December returns are not yet available, but it is likely that production programs will follow the policy decisions of the authorities. Higher hog prices than last year now prevail in Austria, but the policy during 1935 was to reduce hog numbers to the point where they can be maintained on domestic feeds.

Numbers of slaughter hogs in September 1935 were 9.7 percent larger than in June, but 17.9 percent smaller than in September 1934. The September increase was reflected in the Vienna monthly marketings for October and November, which were larger than in the preceding 4 months. Marketings of domestic hogs in 1936, however, are expected to be smaller than in 1935.

While Austria is rated as a fat-deficit country, the supply situation appears to have been less acute than in other Central European deficit countries. Fat consumption probably has declined somewhat as prices have advanced. Butter production, however, has increased. In fact, Austria has a butter surplus and exported both butter and cheese to Germany in the fourth quarter of 1935. The butter situation, the increased imports of fat hogs, and the steady production of margarine have kept fat supplies close to current requirements. There was some tendency to hoard fat as a result of the Italian military activities of last autumn, but steps were taken at once to liberalize the imported supplies of lard. Some special imports were made by the Government, and the import duty on lard was reduced by 2/3 to 10 crowns per quintal (1.6 cents per pound), but imports have been very light in recent months. Butter production has continued to increase and the price of margarine has been reduced. Fat consumption has declined seasonally since January 1, and lard imports are expected to continue light in the immediate future.

Czechoslovakia.- The reduced supplies of domestic hogs in Czechoslovakia during 1935 resulted in imports totaling 193,000 head for the year, against 83,000 head for 1934. Much of the increase over 1934 occurred during the last quarter of the year, according to unofficial advices

covering most of that period. Official slaughter figures for the first
months of 1935 show a total of 3,105,000 head against 3,272,000 head for
the corresponding 1934 period. While imports were not great enough to
bring the slaughter up to the 1934 level, the heavier weights of the imported hogs provided 1935 supplies of pork and fat practically equal to
those of 1934. Total production of hog fat in the first 10 months of 19
is placed at 96,782,000 pounds, of which 21,164,000 pounds were from imp
hogs. The comparable 1934 figures were 91,932,000 pounds and 9,039,000
pounds, respectively.

Prices of domestic hogs around January 1 were about 50 percent hi
than those of a year earlier. Indications are, however, that in spite o
the higher hog prices, the high grain prices and the policy of exchangin
Czecho-industrial goods for fat hogs and fatbacks will permit little cha
in domestic hog production. The Danube Basin countries, notably Hungary
continue as the principal source of fats imported by Czechoslovakia. At
present there is nothing to suggest any relaxation of Czechoslovakia's e
to cultivate the Danubian countries as a source of fat supplies.

The previously reported reductions in Czechoslovakia's lard tarif
have permitted since August marked increases of imports of lard and fatb
Hungary, Yugoslavia, and the Netherlands have been the principal supplie
and the reduced duties also have brought an increase in imports of Ameri
lard. Imports of lard and fatbacks for 1935 were considerably under the
1934 imports, but the value of all imported fats for the first 10 months
exceeded comparable figures for 1934. The lower duty on lard, at 120 cr
per kilo (2.26 cents per pound), originally intended to prevail only unti
January 1, was extended to February 9. No information is available on th
rate after that date. Import contingents for January and February 1936 w
placed at 2,646,000 pounds of lard and fatbacks monthly compared with
4,850,000 pounds for December 1935. Efforts to introduce a tax upon arti
ficial fats have not yet materialized.

Danube Basin

The intentions of Hungarian farmers, as reported on October 1, 193
indicate that about 33 percent more lard-type hogs will be finished and
marketed during the first quarter of 1936 than were sold during the same
period in 1935, according to the Belgrade office of the Foreign Agricultu
Service. The average intended finished weight of fat barrows was reporte
at 375 pounds per head and that of fat sows at 400 pounds. Intended mark
ings of meat-type hogs indicate an increase of 9 percent for January-Marc
1936 in comparison with sales of finished meat hogs during the first 3 mc
of 1935. The average finished weight is expected to be about 285 pounds
head in the case of barrows and 330 pounds in the case of sows.

Hog numbers: By types on reporting farms,
July 1 and October 1, 1934, 1935

Date of census	Lard type	Meat type	Total
	Head	Head	Head
July 1, 1935 .... :	44,259	8,876	53,135
October 1, 1935 .... :	82,115	19,541	101,656
Total for marketing January-March, 1936.... :	126,374	28,417	154,791
July 1, 1934	30,864	8,090	38,954
October 1, 1934 .... :	63,864	17,875	81,739
Total marketed January-March 1935..... :	94,728	25,965	120,693
Percentage January-March 1936 is of January- March 1935...............:	133	109	128

Source: Magyar Statisztikai Szemle.

According to preliminary data, about 33,682,000 pounds of lard were exported from Danube Basin countries during the 1935 calendar year. This is the largest annual lard export from the Basin since the World War, and compares with about 40,565,000 pounds exported in 1926, the second largest post-war export, with 33,069,000 pounds exported in 1934, and with 13,889,000 pounds, the 5-year average for 1929-1933. Of the 1935 lard export total Hungary supplied 53,203,000 pounds, or approximately 84 percent, most of the remainder being of Yugoslav origin. The principal importing countries in 1935 were Germany and Czechoslovakia, but some Hungarian lard was also shipped to England. Large exports in 1935 were made possible primarily as a result of reduced American competition, combined with the negotiation of barter agreements.

Present negotiations between Hungary and Germany, as well as the probability of continued large arrivals of finished lard-type hogs at markets during January-March 1936, indicate that lard exports during the first quarter of 1936 will continue large, although probably smaller than pre-Christmas shipments.

Lard: Exports from Danube Basin countries,
1935 with comparisons

and month	: Bulgaria	: Hungary	: Rumania	: Yug slav
	: 1,000 pounds	1,000 pounds	1,000 pounds	1,0 pou
:September.....:	22	40,483 1/	24	6,
:r.............: 1/	0	4,657 1/	0	1,
)er............: 1/	0	4,149 1/	0	1,
)er............: 1/	0	3,914 1/		1,
·December......:	0	12,720	0	4,
:al............:	22	53,203	24	10,
..............:	0	29,762	0	3,
average.......:	0	11,244	220	2,

>ffice, Foreign Agricultural Service.
:imation.

liminary data show that about 544,787 hogs were exp
:in during the 1935 calendar year, as compared with :
·ted during 1934 and with 550,000 head as the 5-year

Live hogs: Exports from Danube Basin countri
1935 with comparisons

and month	: Bulgaria	: Hungary	: Rumania	: Yug slov
	: Head	Head	Head	Head
-September.....	531	129,032	86,118	151,
er............:	0	17,161	19,219	26,
ber...........: 1/	0	17,715	17,664	20,
ber...........: 1/	0	19,219 2/	19,254 1/	20,
-December.....:	0	54,115	56,137	67,
tal...........:	531	183,147	142,255	218,
..............:	2,000	126,000	76,000	141,
average.......:	1,000	181,000	122,000	246,

ffice, Foreign Agricultural Service.
:imation. 2/ Preliminary.

Although under the 5-year average, 1935 live-hog exports show a considerable advance over those of 1934 on account of a decrease in Central European hog numbers in 1935, combined with the same factors which caused lard exports to increase. The existence of extra-quotas and unused quota-residues transferred to 1936, coupled with Hungarian farmers' reported intentions to market large numbers of finished lard-type hogs during March 1936, indicates a continuation of live-hog exports from the Danube Basin on a relatively large scale during the first quarter of 1936. Austria and Czechoslovakia remained the principal markets for Danubian live hogs during 1935 and will in all probability continue to be in 1936.

Exports of hog carcasses and meats to Germany from Hungary began in September 1935. From September to the end of December about 27,634,000 pounds of hog carcasses and meat from lard-type hogs, equivalent to about 140,000 head, were exported from Hungary, on the basis of several quotas. In January two temporary quotas were fixed, pending announcement of the total contingent for the year. One for 10,000 head was for delivery prior to January 15 and the other, also of 10,000 head, was for shipment before January 20.

Yugoslavia also secured a 40,000-head quota of carcasses and meat for shipments to Germany. According to recent information, deliveries will be made during the winter months, no time limit having been set. In addition to shipments to Germany, Yugoslavia exports pork meat and killed hogs to Austria, on the basis of a weekly quota of about 90,800 pounds. Exports to Germany began in October. During October-November 1935, a total of 3,254,000 pounds of pork was exported from Yugoslavia to all destinations.

Hog carcasses and pork meat: Exports from Danube
Basin countries, 1935

Period	Hungary	Rumania	Yugoslavia
	1,000 pounds	1,000 pounds	1,000 pounds
1935			
January-September........:	1,569	0	1/
October.................:	6,018	0	2,395
November................:	9,813	1,006	858
December................:	9,792	1/	1/
Total...............:	27,193	1/	1/

Belgrade office, Foreign Agricultural Service.
1/ Not available.

Besides carcass and meat quotas, a number of new quotas have been obtained by Danubian countries covering the movement of live hogs, fat sides and lard to Czechoslovakia and Germany.

Hogs and pork products: Indices of foreign supplies and demand

Country and item	Unit	1909-10 to 1913-14 average	1924-25 to 1928-29 average	Oct. - Dec. 1932-33	1933-34	1934-35	1935-
UNITED KINGDOM:							
Supplies,domestic fresh pork,London	1000 pounds			19,897	28,710	23,309	24,145	28,3
Imports -							
Bacon -							
Denmark ....:	"	59,816	123,760	205,507	129,292	111,771	100,1
Irish Free State:	"		17,921	7,311	8,833	13,468	15,2
United States ..:	"	44,343	23,451	1,004	1,910	1,225	6
Canada ....:	"	8,930	21,557	2,687	19,834	23,739	22,4
Others ....:	"	11,247	38,198	105,075	71,132	50,029	45,2
Total ....:	"	124,336	224,887	321,585	231,001	200,232	183,6
Ham, total ......:	"	20,474	28,045	22,013	21,079	17,257	17,2
Lard, total .....:	"	57,050	57,495	58,762	74,563	66,879	34,9
DENMARK:							
Exports -							
Bacon ....:	"		123,103	202,657	138,968	111,914	102,1
CANADA:							
Slaughter -	1000's						
Hogs,inspected ..:	"	450	738	707	765	782	7
GERMANY:							
Production -							
Hog receipts 14 cities ......:	"		812	799	770	870	3
Hog slaughter 36 centers .....:	"	1,111	1,010	1,081	1,057	1,174	5
Imports -	1000						
Bacon, total ....:	pounds	868	5,932	9,369	8,500	10,843	6,5
Lard, total .....:	"	54,037	51,197	65,992	39,707	16,635	27,7
UNITED STATES:							
Slaughter -							
Hogs,inspected ..:	1000's	8,806	12,538	11,967	12,089	11,765	7,4
Exports -							
Bacon -	1000						
United Kingdom .:	pounds	32,530	14,570	864	714	643	2
Germany ....:	"	729	2,693	372	1,415	0	
Cuba ....:	"	1,833	5,505	952	941	1,294	2
Total ....:	"	45,196	33,236	4,736	7,144	2,578	7
Hams, shoulders							
United Kingdom .:	"	30,316	30,981	13,108	14,910	11,138	9,6
Total ....:	"	35,684	37,975	15,835	17,654	14,349	11,3
Lard -							
United Kingdom .:	"	39,297	51,563	59,508	75,683	46,667	13,5
Germany ....:	"	34,485	43,221	43,035	33,625	1,828	8
Cuba ....:	"	8,857	20,237	1,932	2,757	8,767	3,5
Netherlands ....:	"	8,375	10,313	8,985	11,455	9	
Total ....:	"	112,662	174,048	139,370	152,153	62,779	18,5

Hogs and pork products: Foreign and domestic average prices per 100
pounds for the month indicated, and stocks at the end of the month

Item	1909-1913 average	1925-1929 average	Dec. 1934	Nov. 1935	Dec. 1935
PRICES -	Dollars	Dollars	Dollars	Dollars	Dollars
Hogs, Chicago, basis packers' and shippers' quotations ....:	7.50	9.76	5.89	9.31	9.57
Corn, Chicago, No. 3 Yellow ....:	.98	1.46	1.66	1.11	1.05
Hogs, heavy Berlin live weight ....:	11.63	15.73	16.37	17.70	17.70
Barley, Leipzig ....:	1.70	2.27	3.01	3.15	3.18
Lard -					
Chicago ....:	10.71	14.00	11.97	14.38	13.62
Liverpool ....:	12.10	13.89	11.18	15.50	15.06
Hamburg ....:	11.92	14.54	---	16.09	14.39
Cured pork -					
Liverpool -					
American short cut green hams	14.30	25.16	19.18	20.13	20.28
American green bellies		21.27	Nominal	Nominal	Nominal
Danish Wiltshire sides·	14.10	23.07	18.32	18.66	18.09
Canadian green sides..:	13.34	20.97	16.70	16.04	15.34
	1,000 pounds	1,000 pounds	1,000 pounds	1,000 pounds	1,000 pounds
STOCKS -					
United States -					
Processed pork 1/.....:		555,885	687,563	253,209	323,633
Lard in cold storage...:		62,928	118,107	37,906	52,718

1/ Dry salt cured and in process of cure; pickled, cured, and in process of cure, and frozen.

HOG-FEED PRICE RATIOS AND HOG SLAUGHTER, UNITED STATES, GERMANY, AND DENMARK, 1924 TO DATE

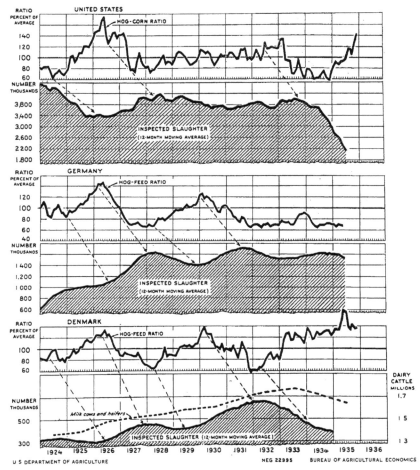

U S DEPARTMENT OF AGRICULTURE   NEG 22995   BUREAU OF AGRICULTURAL ECONOMICS

FIGURE 1.- IN THE UNITED STATES AND OTHER IMPORTANT HOG-PRODUC-
ING COUNTRIES CHANGES IN THE HOG-FEED PRICE RATIO ARE USUALLY FOLLOW-
ED BY CHANGES IN HOG SLAUGHTER FROM ONE TO TWO YEARS LATER, AS INDI-
CATED BY THE SLANTING ARROWS IN THE ABOVE FIGURE. IN DENMARK AND
UNITED STATES THE HOG-FEED PRICE RATIO IS NOW VERY FAVORABLE FOR AN
INCREASE IN HOG PRODUCTION. IN THESE TWO COUNTRIES AND IN GERMANY
AN INCREASE IN PRODUCTION NOW APPEARS TO BE UNDER WAY.

PORK AND LARD EXPORTS FROM THE UNITED STATES, 1900 TO DATE

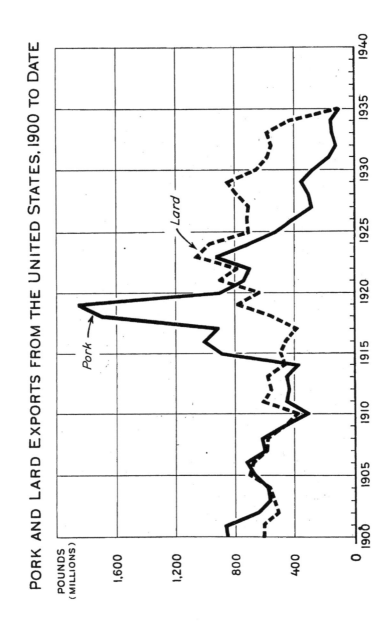

UNITED STATES DEPARTMENT OF AGRICULTURE
Bureau of Agricultural Economics
Division of Statistical and Historical Research
Washington

HP-76

March 26, 1936

WORLD HOG AND PORK PROSPECTS

Summary

Commercial slaughter supplies of hogs in the United States during the remainder of the present hog marketing year, March through September 1936, probably will be from 30 to 35 percent greater than a year earlier. Most of this increase in slaughter supplies is likely to occur after May 1 when marketings of fall farrowed pigs get under way in large volume. The 1935 fall pig crop was 31 percent greater than that of 1934. With supplies increasing, and any improvement in demand which may occur unlikely to be sufficient to offset the larger supplies, domestic hog prices are likely to decline materially in the early summer, and in the late summer probably will not reach the high level of a year earlier.

The relationship of hog prices to corn prices in the United States in the last 6 months has been very favorable for increased hog production. The hog-corn price ratio in February (19.3) was the highest in over 2 years. This favorable price relationship now prevailing, and the fact that hog prices have held up well for more than 2 years, probably will result in a considerable increase in the number of pigs produced in 1936 compared with 1935. The number of hogs on farms at the beginning of this year was 9 percent greater than a year earlier.

An increase in hog production in Canada in 1936 also is expected. It is reported that spring farrowings this year will be increased in all Canadian provinces as a result of favorable relationship between hog prices and feed prices prevailing in 1935. Marketings of hogs in Canada in 1935 were somewhat smaller than in other recent years.

The British quota for imports of bacon and hams from
countries has been fixed for March and April at a rate 8 per
in those months last year, but 3 percent greater than the mo
prevailing from October to February 1935-36. The share of t
is this quota continues to be 8.1 percent.

Lard exports from the Danube Basin continued large in
Most of such lard exports have been shipped from Hungary, an
been the most important outlet for these shipments. It is e
exports of Hungarian lard to Germany and Czechoslovakia will
for several months. Hog feeding operations in Hungary have
large in recent months.

In view of these and other conditions, no material im
the export demand for hog products in the near futures is ant
although some increase in exports as a result of increasing
production is likely to occur.

United States

Supplies of hogs for commercial slaughter during the r
the current hog marketing year, up to September 30, 1936, pro
from 25 to 30 percent larger than a year earlier in terms of
slaughtered. However, with average weights continuing heavi
year the total live weight of hog slaughter under Federal ins
March to September 1936 probably will be 30 to 35 percent gre
the corresponding period of 1935. Most of the increase in ho
in the period above mentioned is likely to occur after May 1,
ings in the summer months are mostly fall farrowed pigs and t
pig crop was 31 percent larger than that of 1934. With such
supplies hog prices during May and June are likely to decline
and prices in the later summer may not advance to the high le
earlier.

The level of hog prices in the last 6 months has been
in relation to corn prices. The hog-corn price ratio in the
States in February based on farm prices as of the 15th of the
19.3, one of the highest ratios on record. The favorable pri
recent months, undoubtedly will provide an effective stimulus
hog production. A substantial increase in the 1936 spring pi
indicated by the December 1935 pig crop report. In view of p

level of hog production an increase in the number of pigs produced in the
fall of 1936 may also occur, depending, of course, upon the outturn of the
1936 corn crop.

The advance in hog prices which began in early January continued
during the first half of February but prices declined during the second
half of the latter month.   A moderate upturn in hog prices occurred in
early March. The weekly average price of hogs at Chicago rose from $10.01
the last week in January to $10.70 the second week in February and then
declined to $9.99 in the closing week of the month. The average price
of hogs at Chicago in February of $10.37 was about 50 cents higher than
the average for January and about $2.00 higher than that of February last
year.

Hog slaughter under Federal inspection during February, totaling
2,319,000 head, was about 4 percent less than the very small slaughter of
February last year and was the smallest for the month since 1903. Inspected
slaughter in February was about 1,100,000 head smaller than that in January.
Severe winter weather in most of the Corn Belt in early February, however,
tended to restrict hog marketings.

Average weights of hogs marketed in February were lighter than those
in January but were heavier than in February last year. The average weight
at the seven principal markets was 228 pounds compared to 232 in January and
218 pounds in February 1935. The decrease in weights in February as compared
with a month earlier probably was the result of a smaller than usual proportion of packing sows marketed and also the poor gains made by hogs in the
last 2 months because of the unfavorable weather. For the first 5 months of
the present hog marketing year, October 1935 to February 1936, inspected
hog slaughter totaled 13,180,000 head which was 25 percent smaller than the
slaughter for the corresponding months last year and 39 percent less than
the 5-year average for the corresponding period.

Prices of fresh pork declined sharply during most of January as
slaughter supplies increased, but nearly all of this decline was recovered
in the first half of February as hog slaughter was curtailed. During
the second half of February, however, fresh pork prices again declined and
by the end of the month they were near the level of early January. Prices
of cured pork after declining sharply in January were about steady during
February. The composite wholesale price of hog products in New York in
February was $20.84 per 100 pounds compared with $21.92 in January and
$19.51 in February last year. Prices of lard continued to weaken during
February, the average wholesale price of refined lard at Chicago averaging
$12.06 for the month compared with $14.44 for February a year earlier.

Total exports of pork in January were smaller than in the preceding
month but exports of lard showed an increase over those of a month earlier.
Shipments of both pork and lard from the principal ports in February were
smaller than in January and continued much below those of a year earlier.
Exports of pork in January totaled 4,770,000 pounds which was less than
half the quantity exported in January 1935.

Exports of hams and shoulders in January amounted to 3,152,000 pounds which was about 400,000 pounds smaller than in December and about 1,000,000 pounds smaller than in January 1935. Bacon exports continued small in January, amounting to only 207,000 pounds. A large part of the decrease in pork exports in January compared with a year earlier was occasioned by the decrease in shipments of fresh frozen pork.

Lard exports in January, totaling 10,161,000 pounds, were 29 percent greater than in December, but they were considerably smaller than in January last year. Exports of lard to Germany in January, amounting to 782,000 pounds, were larger than in any month since December 1934, but they were very small in relation to the monthly lard exports to that country in years prior to 1934. Exports of lard to both Great Britain and Cuba in January were larger than in December.

A table on page 5 shows the preliminary estimates of the number of hogs on farms in the United States on January 1, 1936 and the revised estimates of numbers from 1930 through 1935. Hog numbers are also shown in this table for the same years for the several geographic divisions of the country. It will be observed that the number of hogs on farms on January 1 this year was 9 percent greater than a year earlier but was still very small in relation to the number in other post-war years. The largest increase in numbers reported was in the North Central (Corn Belt) States, where numbers were 13 percent larger on January 1, 1936 than a year earlier. Increases however, were reported in all of the major geographic divisions. This increase in hog numbers is largely a reflection of the increase in the 1935 fall pig crop, since the 1935 spring pig crop was smaller than that of 1934. The average value of hogs on farms per head on January 1 was $12.68 compared with $6.31 a year earlier and $4.09 2 years earlier. The aggregate value of all hogs on farms was estimated to be $540,000,000, which was more than twice as large as the aggregate value a year earlier and was the largest total value of hogs on farms reported since January 1931.

Canada

Some increase in hog production in Canada during 1936 is expected, according to the Canadian Department of Agriculture in its recent publication entitled "The Agricultural Situation and Outlook for 1936". The increase will probably be small during the first 6 months but somewhat larger during the second 6 months. The indicated increase in hog output may be expected to result in some increase in exports. The increase in exports, however, may be limited because of the possibility of increased domestic consumption of pork as a result of improved consumer purchasing power and anticipated higher prices of beef.

Indications are for an increase in spring farrowings in practically all provinces as a result of high prices for hogs during 1935, generally low feed prices, and the relatively favorable supply and distribution of feed throughout the Dominion.

United States: Number of hogs, including pigs, in the North Central States, and other States on January 1, 1930-1936

States	1930	1931	1932	1933	1934	1935	1936	:1936 as :a per- :centage :of 1935
	Thou-sands	Thou-sands	Thou-sands	Thou-sands	Thou-sands	Thou-sands	Thou-sands	Per-cent:
est North Central:								
Iowa ....:	10,200	10,509	10,700	10,140	10,200	6,250	7,250	116
Mo. ....:	3,750	3,488	4,100	4,674	4,113	2,400	2,712	113
Nebr. ....:	5,010	4,820	5,334	4,534	5,010	2,034	2,136	105
Minn ....:	3,494	3,665	3,884	3,496	3,321	1,900	2,299	121
Kans ....:	2,826	2,487	3,073	3,165	2,430	1,200	1,248	104
S. Dak.......:	2,800	3,000	1,950	2,048	1,229	600	840	140
N. Dak.......:	730	766	751	638	475	232	283	122
Total.....:	28,810	28,735	29,792	28,695	26,778	14,616	16,768	114.7
ast North Central:								
Ill. ....:	4,415	4,415	4,900	5,537	5,260	3,510	3,931	112
Ind. ....:	2,637	2,637	2,953	3,750	3,900	2,675	2,942	110
Ohio ....:	2,462	2,330	2,485	3,130	3,035	2,160	2,333	108
Wis. ....:	1,422	1,536	1,560	1,506	1,364	1,064	1,234	116
Mich. .. ... :	630	542	661	793	730	512	594	116
Total... .:	11,566	11,460	12,559	14,716	14,289	9,921	11,034	111.2
otal North Central	40,376	40,195	42,351	43,411	41,067	24,537	27,802	113.3
outh Central.....:	7,674	7,111	8,755	10,327	9,618	7,716	7,768	100.7
outh Atlantic....:	4,161	4,101	4,409	4,672	4,520	4,092	4,146	101.3
estern ....:	2,284	2,298	2,646	2,514	2,277	1,650	1,735	105.2
orth Atlantic....:	1,210	1,130	1,140	1,203	1,139	1,009	1,090	108.0
nited States . .:	55,705	54,835	59,301	62,127	58,621	39,004	42,541	109.1

ivision of Statistical and Historical Research.   Compiled from reports of he Division of Crop and Livestock Estimates.

Pork and lard: Exports from the United States, January to December, 1933 to 1935

Year and month	Pork 1/	Lard, incl. natural lard:			Bacon:			Hams and shoulder	
		Total	To Germany	To United Kingdom	Total 2/	To Germany	To United Kingdom 2/	Total	To United Kingdom 2/
	1,000 pounds	1,000 pounds	1,000 pounds	1,000 pounds	1,000 pounds	1,000 pounds	1,000 pounds	1,000 pounds	1,000 pounds
1933 –									
Jan.	9,687	78,997	28,233	28,775	2,023	625	243	4,580	3,88
Feb.	7,497	58,264	15,051	31,513	1,196	48	168	3,753	3,10
Mar.	10,239	48,113	7,827	26,761	1,278	114	118	5,707	4,84
Apr.	11,459	39,180	8,637	19,240	979	11	268	7,716	6,94
May	9,877	46,277	12,129	22,414	911	19	154	6,508	5,89
June	13,881	38,213	4,397	23,223	1,162	24	239	9,619	8,77
July	14,483	36,628	2,324	23,406	1,626	8	264	9,359	8,33
Aug.	13,045	36,195	4,425	21,277	1,841	20	304	7,531	6,88
Sept.	12,136	49,020	10,158	24,276	2,238	43	467	6,152	5,65
Oct.	11,568	50,296	13,695	22,493	2,304	54	325	5,745	5,06
Nov.	15,921	47,784	11,140	22,080	2,590	824	205	7,626	6,52
Dec.	12,242	55,271	8,790	31,197	2,250	537	184	4,283	3,32
Total	142,035	584,238	126,806	296,655	20,398	2,327	2,939	78,579	69,22
1934 –									
Jan.	11,033	51,584	5,735	30,610	1,702	95	181	3,188	2,63
Feb.	13,604	37,111	2,386	23,263	2,348	671	199	4,634	4,03
Mar.	12,269	39,845	3,860	26,122	1,783	209	225	5,390	4,66
Apr.	10,119	39,643	3,135	21,692	1,215	10	265	5,044	4,35
May	13,319	66,623	5,254	39,492	1,936	47	353	5,750	4,83
June	14,839	41,413	1,831	28,320	1,337	24	266	6,786	6,03
July	17,382	33,860	2,561	21,743	1,909	22	366	9,638	8,95
Aug.	15,965	29,755	96	21,003	1,798	0	223	6,950	6,03
Sept.	9,949	31,701	0	22,712	1,489	0	159	3,375	2,67
Oct.	8,641	27,096	360	20,135	903	0	183	4,346	3,56
Nov.	14,058	19,965	512	14,845	874	0	243	6,648	5,35
Dec.	9,375	16,295	956	11,746	888	3	217	3,355	2,21
Total	150,553	434,891	26,686	281,683	18,1				
1935 –									
Jan.	9,641	17,777	497	12,833	880	0	163	4,196	3,39
Feb.	8,158	16,007	188	12,126	637	0	121	3,501	3,01
Mar.	8,543	10,781	3/	7,892	590	3/	115	4,809	3,99
Apr.	7,417	7,369	0	4,506	503	0	106	4,817	4,20
May	10,463	9,831	0	7,065	618	0	126	6,782	6,09
June	8,078	6,963	0	3,762	494	0	80	6,144	5,53
July	8,461	4,953	0	1,773	701	0	81	5,832	5,18
Aug.	6,785	3,470	3/	623	393	0	58	4,776	4,09
Sept.	4,659	1,553	0	498	334	0	60	3,151	2,71
Oct.	4,656	2,769	190	2,017	233	3/	69	3,071	2,59
Nov.	6,895	7,988	334	5,750	207	3/	83	4,723	4,15
Dec.	4,934	7,898	336	5,861	278	5	128	3,579	2,88
Total	88,680	97,359	1,545	64,706	5,868	5	1,190		

Division of Statistical and Historical Research. Compiled from reports of the United States Department of Commerce. Totals computed from rounded numbers.
1/ Includes fresh or frozen, pickled, cured, and canned pork.
2/ Included in total pork (first column)
3/ Less than 500 pounds.

Hog numbers in specified exporting and importing countries, 1921 to date

Year	Non-European			European				
	United States Jan. 1	Canada June 1	Denmark July 15	Nether-lands May-June	Irish Free State June 1	Poland June 30	Sweden Sept. 15	Hungary Spring
	Thousands	Thousands	Thousands	Thousands	Thousands	Thousands	Thousands	Thousands
1909-913 1/	53,300	3,350	2,715	1,305	1,046	5,487	1,023	3,322
21 ...	59,942	3,855	1,430	2/ 1,519	891	3/ 5,287		---
22 ...	59,349	3,916	1,899	---	938			2,473
23 ...	69,304	4,405	2,855	---	1,186			2,133
24 ...	66,576	5,069	2,868	---	987			2,458
25 ...	55,770	4,426	2,517	---	732			2,633
26 ...	52,105	4,360	3,122	---	884			2,520
27 ...	55,496	4,695	3,731	---	1,178	3/ 6,329		2,387
28 ...	61,873	4,497	3,363	---	1,183		1,387	2,662
29 ...	59,042	4,382	3,618	---	945	4,829		2,582
30 ...	55,705	4,000	4,872	2/ 2,018	1,052	6,047	1,761	2,362
31 ...	54,835	4,717	5,453	4/ 2,434	1,227	7,331	1,724	2,715
32 ...	59,301	4,639	4,886	4/ 2,244	1,108	5,844	1,465	2,361
33 ...	62,127	3,801	4,390	5/ 2,022	931	5,753	1,713	1,899
34 ...	58,621	3,654	3,057	6/ 1,875	968	7,091	1,529	2,502
35 ...	39,004	3,549	3,034	3/ 1,629	1,107	6,703		3,176
36 ...	42,541							

	Importing countries				
	Great Britain June 1	Northern Ireland June 1	Germany exc. Saar, Jan 1 7/	France Jan. 1 7/	Czechoslovakia Jan. 1 7/
	Thousands	Thousands	Thousands	Thousands	Thousands
1909-913 1/	2,544	215	22,533	7,529	2,516
21 ...	2,650	105	14,153	4,941	2/ 2,201
22 ...	2,450	118	15,818	5,166	
23 ...	2,798	196	14,678	5,196	
24 ...	3,427	140	---	5,406	
25 ...	2,798	112	16,895	5,802	
26 ...	2,345	158	16,200	5,793	2/ 2,539
27 ...	2,889	236	19,424	5,777	---
28 ...	3,167	229	22,899	6,019	---
29 ...	2,509	192	20,106	6,017	---
30 ...	2,453	216	19,944	6,102	---
31 ...	2,945	236	23,442	6,329	2/ 2,776
32 ...	3,350	220	23,808	6,398	2,576
33 ...	3,236	271	22,859	6,488	2,621
34 ...	3,525	380	23,890	6,769	3,430
35 ...	4,066	458	23,170	7,044	3,035
36 ...			22,699		

vision of Statistical and Historical Research; compiled from official records of the International Institute of Agriculture and reports of United States Government presentatives abroad. 1/ Average for 5 years for present boundaries, otherwise for any year or years within this period for which data are available. 2/ Census. November. 4/ Estimates based on percentage changes from one year to the other furnished by United States representative. 5/ May. 6/ August. 7/ Estimates ported as of December have been considered as of January 1 of following year.

Pork and lard: Exports from the United States, January to December,
1933 to 1935

Year and month	Pork 1/	Lard, incl. netural lard: Total	To Germany	To United Kingdom	Bacon: Total	To Germany	To United Kingdom 2/	Hams and shoul: Total	To Unit King 2/
	1,000 pounds	1,000 pounds	1,000 pounds	1,000 pounds	1,000 pounds	1,000 pounds	1,000 pounds	1,000 pounds	1,0 pou
1933 -									
Jan.	9,687	78,997	28,233	28,775	2,023	625	243	4,580	3
Feb.	7,497	58,264	15,051	31,513	1,196	48	168	3,753	3
Mar.	10,239	48,113	7,827	26,761	1,278	114	118	5,707	4
Apr.	11,459	39,180	8,637	19,240	979	11	268	7,716	6
May	9,877	46,277	12,129	22,414	911	19	154	6,508	5
June	13,881	38,213	4,397	23,223	1,162	24	239	9,619	8
July	14,483	36,628	2,324	23,406	1,626	8	264	9,359	8
Aug.	13,045	36,195	4,425	21,277	1,841	20	304	7,531	6
Sept.	12,136	49,020	10,158	24,276	2,238	43	467	6,152	5
Oct.	11,568	50,296	13,695	22,493	2,304	54	325	5,745	5
Nov.	15,921	47,784	11,140	22,080	2,590	824	205	7,626	6
Dec.	12,242	55,271	8,790	31,197	2,250	537	184	4,283	3
Total	142,035	584,238	126,806	296,655	20,398	2,327	2,939	78,579	69
1934 -									
Jan.	11,033	51,584	5,735	30,610	1,702	95	181	3,188	2
Feb.	13,604	37,111	2,386	23,263	2,348	671	199	4,634	4
Mar.	12,269	39,845	3,860	26,122	1,783	209	225	5,390	4
Apr.	10,119	39,643	3,135	21,692	1,215	10	265	5,044	4
May	13,319	66,623	5,254	39,492	1,936	47	353	5,750	4
June	14,839	41,413	1,831	28,320	1,337	24	266	6,786	6
July	17,382	33,860	2,561	21,743	1,909	22	366	9,638	8
Aug.	15,965	29,755	96	21,003	1,798	0	223	6,950	6
Sept.	9,949	31,701	0	22,712	1,489	0	159	3,375	2
Oct.	8,641	27,096	360	20,135	903	0	183	4,346	3
Nov.	14,058	19,965	512	14,845	874	0	243	6,648	5
Dec.	9,375	16,295	956	11,746	888	3/	217	3,355	2
Total	150,553	434,891	26,686	281,683	18,182	1,078	2,880	65,104	55
1935 -									
Jan.	9,641	17,777	497	12,833	880	0	163	4,196	3
Feb.	8,158	16,007	188	12,126	637	0	121	3,501	3
Mar.	8,543	10,781	3/	7,892	590	3/	115	4,809	3
Apr.	7,417	7,369	0	4,506	503	0	106	4,817	4
May	10,463	9,831	0	7,065	618	0	126	6,782	6
June	8,078	6,963	0	3,762	494	0	80	6,144	5
July	8,461	4,953	0	1,773	701	0	81	5,832	5
Aug.	6,785	3,470	3/	623	393	0	58	4,776	4
Sept.	4,659	1,553	0	498	334	0	60	3,151	2
Oct.	4,656	2,769	190	2,017	233	3/	69	3,071	2
Nov.	6,885	7,988	334	5,750	207	3/	83	4,723	4
Dec.	4,934	7,898	336	5,861	278	5	128	3,579	2
Total	88,680	97,359	1,545	64,706	5,868	5	1,190	55,381	47

Division of Statistical and Historical Research. Compiled from reports of the
United States Department of Commerce. Totals computed from rounded numbers.
1/ Includes fresh or frozen, pickled, cured, and canned pork.
2/ Included in total pork (first column).
3/ Less than 500 pounds.

Hog numbers in specified exporting and importing countries, 1921 to date

Exporting countries

	Non-European			European				
ir	United States Jan. 1	Canada June 1	Denmark July 15	Nether-lands May-June	Irish Free State June 1	Poland June 30	Sweden Sept. 15	Hungary Spring
.909-	Thou-sands	Thou-sands	Thou-sands	Thou-sands	Thou-sands	Thou-sands	Thou-sands	Thou-sands
1/ :	53,300	3,350	2,715	1,305	1,046	5,487	1,023	3,322
... :	59,942	3,855	1,430	2/ 1,519	891	3/ 5,287		---
... :	59,349	3,916	1,899	---	938			2,473
... :	69,304	4,405	2,855	---	1,186			2,133
... :	66,576	5,069	2,868	---	987			2,458
... :	55,770	4,426	2,517	---	732			2,633
... :	52,105	4,360	3,122	---	884			2,520
... :	55,496	4,695	3,731	---	1,178	3/ 6,329		2,387
... :	61,873	4,497	3,363	---	1,183		1,387	2,662
... :	59,042	4,382	3,618	---	945	4,829		2,582
... :	55,705	4,000	4,872	2/ 2,018	1,052	6,047	1,761	2,362
... :	54,835	4,717	5,453	4/ 2,434	1,227	7,321	1,724	2,715
... :	59,301	4,639	4,886	4/ 2,244	1,108	5,844	1,465	2,361
... :	62,127	3,801	4,590	5/ 2,022	931	5,753	1,713	1,899
... :	58,621	3,654	3,057	6/ 1,875	968	7,091	1,529	2,502
... :	39,004	3,549	3,034	3/ 1,629	1,107	6,703		3,176
... :	42,341							

Importing countries

	Great Britain June 1	Northern Ireland June 1	Germany exc. Saar, Jan 1 7/	France Jan. 1 7/	Czechoslovakia Jan. 1 7/
909-	Thousands	Thousands	Thousands	Thousands	Thousands
1/ :	2,544	215	22,533	7,529	2,516
... :	2,650	105	14,153	4,941	2/ 2,201
... :	2,450	118	15,818	5,166	
... :	2,798	196	14,678	5,196	
... :	3,427	140	---	5,406	
... :	2,798	112	16,895	5,802	
... :	2,345	158	16,200	5,793	2/ 2,539
... :	2,889	236	19,424	5,777	---
... :	3,167	229	22,899	6,019	---
... :	2,509	192	20,106	6,017	---
... :	2,453	216	19,944	6,102	---
... :	2,945	236	23,442	6,329	2/ 2,776
... :	3,350	220	23,808	6,398	2,576
... :	3,236	271	22,859	6,488	2,621
... :	3,525	380	23,890	6,769	3,430
... :	4,066	458	23,170	7,044	3,035
... :			22,699		

ion of Statistical and Historical Research; compiled from official records of
nternational Institute of Agriculture and reports of United States Government
sentatives abroad.   1/ Average for 5 years for present boundaries, otherwise
ny year or years within this period for which data are available.   2/ Census.
vember.   4/ Estimates based on percentage changes from one year to the other
rnished by United States representative.   5/ May.   6/ August.   7/ Estimates
ted as of December have been considered as of January 1 of following year.

Hogs: Slaughter in certain exporting and
countries, 1921 to

Year	Exporting			
	Non-European			
	United States :inspected :slaughter	Canada inspected slaughter	Denmark xport slaughter	Netherlands slaughte for con sumptio & expor
	Thousands	Thousands	Thousands	Thousan
1921	38,982	1,636	1,641	---
1922	43,114	1,927	2,215	---
1923	53,334	2,256	3,414	1,785
1924	52,873	2,914	4,024	2,768
1925	43,043	2,642	3,766	2,810
1926	40,636	2,491	3,838	2,440
1927	43,633	2,540	5,098	3,041
1928	49,795	2,547	5,373	3,077
1929	48,445	2,353	4,994	2,415
1930	44,266	1,926	6,132	2,746
1931	44,772	2,243	7,320	3,661
1932	45,245	2,723	7,841	3,560
1933	47,226	2,802	6,392	2,777
1934	43,876	2,872	4,898	2,525
1935	26,058	3/2,826	4/4,212	

	Importing coun		
	Great Britain sold off farms for slaughter	Northern Ireland: purchased for curing	(il
	Thousands	Thousands	T.
1921	3,312	212	
1922	3,504	232	
1923	3,715	256	
1924	4,406	298	
1925	4,172	269	
1926	3,461	280	
1927	3,639	355	
1928	4,449	394	
1929	4,053	353	
1930	3,661	377	
1931	4,080	391	
1932	4,687	378	
1933	4,787	370	
1934		414	
1935		5/ 509	3/

Hogs: Slaughter in certain exporting and importing hog producing
countries, 1921 to date   cont'd

NOTES:
Division of Statistical and Historical Research; compiled from official records and from reports of United States Department of Agriculture representatives abroad. Sweden is a more important exporting country than Hungary, and France is more important as an importing country than Czechoslovakia; but these are not included owing to lack of annual official slaughter statistics.
1/ Purchased by curers in Leinster, Munster, and Connacht, later formed into Irish Free State with part of Ulster. This also corresponds to number purchased alive, which constitutes most of the number bought by curers in Irish Free State, curers in Northern Ireland purchasing their hogs on a dressed weight basis.
2/ Estimate based on percentage that purchases by curers in Irish Free State represents of purchases by curers in all Ireland.
3/ Preliminary estimate for year based on slaughter for 11 months.
4/ Preliminary estimate based on slaughter for 6 months alone.
5/ Estimate for year based on weekly reports.
6/ Estimate for year based on figures for 8 months.

        Increased hog marketings in 1936 are expected, especially in Ontario, Quebec, and Alberta, all important hog producing provinces. In Ontario, where about 35 percent of the total number of hogs in Canada is found, conditions are now very favorable for an expansion of hog production from the recent low level, with supplies of coarse grain crops ample. In the prairie provinces the increases in marketings in 1936 will probably be somewhat restricted by the low quality of the feed supply and the scarcity of breeding stock on farms last spring.

        Canadian hog prices during 1936 are expected to remain fairly high despite the expected increase in the volume marketed.

        Hog prices in Canada remained at practically the January level throughout February 1936. The average price of bacon hogs at Toronto for the 4-week period ended February 27 was $8.64 per 100 pounds weighed off cars and was the same as for the preceding 4-week period. During the week ended February 20 the price went as high as $8.95 per 100 pounds, but it fell to $8.45 in the last week of the month. The Toronto average price for the month of January on a fed and watered basis was $8.44 per 100 pounds compared with $8.32 in December and $8.58 in January a year ago.

        Supplies during the 4 weeks of February as represented by live hogs graded at stockyards and packing plants amounted to only 236,489 head, a decrease of 27,000 compared with the same period last year. Gradings of live hogs at stockyards and packing plants for the first 9 weeks of 1936 amounted to 498,000 head, a decrease of 11 percent compared with the same period of 1935. About half of this apparent decrease, however, may be accounted for by an increase in the grading of hog carcasses, a new service in Canada which is known as "rail grading". The custom of grading dressed carcasses, as done in certain European countries, will make it possible to eliminate many of the conditions which now are sources of serious loss to Canadian producers, it is believed.

Live hog grading was begun in 1922 in Canada as a result of a decision of the Hog Conference of 1921 and has accomplished much along the lines of uniformity of type and finish, according to an article published in the Industrial Development Council of Canadian Meat Packers.

The experimental grading of hog carcasses in 1935 amounted to 115,000 head in addition to the 2,854,000 live hogs graded. The carcasses at present are classified as follows: Grades A - E (A representing the choice grade); light; heavy, extra heavy, and sows. Of the total number of 115,000 carcasses graded in 1935, 55,000 or 48 percent were classified as B grade and 40,000 or 35 percent as A grade. Of the total number of 2,854,000 live hogs graded, 1,201,000 or 42 percent were graded as bacon hogs (the second grade) and 654,000 or 23 percent as select bacon hogs.

In January only 12,056,000 pounds of bacon were exported to the United Kingdom, a decrease of 11 percent as compared with the same month of 1935. Lard exports to the United Kingdom continued large, amounting to 1,659,000 in January or 4 times as large as in the same month of 1935. Fresh frozen pork exports to the United States were about three times as large as in January 1935; the total, however, was relatively small, amounting to only 133,000 pounds. There was also an increase from 24,000 pounds to 536,000 pounds in exports of pork to the United States. The live hog exports to the United States in January alone reached 2,501 head, or about one-fifth of the total live hog exports to the United States from Canada last year.

United Kingdom and Irish Free State

The total quota for cured pork imports into Great Britain for the current period, February 26 to April 30, amounts to 103,296,000 pounds. This is a reduction of about 8 percent from the rate for the same period a year ago. It represents, however, an increase of approximately 3 percent over the rate prevailing in the period October 1 - February 25, 1935-36. The United States share is still 8 percent of the total, amounting for the whole period to 8,264,000 pounds. This amount also represents an increase of 3 percent over the rate in effect in the October-February period and an 8-percent decrease below that for the same period of last year. In addition, the United States is allowed the usual 0.1 percent of the total quota, or 103,296 pounds, as an adjustment for consignments made through Canadian ports. On account of the unusual supply conditions in the United States, however, it is unlikely that the United States quota can be fully utilized during the next few months.

The new quotas are based on the percentage allocations to the various countries concerned, established March 29, 1934. These percentages were arrived at after a period of experimentation and are the result of an attempt to permit imports from all major suppliers in the same relative proportion as imports were from those countries before the inauguration of the quota system. No fixed basic period was used, since no one period was acceptable to all of the interested countries as representative of their normal trade. The position of the United States, for example, during the period of largest total cured pork imports into the United Kingdom, 1932, was relatively much less important than it had been during the years 1924 to 1929. The trade of certain of the Baltic States, and in particular Poland, on the other hand, only became significant after 1929. Therefore the reduction in imports since 1932 effected by the quota system was relatively much greater for most of the quota countries than it was for the United States. The reduction in imports from the United States, using the period 1924-25 to 1928-29 as a base, however, was much greater. As will be seen from the table on page 13, the decrease in the rate of imports into the United Kingdom effected by the quota system from the rate of optimum years is approximately 56 percent for the United States and the quota countries as a whole.

The fresh pork quota for the United States for the second quarter of 1936 has been announced as 2,844,800 pounds. The frozen pork which may be imported from the United States for curing is limited to 772,800 pounds for the last three quarters of 1936, or 257,600 pounds a quarter. This is the same as the rate prevailing since last October, but a reduction of 12 percent from that of a year ago. The total fresh pork quota, of which the quota of pork imported for curing is a part, is the same as the corresponding quota for last year. See table, page 14.

Liverpool bacon quotations advanced slightly during February, Danish Wiltshire sides reaching an average of $20.58 per 100 pounds for the month. This was an increase of £1.15 over the January average and of $1.76 over that of a year earlier. Quotations for Canadian green sides likewise showed an increase, averaging $17.82 per 100 pounds for the month, $1.37 above the January average and $2.60 higher than the February 1935 figure. American green bellies made an average of $15.27 per 100 pounds for February, which was only a few cents above that for January or for February of last year.

British imports of Danish bacon amounted to a little less than 32,000,000 pounds. The total for the period October to February of 132,000,000 pounds represented a decline from comparable 1934-35 imports of 11 percent and from the record 1931-32 shipments of 55 percent. This is closely in line with the reductions made in the total import quota. The Danish share of total actual imports for the period was 54 percent as against 55 percent during the same period the previous year and 69 percent during October-January 1931-32.

Imports of bacon into the United Kingdom from the Irish Free State for the first 4 months of the current season amounted to over 19,600,000 pounds and were 15 percent above corresponding imports of the 1934-35 season. They represented an increase of approximately 121 percent over comparable imports during the first 4 months of the 1932-33 season.

October-January imports from Canada at 31,000,000 pounds represented a decrease of 15 percent from the record imports of the same months of 1934-35. However, they were nearly 8 times as large as comparable 1931-32 imports. Of total bacon imports into the United Kingdom for the first 4 months of this season, 21 percent was supplied by Empire countries as against 4 percent in comparable months of 1931-32.

Imports into the United Kingdom from the United States record low point of 81,000 pounds for the month of February. for the current season at 681,000 pounds stood 54 percent bel 1934-35 imports, 80 percent below those of 1931-32, and 99 pe the 1909-10 to 1913-14 average.

Total bacon imports at less than 243,000,000 pounds fo October-January represented a decrease of 10 percent from tho ago and were 43 percent below imports for the first 4 months.

Ham prices did not improve during February. At an ave per 100 pounds, they were 52 cents below the January average below that of February 1935. Total ham imports for the seaso January, amounted to approximately 22,000,000 pounds, a decre percent from imports for the comparable period last year and from those of 1932-33. Ham imports from the United States at 11,700,000 pounds accounted for less than 53 percent of the t compared with 60 percent during October-January of 1934-35 an percent during the same period of 1929-30. The proportion of supplied by Canada in January 1936 was over 41 percent.

Quotations for refined lard on the Liverpool market con steady decline from the high point of $17.08 per 100 pounds re August 1935 and averaged for the month of February $12.99. Al average is 49 cents less than the January average and 44 cents the comparable one for last year, it is still $5.34 higher th February 1934 figure.

Lard imports into the United Kingdom for the first 4 mo1 1935-36 season totaled 50,578,000, of which the United States 1 32 percent. Comparable figures for the same period of 1934-35 82,530,000 pounds and 83 percent. United States imports for J1 at 7,000,000 pounds were nearly double those of December but w1 much below usual monthly shipments. Brazil, which prior to 193 a negligible amount of lard to the British market, supplied 16 of the January imports. Other foreign countries, principally F furnished 21 percent and Empire sources 17 percent, over half c originated in Canada.

British cured pork import quotas: Weekly rates for imports from the United States and all quota countries, March 29, 1934 to April 30, 1936, with comparisons. 1/

Period	United States				Period	Total		
	Weekly quota rate :1,000 pounds:	Percentage of progressive reductions in quotas : Percent	Percentage of reductions from 1932 imports : Percent	Percentage of reductions from average 1924-25, 1928-29 imports : Percent		Weekly quota rate :1,000 pounds:	Percentage of progressive reductions in quotas : Percent	Percentage of reductions from 1932 imports : Percent
Imports:								
Average								
1924-25,	2,009							
1928-29								
1932	1,162			42.2		25,163		
Quotas:								
1934					1934			
Mar.29-July ....:	1,123	3.4	3.4	44.1	Mar.29-July	14,043	44.2	44.2
Aug.-Dec. ......:	1,030	8.3	11.4	48.7	Aug.-Dec.	12,877	8.3	43.8
1935					1935			
Jan.-Apr. ......:	964	6.5	17.0	52.0	Jan.-Apr.	12,044	6.5	52.1
May-June ....:	932	3.4	19.3	53.6	May-June	11,650	3.3	53.7
July-Sept. .....:	978:2/	4.9	15.3	51.3	July-Sept.	12,224:2/	4.9	51.4
Oct.-Dec. ......:	855	12.6	26.4	52.5	Oct.-Dec.	10,716	12.3	57.4
1936					1936			
Jan.-Feb. 25 ...:	865:2/	1.1	25.6	57.0	Jan.-Feb.25	10,831:2/	1.1	57.0
Feb.26-Apr. ...:	891:2/	3.0	23.3	55.7	Feb.26-Apr.	11,113:2/	2.6	55.8

1/ These rates are calculated by dividing total allocations by the number of weeks in the period, taking fractions of weeks into account. A slightly different result is obtained for individual priods if fractions of weeks are disregarded in making computations. 2/ Increase.

British cured pork import quotas: Allocations to principal countries,
March 29, 1934 - April 30, 1936

Country	1934 Mar.29-July 31 1/	Aug.1-Dec.31	1935 Jan.1-Apr.30	May 1-June 30	July 1:Sept.30	Oct.1-Dec.31	1936 Jan.1-Feb.25	Feb.26-Apr.30	Percentage of total quota
	1,000 pounds	1,000 pounds	1,000 pounds	1,000 pounds	1,000 pounds	1,000 pounds	1,000 pounds	1,000 pounds	Per-cent
Denmark 2/	159,260	178,753	131,084	65,542	101,993	89,227	54,909	65,593	63.50
Netherlands	23,826	26,742	19,611	9,805	15,259	6,604	8,215	9,813	9.50
Poland	19,939	22,379	16,411	8,206	12,769	13,349	6,875	8,212	7.95
Sweden	11,788	13,231	9,702	4,851	7,549	11,171	4,064	4,855	4.70
Lithuania .	7,399	8,304	6,090	3,045	4,738	4,145	2,551	3,047	2.95
Estonia ...	1,881	2,111	1,548	774	1,207:3/	1,118:3/	688	775	.75
Finland ...	1,003	1,126	826	413	642:3/	596:3/	367	413	.40
Latvia	1,756	1,971	1,445	723	1,124:3/	1,043:3/	641	723	.70
U.S.S.R. ..	2,132	2,393	1,755	877	1,365:3/	1,267:3/	780	878	.85
Argentina .	1,756	1,971	1,445	723	1,124:3/	1,043:3/	641	723	.70
U.S. 4/ ...	20,064	22,520	16,515	8,257	12,850	11,241	6,917	8,264	8.00
Total ...	250,804	281,501	206,432	103,216	160,620	140,804	86,648	103,296	100.00

1/ First period of present percentage allocations.
2/ Unadjusted to bring the Danish share in total imports from foreign sources
up to 62.5 in accordance with the Anglo-Danish trade agreement.
3/ Includes small percentage of the Danish allowance for previous undershipments.
4/ The United States, in addition, is permitted to ship 0.1 percent of total,
representing adjustments made on account of exports of American pork moving
via Canada and credited to that country in British import records.

British frozen pork quota: Allocations to the United States
for curing, 1935 and 1936

Period	1935 Total	Part for curing	1936 Total	Part for curing	Percent total 1936 is of total 1935
	Pounds	Pounds	Pounds	Pounds	Percent
Jan. 1 - Mar. 31	4,584,496:1/	294,000	4,584,496	257,600	100
Apr. 1 - June 30	2,844,800:1/	294,000	2,844,800:2/	257,600	100
July 1 - Sept. 30	2,834,608	294,000			
Oct. 1 - Dec. 31	4,916,016	257,600			
Total	15,179,920	1,139,600			

1/ January 1 - April 30, 392,000 pounds; May 1 - June 30, 196,000 pounds. Same
periods of allocation for pork for curing as for cured pork.
2/ Allocation made for April-December 1936 of 772,800 pounds.

Germany

The slight upward tendency of recent months in German hog receipts and slaughter was continued through January, according to reports from the Berlin office of the Foreign Agricultural Service. Regulations restricting direct marketing and some increase in hog numbers are having some effect upon the volume of business conducted through regular trade channels, but the volume continues considerably below that of a year ago.

There has been little change in the German fat situation in recent weeks. Domestic supplies remain deficient and imports, while larger than last year, are confined almost entirely to receipts from countries with which Germany has compensation agreements.

Hungary continues in the position of principal lard supplier attained a few months ago, with Denmark in second place. Of the 6,900,000 pounds imported from all countries in January, Hungary, and Denmark shared almost equally in 73 percent of the total. Yugoslavia, Netherlands, Sweden, Argentina, and the United States divided the remainder, with imports of American lard amounting to only 50,000 pounds. Monthly lard imports since September 1935 have been larger than in the corresponding months of a year earlier. For the October-January period of the current season, total lard imports were 41 percent larger than the corresponding 1934-35 figures, but they were less than half the usual volume of a few years ago.

Total lard imports for the calendar year 1935 were 26 percent smaller than the 1934 imports. In 1935, Denmark displaced the United States as principal supplier, with Hungary in second place.

Lard: Imports into Germany, by countries of origin, 1934 and 1935

Country	1934		1935	
	Imports	Percentage of total	Imports	Percentage of total
	1,000 pounds	Percent	1,000 pounds	Percent
Denmark ....:	22,972	25.2	26,149	39.1
Hungary ....:	12,555	13.8	22,028	32.9
Yugoslavia ....:	1,323	1.4	7,551	11.3
France ....:	---	---	3,805	5.7
United States ....:	49,116	53.9	3,150	4.7
Latvia ....:	220	.2	1,916	2.9
Netherlands ......:	3,422	3.7	1,204	1.8
Sweden ....:	913	1.0	611	.9
Others ....:	670	.8	452	.7
Total ....:	91,191	100.0	66,866	100.0

Foreign Agricultural Service Division.

Imports of cured pork into Germany in December and January were somewhat larger than those of a year earlier. The January figures on bacon imports were about the same size as for other recent years except 1935, with the Netherlands in its usual position of principal supplier and Hungary second. For the first 4 months of the 1935-36 season, however, total bacon imports were 16 percent smaller than in the corresponding 1934-35 period.

Germany continues to encourage the importing of lard and pork from the Danube Basin countries. So far, Hungary has been the chief beneficiary of this policy, especially in connection with lard. Hungary is the leading Danubian exporter of hogs and pork products. The other countries, however, have profited somewhat from the current German trade in those items.

Danube Basin

Lard exports from the Danube Basin in January and February totaled about 55,000 quintals (12,125,300 pounds) against about 53,000 quintals (11,684,400 pounds) exported in the corresponding 1935 months, according to the Belgrade office of the Foreign Agricultural Service. Hungary accounted for about 90 percent of the current export figure. Hungary secured a lard quota from Germany for the 2 months amounting to 5,754,000 pounds. Shipments were made also to Czechoslovakia and the United Kingdom. A trial shipment also went to Belgium. The indications are for continued large shipments of Hungarian lard to Germany and Czechoslovakia. The movement to the United Kingdom, however, is likely to decline if Liverpool prices continue to decline. During 1935 Hungary supplied about 83.5 percent of the total Danube lard exports and Yugoslavia about 16 percent.

Fresh pork exports in January and February from Danubian countries showed a material decline from the average monthly shipments of the last quarter of 1935. Total exports in the latter period reached 63,429,000 pounds, of which 95 percent went to Germany. About 70 percent of the total exports originated in Hungary, which sent all of its exports to Germany; 21 percent was supplied by Yugoslavia; Rumania provided most of the remaining 9 percent.

The January-February exports of Danubian live hogs exceeded 100,000 head. The monthly exports of around 50,000 head compare with about 35,000 head a year ago. Prices in Prague and Vienna, important markets for Danubian hogs in Czechoslovakia and Austria tended to decline during February, while shipments to those markets decreased. The 1935 total exports of live hogs from the Basin is now placed at 543,000 head against about 345,000 head in 1934 and an average of 550,000 for the years 1929-1933. The heavy 1935 shipments were accompanied by a record export movement of lard.

Hog feeding is reported as having been unusually large in February for this season of the year. The unusually mild winter sustained Central European demand, and availability of imported feeds at favorable prices have contributed to continued feeding operations. Loss of the Italian market for fat cattle from Yugoslavia through sanctions has concentrated attention on hog feeding in that country.

Hogs and pork products: Indices of foreign supplies and demand

Country and item	Unit	1909-10 to 1913-14 average	Oct.-Jan. 1924-25 to 1928-29 average	1932-33	1933-34	1934-35	1935-36
UNITED KINGDOM:							
Supplies–							
Domestic fresh	1000						
pork, London ...	pounds		25,709	37,294	30,332	31,996	36,953
Imports–							
Bacon–							
Denmark ....:	"	79,193	166,731	262,814	169,398	148,637	132,064
Irish Free							
State ....:	"		22,646	8,904	11,669	17,138	19,669
United States .:	"	61,449	35,479	1,391	2,162	1,472	681
Canada ....:	"	12,520	28,133	5,159	28,908	36,411	31,112
Others ....:	"	14,259	50,937	139,917	91,172	67,347	59,793
Total ....:	"	167,421	303,926	418,187	303,310	271,005	243,319
Ham, total .....:	"	28,238	38,588	29,123	25,822	22,269	22,105
Lard, total ....:	"	77,367	83,626	83,143	109,508	82,530	50,578
DENMARK:							
Exports–							
Bacon ....:	"		165,561	261,662	177,080	147,060	
CANADA:							
Slaughter–							
Hogs,inspected...	1000's	603	1,006	954	1,035	1,064	1,064
GERMANY:							
Production–							
Hog receipts							
14 cities .....:	"		1,073	1,074	1,066	1,157	589
Hog slaughter							
36 centers ....:	"	1,486	1,334	1,459	1,455	1,571	811
Imports–	1000						
Lard, total ....:	pounds	69,965	72,653	89,516	54,035	24,494	34,636
Bacon, total ...:	"	1,110	7,360	12,118	11,278	11,480	9,542
UNITED STATES:							
Slaughter–							
Hogs,inspected .:	1000's	12,162	17,780	16,667	17,480	14,812	10,860
Exports–							
Bacon–	1000						
United Kingdom.:	pounds	45,422	22,098	1,107	895	806	311
Germany ....:	"	828	3,762	997	1,510	0	0
Cuba ....:	"	2,495	7,549	1,262	1,181	1,809	325
Total ....:	"	62,797	48,729	6,759	8,846	3,458	925
Ham,shoulders– :							
United Kingdom.:	"	43,978	44,350	16,989	17,547	14,537	12,416
Total ....:	"	50,982	54,263	20,415	20,842	18,545	14,525
Lard–							
United Kingdom.:	"	56,277	74,412	88,218	106,239	59,466	20,329
Germany ....:	"	46,157	63,074	70,934	39,356	2,325	1,642
Cuba ....:	"	11,806	28,371	2,924	3,707	12,493	5,547
Netherlands ...:	"	13,684	15,616	17,735	13,917	9	0
Total ....:	"	157,612	249,157	217,477	203,355	80,446	28,633

Hogs and pork products: Foreign and domestic average prices per 100
pounds for the month indicated, and stocks at the end of each month

Item	1909-1913 average	1925-1929 average	Jan. 1935	Dec. 1935	Jan. 1936
	Dollars	Dollars	Dollars	Dollars	Dollars
PRICES -					
Hogs, Chicago, basis packers' and shippers' quotations ....:	7.26	10.37	7.70	9.57	9.85
Corn, Chicago, No. 3 Yellow ....:	1.00	1.64	1.62	1.05	1.08
Hogs, heavy, Berlin, live weight ....:	11.52	14.87	16.57	17.70	17.70
Potatoes, Breslau feeding ....:	.32	.61	.85		
Barley, Leipzig ....:	1.74	2.49	3.04	3.18	3.23
Lard -					
Chicago ....:	10.28	14.65	13.82	13.62	12.15
Liverpool ....:	11.50	15.29	12.98	15.06	13.48
Hamburg ....:	15.48	15.84	26.56	14.39	13.14
Cured pork -					
Liverpool -					
American short cut green hams ....:	13.70	24.71	20.37	20.28	19.23
American green bellies:		21.40	15.55	Nominal	15.19
Danish Wiltshire sides ....:	14.10	22.40	19.10	18.09	19.43
Canadian green sides..:	13.17	20.22	16.01	15.34	16.45
	1,000 pounds	1,000 pounds	1,000 pounds	1,000 pounds	1,000 pounds
STOCKS -					
United States -					
Processed pork 1/ .....:		683,564	667,984	326,777	436,042
Lard in cold storage....:		94,200	112,497	52,718	75,669

1/ Dry salt cured and in process of cure; pickled, cured, and in process of
cure; and frozen.

HOGS SLAUGHTER IN SPECIFIED IMPORTING COUNTRIES, 1921 TO DATE

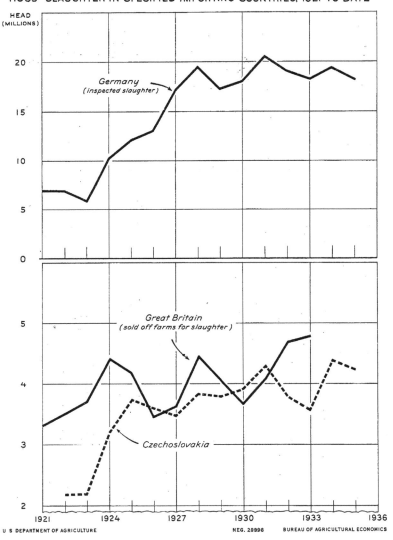

FIGURE 1

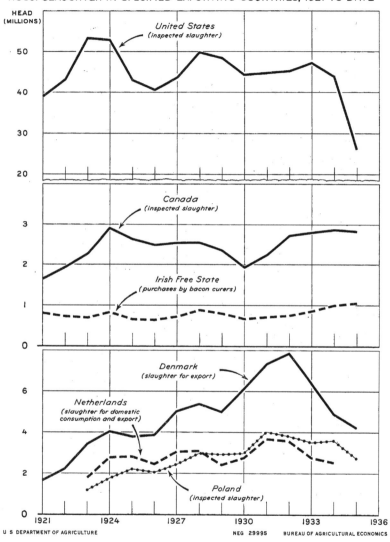

FIGURE 2

HP-77

WORLD HOG AND PORK PROSPECTS

April 20, 1936

Summary

In each month during the remainder of the present hog marketing
year (up to September 30, 1936) United States hog slaughter probably will
be larger than in the corresponding month last year. A material increase
in slaughter supplies compared with a year earlier is likely in the summer
months, June to September. Last year, however, inspected hog slaughter
during the summer was the smallest in more than 25 years. Although the
number of hogs slaughtered under Federal inspection during the 1935-36
marketing year probably will not be as large as the number slaughtered in
1934-35, the heavier average weights probably will cause the total tonnage
of federally inspected hog products produced this year to be larger than
in 1934-35.

Imports of all hog products into the United Kingdom in the last
6 months have been somewhat smaller than a year earlier and materially
smaller than 2 years earlier. The decrease in British imports of bacon
and ham in the last 2 years has been primarily the result of Governmental
restrictions on imports of such products from non-Empire countries. The
decrease in lard imports into Great Britain in the last year has been due
chiefly to the decreased hog production in the United States resulting
from the 1934 drought. For many years prior to 1935 the United States
supplied the bulk of the British imports of lard. In the period October
1935 - February 1936, lard imports into Great Britain from the United
States represented only 33 percent of the total imports. A year earlier
this proportion was 81 percent and 2 years earlier 91 percent.

The restrictions on imports into the British market were adopted largely to aid British pig producers. Recent Census returns indicate that hog numbers in England and Wales at the end of 1935 were 46 percent larger than in early 1933, which was about the time the import restrictions became effective. The number of hogs in Germany in early March 1936 was 5 percent larger than the number on hand the year earlier. Germany reported an increase in nearly all classes of hogs. The number of bred sows in early March 1936 was 14 percent greater than in March 1935. Thus, German hog numbers may show a further increase as the present year advances.

As hog slaughter in this country in 1936 increases from the present low level, it is probable that exports of hog products will also increase. It is not likely, however, that exports of pork and lard in 1936 will reach a level equal to the 1930-1934 average, since domestic slaughter supplies of hogs this year will be much below average. Although restrictions to imports constituted the principal factor in the decrease in exports of hog products from 1931 to 1934, such restrictions in most countries are not sufficiently severe to prevent a moderate increase from the current low level in the exports of pork and lard from the United States. This is especially true in view of the concessions secured by the United States on hog products in several trade agreements, notably in the case of Cuba.

United States

In each month during the remainder of the present hog marketing year (up to September 30, 1936) hog slaughter probably will be larger than in the corresponding month of last year. A material increase in slaughter supplies compared with a year earlier is likely in the summer months, June to September, in view of the large increase in the 1935 fall pig crop. Since the number of hogs slaughtered under Federal inspection in the first half of the 1935-36 marketing year was much smaller than in 1934-35, the increase in the number of head slaughtered in the next 6 months probably will not be large enough to offset the decrease in the first 6 months of the year. Average weights of hogs marketed thus far in 1935-36 have been materially heavier then a year earlier, and weights in the last half of the year are likely to continue heavier than last year. Thus the total tonnage of federally inspected hog products produced in 1935-36 may be slightly larger than the production in 1934-35.

The trend of hog prices in the next 3 months, April through June, is likely to be downward in view of the probable increase in marketings in this period. As supplies of hogs for slaughter are seasonally reduced in the late summer, some advance in hog prices probably will occur at that time. The extent of this late summer advance, however, will depend partly upon changes in consumer demand between now and the late summer and partly upon how large slaughter supplies of other livestock are in that period.

Prices of hogs rose steadily during March despite the increased marketings in the last half of the month, and at the end of the month a large part of the decline which occurred in late February had been regained. The weekly average price of hogs at Chicago declined from $10.70 per 100 pounds for the second week in February to $9.99 in the last week of that month, but the rise during March brought this average to $10.42 for the week ended March 28. The average price of hogs at Chicago in March was $10.24 per 100 pounds, compared with $10.37 in February and $9.09 in March 1935. The advance in prices during March was slightly greater for heavy weight hogs than for light weights. The spread between the price of heavy weight and medium weight hogs was relatively narrow during the month, as is usual for this season of the year. In March last year, however, prices of heavy weight hogs were slightly higher than prices of the medium weights, whereas this year the situation has been more nearly normal, with medium weight hogs commanding a premium over heavy weights.

Hog slaughter under Federal inspection in March, amounting to about 2,617,000 head, was 13 percent larger than in February, when marketings were retarded because of unfavorable weather conditions. Slaughter in March is usually smaller than that of February. Although inspected slaughter in March was about 21 percent greater than the very small slaughter of March 1935, it was smaller than the slaughter for that month in any other post-war year. The increase in hog marketings which occurred after the middle of March was largely the result of improved weather and road conditions. In the first 6 months of the current hog marketing year, October 1935 to March 1936, the total inspected slaughter of 15,796,000 head was about 20 percent less than that of the corresponding period in 1934-35.

Average weights of hogs marketed were considerably heavier in March than in February, probably because of the improved feeding conditions accompanying the return of more favorable weather in the principal hog producing areas. The average weight of hogs at the seven leading markets was 240 pounds in March, compared with 228 pounds in February and 224 pounds in March 1935. The increase in average weights as compared with a year earlier was due chiefly to the fact that the hog-corn price ratio has been more favorable for hog feeding this year than last.

Corn prices tended to decline during most of March, and with the advance in hog prices the hog-corn price ratio increased during the month. The average price of No. 3 Yellow corn at Chicago for March was 60.8 cents per bushel compared with 61.3 cents in February and 83.3 cents in March 1935. Based on average farm prices for the 15th of the month, the hog-corn price ratio in the North Central States was 18.8 in March compared with 19.3 in February and 11.0 in March a year earlier.

After weakening during the second half of February, wholesale prices of fresh pork advanced during most of March, although there was a tendency for prices of some cuts to decline toward the end of the month. Prices of cured pork during most of March were about steady compared with prices in February, but advanced during the last week of the month, probably because of a strong demand for cured meats for the Easter trade. The composite wholesale price of hog products in New York in March was $20.75 per 100 pounds, compared with $20.84 in February and $20.47 in March 1935. Prices of lard at Chicago rose steadily through March after declining in January and February, but the average wholesale price of refined lard at Chicago in March was $11.88 per 100 pounds, compared with $12.06 in February. In March last year the average price of refined lard at Chicago was $15.50.

Exports of both pork and lard declined materially in February, with total exports of pork being the smallest for the month in many years. Exports of lard in February were very small, but were larger than the monthly exports of last summer and fall. Exports of both pork and lard in February were equal to less than half of the volume of such products exported in the same month a year earlier. Shipments of both pork and lard from the principal ports in March were larger than in February.

Exports of hams and shoulders in February, totaling 2,144,000 pounds, were 32 percent smaller than the quantity exported in January and were smaller than for any other month of the post-war period. The decrease in the exports of these cuts apparently accounts for most of the decrease in pork exports compared with the preceding month. Some increase in exports of canned pork was reported in February, but the quantity of such exports are small relative to the total pork exports. Bacon exports also declined in February, the total of 186,000 pounds being almost an insignificant item in export trade. For many years prior to 1930 exports of bacon were larger than those of any other form of pork. Exports of fresh pork, which were relatively large in 1934, have declined greatly since early 1935.

Lard exports in February, amounting to 7,570,000 pounds, were more than 25 percent smaller than those in January. A decline in the exports of lard to the United Kingdom accounted for most of the decrease in total lard exports during February. Lard exports to Cuba and the Netherlands in February were slightly larger than in January. Exports of lard to Germany in February, although larger than those of the same month a year earlier, were smaller than the shipments in January and much smaller than the monthly shipments of lard to that country in the post-war years prior to 1934.

As hog slaughter in this country increases during the remainder of 1936, it is probable that exports of pork and lard will show some increase from the present low level. It is not likely, however, that total exports of hog products in 1936 will return to the level of exports prevailing in the years from 1930 to 1934. The large decrease in exports since early 1935 was primarily the result of the material decrease in domestic slaughter

roplies of hogs rather than to import restrictions which had reduced ex-
irts from 1931 to 1935. Although these import restrictions for the most
irt remain in effect, exports of hog products from the United States can
: increased somewhat without being affected by restrictive measures.

Canada

The price of bacon hogs at Toronto during the 4-week period ended
irch 26 was $8.49 American currency per 100 pounds weighed off cars and
is about 10 cents below the February price. In March 1935 the price was
3.09 per 100 pounds, in March 1934 $9.09 and in March 1933 only $4.27.
ie price of good and choice hogs of similar weights, i.e., 180 to 220
punds, at Chicago, during the 4 weeks ended March 28 was $10.59 per 100
punds compared with $9.17 a year ago.

The price of hogs at Chicago made a sharp advance in 1935, the
rerage price for the year being $5.24 per 100 pounds higher than in 1934.
inadian hog prices, however, made the sharpest gain of recent years in
)34 when the average price of bacon hogs at Toronto was $3.45 per 100
punds above 1933.

The greatest factor in the advance of hog prices in Canada since
)33 was the favorable outlet to the British market provided by the generous
icon quota granted Canada in the Ottawa agreement of 1932. In the United
tates hog prices rose principally as a result of improved demand and greatly
iduced supplies resulting from the severe drought of 1934. The average
rice of hogs at Chicago was higher for the year 1935 than it was in Canada
y about 80 cents per 100 pounds and for the first 3 months of 1936 it was
1.83 higher than for hogs of similar weights in Canada.

Gradings of live hogs and hog carcasses combined, in Canada for the
weeks ended March 26 amounted to 254,179 compared with 235,515 a year
go, an increase of 8 percent. Gradings of live hogs and hog carcasses
or the first 13 weeks of this year amounted to 783,860 head compared with
)2,323 head a year ago, a decrease of 2 percent. Ontario was the only
rovince so far showing increased supplies. Increases also are to be ex-
2oted later in Quebec and Alberta.

Despite the smaller total number of hogs graded in Canada so far
his year, exports of live hogs and of pork products from Canada increased
lightly in the first 2 months of 1936. The total quantity of pork products
xported during that period (live hogs converted to a dressed meat basis)
1s approximately 31,536,000 pounds, compared with 30,279,000 pounds for
he same period a year ago, an increase of 4 percent. Whereas exports to
he United Kingdom in January and February 1936, totaling 28,000,000 pounds,
2creased 2 percent, there was an increase in exports to the United States
2 3,248,000, an increase of 29 percent above a year ago during the same
eriod (live hogs converted to a meat basis).

Attracted by favorable prices in the United States, Canada shipped
bout 8,000 live hogs to this country in the first 2 months of this year
ompared with practically none last year during the corresponding period.
hipments of live hogs to this country during the entire year 1935 reached
5,000 head, whereas such shipments did not exceed 2,000 head annually

during the years 1929 to 1934. The largest live hog exports to this
country from Canada occurred in 1914 when the number reached 215,000 head,
the next largest exportation being 195,000 head in 1927. Exports of bacon
and pork from Canada to the United States for the first 2 months of 1936
amounted to 1,836,000 pounds, compared with only 251,000 pounds in the
corresponding period of 1935.

Bacon exports to the United Kingdom from Canada amounted to only
11,050,000 pounds in February and were about 1,000,000 pounds smaller than
in January and almost 4,000,000 smaller than in February 1935. Approximately 98 percent of the total Canadian bacon exports went to the United
Kingdom. Combining exports of bacon and hams, pork, and lard, exports to
the United Kingdom in the first 2 months of 1936 declined 2,000,000 pounds
or 6 percent.

Exports of bacon from Canada to all countries for the first 2 months
of the year 1936 showed a decrease of 17 percent to 23,462,000 pounds.
There has been a substantial increase in lard exports, principally to the
United Kingdom, the quantity in February 1936 amounting to 2,669,000 pounds
or almost 4 times the quantity exported in February a year ago. Total lard
exports from Canada in the first 2 months of 1936 amounted to 4,349,000
pounds against only 1,140,000 a year earlier.

United Kingdom and Irish Free State

The United States shipments of bacon and ham to the British market
continue at low levels, British import figures in February 1936 reported
at very little over 2,000,000 pounds. Bacon imports from the United States
were negligible, and ham imports for the first time were second in absolute
quantity to those from another source - Canada.

The United States cured-pork quota as announced for the first 4
months of the year amounts to approximately 16,149,000 pounds, or over
8,000,000 pounds for the period January-February. For the past 2 years,
however, United States shipments for the first 4 months by special arrangement have been at the rate of 28 percent of the year's quota rather than 33
percent, allowing for seasonally heavier shipments during the summer months.
On account of the unusual supply conditions in the United States, the British
Government has also granted United States shippers a 2,800,000-pound abate-
ment to cover estimated shortages during the first 4 months of 1936. Considering the seasonally reduced rate and the allowance granted, shipments
for the first 4 months should amount to nearly 10,800,000 pounds, or around
5,400,000 pounds during the period January-February. Actual imports from
the United States into the United Kingdom for January and February have
totaled 4,472,000 pounds, or 54 percent of the original quota and only 83
percent of the adjusted allotment of 5,400,000. It will be necessary,
therefore, for United States shipments to average over 3,000,000 pounds
monthly during March and April to make up the deficiency now existing even
in the greatly reduced allotment indicated. (see table, page 7).

Liverpool bacon quotations remained firm during the month of March,
with the average price of Danish Wiltshire sides at $20.56 per hundred
pounds and Canadian green sides at $17.87. Both March averages were
approximately 17 percent above corresponding 1935 figures and were the
highest since March 1930. American green belly quotations were nominal.

United Kingdom: Cured pork import allotments to the United States
and monthly imports from the United States,
1933-1936

Month	1933		1934		1935		1936	
	Quota	Imports	Quota	Imports	Quota 1/	Imports	Quota 1/	Imports
	1,000 pounds	1,000 pounds	1,000 pounds	1,000 pounds	1,000 pounds	1,000 pounds	1,000 pounds	1,000 pounds
Jan......:	4,480	4,328	3,764:	2,730	4,322	3,020	4,308:	2,324
Feb.....:	4,756	3,466	3,399:	2,322	3,904	3,017	3,989:	2,148
Jan-Feb..: total...:	9,236	7,864	7,163:	5,052	8,226	6,037	8,297:	4,472
Mar......:	6,174	3,464	3,857:	5,236	4,322	3,409	3,090:	
Apr......:	5,492	5,887	4,876:	5,081	4,182	4,699	3,862:	
May......:	5,643	7,690	5,038:	4,948	4,243	5,006	:	
June.....:	5,707	6,293	4,876:	5,267	4,111	5,916	:	
July.....:	7,108	10,640	5,038:	9,866	4,384	6,257	:	
August...:	6,944	5,776	4,560:	7,173	4,384	4,349	:	
Sept.....:	5,704	7,241	4,560:	3,717	4,243	3,510	:	
Oct......:	4,612	5,594	4,561:	3,690	3,835	2,437	:	
Nov......:	3,888	5,794	4,560:	4,249	3,712	2,903	:	
Dec......:	3,764	4,220	4,561:	3,799	3,835	4,682	:	
Total...:	64,272	70,472	53,650:	58,078	49,483	49,205	:	

Foreign Agricultural Service Division.
1/ Figures do not reflect the special agreement allowing the United States to
ship 28 percent of estimated annual quota during first 4 months, 47 percent
during second 4 months, and 25 percent during last 4 months of the year.

Imports of Danish bacon in February, at about 30,000,000 pounds, were
nearly 2,000,000 pounds under January receipts. The total for the period
October-February, at a little over 162,000,000 pounds, was 10 percent below
corresponding 1934-35 imports and 56 percent less than those of the peak season
of 1931-32. Danish imports represented 54 percent of the total bacon imports
for the current season to February 29, the same as in the corresponding periods
of the 2 immediately preceding seasons, as against 63 percent during October-
February 1932-33 and 69 percent in 1931-32.

During the current season to the end of February, imports of Irish Free
State bacon into the United Kingdom have exceeded comparable 1934-35 imports
by nearly 3,000,000 pounds and have been higher than for any similar period
since 1928-29.

n imports from Canada have been maintained at the
e of over 8,500,000 pounds since November 1935, t
tober 1935 to February 1936 standing at nearly 40
represents a reduction of 15 percent from compar
rts but a 6 percent increase over imports of the
iod. The current figures are nearly 6-3/4 times
imports.

l bacon imports of 300,000,000 pounds into the Un
season to the end of February showed a decrease
ures of 9 percent and from imports of 1931-32 of

rpool quotations on American short cut green hams
ke an average of $19.65 per hundred pounds for th
;71 for January and $18.22 for February 1935. Im
es totaled less than 14,000,000 pounds for the pé
-1936. This represents a reduction of 15 percent
a year earlier and of 32 percent from those of 19
February period imports from the United States re
of the total ham imports. For the corresponding
ion of the total imports represented by shipments
59 percent and for 1933-34, 61 percent. Canadian
f February were 11 percent above those from the U
45 percent of total imports of ham into the Unit
percent from the United States. The remaining 14
incipally by the Irish Free State, Argentina, and

rpool lard quotations during March remained stead;
pounds. The average for the month was 70 cents 1
e, but nearly double that of March 1934. Lard im
pounds from the United States for the 5 onths Oc
h 81,000,000 pounds in the corresponding 1934-35
pounds in 1933-34. The United States share decl
3-34 to 81 percent in 1934-35 and to 33 percent i:
he current season. Total lard imports into the U:
to February 29 were 33 percent below those of Oc
51 percent below 1933-34 imports. Canada ranked
hipments of lard to the United Kingdom during Feb:
of the total, with Brazilian shipments amounting
l for the month.

ipts of British and Irish fresh pork at London Ce:
uary were 3,000,000 under January figures and for
were below corresponding monthly receipts of a y
he season to February 29, however, is still some !
ole total for 1934-35.

ecember 4, 1935 a voluntary census of livestock n
as made in order to obtain further information co:
listribution of livestock throughout England and 1
winter and to assist in estimating the probable f
ed meat. The result of the survey indicates a st
og numbers.

The number of hogs on December 4, 1935 was estimated at 4,113,000, according to statistics published in the Agricultural Market Report of March 6, 1936. This is an increase of 8 percent above the June 1935 estimate with which it is obviously not strictly comparable as the estimates were at different times of the year. There is usually a decline in number between June and December, but this year there appears to have been an increase.

A comparison of the December 1935 estimate with that of February 1933 shows an increase of 46 percent since that date, whereas since January 1930 there has been an increase of almost 100 percent in hog numbers.

The number of sows kept for breeding, including bred gilts, in December 1935 was reported at 507,000 and was 3 percent larger than in February 1933 and 67 percent above the January 1930 estimate. The rate of increase between 1933 and 1935, however, appears to be less than between the year 1930 and 1933.

There has been a fairly large increase in hogs other than breeding stock. The number of other hogs (butcher hogs) of all ages was 3,556,000 on December 4, 1935, an increase of 8 percent above the number on hand in June. As compared with February 1933 there is an increase of 46 percent and as compared with January 1930, an increase of 91 percent. An increase in slaughter supplies in 1936 is suggested by these figures.

Marketings of fat hogs at the representative English and Welsh markets during the first 12 weeks of 1936 amounted to 229,000, an increase of 7 percent above the corresponding period of 1935.

England and Wales: Number of hogs on December 4, 1935 with comparisons

Month and year	Sows kept for breed- ing (incl. pregnant gilts)	Boars being used for service	Other hogs Under 2 months	2 months and above	Total hogs
	Thousands	Thousands	Thousands	Thousands	Thousands
June 1922.:	307	22	2,038		2,367
Jan. 1930.:	304	21	1,828		2,153
June 1930.:	315	21	1,974		2,310
June 1931.:	402	26	2,355		2,783
June 1932.:	425	29	2,730		3,184
Feb. 1933.:	402	29	2,392		2,823
June 1933.:	406	29	819	1,815	3,069
June 1934.:	450	31	989	1,870	3,320
June 1935.:	494	40	1,205	2,074	3,813
Dec.4,1935:	507	41	1,046	2,519	4,113

Compiled from Agricultural Market Report, March 6, 1936.

As in the case of England and Wales i
numbers in Northern Ireland between June 193
the same trend was noticed between June 193

The number of hogs on January 1, 1936
mated at 488,000 an increase of 22 percent a
above January 1934 and 130 percent above Jar
in 1935 was greater than in 1934 or the incr
January 1934.

The number of sows kept for breeding
increase of 24 percent above the number on b
a further increase in hog numbers in 1936.

Between June 1935 and January 1936 tl
in hogs other than breeding stock. The numb
or 21 percent above the number on hand on De
slaughter supplies in 1936 than in 1935. Du
the number of hogs bought for curing in Nort
head, an increase of 48 percent above the sa

Northern Ireland: Number of hogs on Janu

Year and month	:Sows kept :for breed- :ing (incl. . pregnant : gilts)	Boars being used for service	Under 3 mos.
	: Thousands	: Thousands	: Thousan
June 1930 :	20 :	1/ :	
Jan. 1931 :	--- :	--- :	
June 1931 :	22 :	1/ :	
June 1932 :	20 :	1/ :	
June 1933 :	26 :	1/ :	
Jan. 1934 :	--- :	--- :	
June 1934 :	40 :	1/ :	
Dec. 1, 1934 :	42 :	1 :	199
June 1935 :	48 :	1 :	234
Jan. 1, 1936 :	52 :	2 :	229

Compiled from Agricultural Statistics, Int
May 1934, and mimeographed sheet dated Febru
Northern Ireland, Minister of Agriculture.
1/ Included with other hogs 6 months and ove
2/ Boars included.

Denmark

The hog industry in Denmark is probably in a more satisfactory condition than in any other important hog-producing country in Europe, according to Agricultural Commissioner H. E. Reed at Berlin. Between 1932 and 1934 hog numbers were reduced approximately 40 percent and since the middle of 1934 hog production has been in line with market possibilities. The adjustments which have taken place in the Danish hog industry have largely been the result of measures adopted in 1933 following Great Britain's quantitative restrictions on imports of cured pork. Considering the uncertainties which have existed as to the tonnage which could be exported to Great Britain, together with the fact that the Danish control measures have been applied directly to marketings and not to production, the adjustments have been a real achievement. While the present situation appears satisfactory, future trends in Danish hog production are not clear and, as is the case with other European hog-exporting countries, much depends upon economic and political developments in Europe.

Danish inspected hog slaughter in 1935, at 4,331,000 head, was 11.5 percent smaller than in 1934, and 44.7 percent below the high point reached in 1932, according to Vice Consul E. Gjessing at Copenhagen. Danish prices of export bacon were higher during 1935 than in 1934, averaging 158.85 crowns per 100 kilos ($15.77 per 100 pounds). The total export value of all hog products in 1935 amounted to 427,000,000 crowns ($93,442,118) compared with 450,600,000 crowns ($101,385,000) in 1934, and 464,000,000 crowns ($92,298,000) in 1933.

About 84 percent of the hogs slaughtered in 1935 were sent to British bacon markets, as against about 81 percent in 1934. Shipments to Great Britain averaged about 74,000 hogs weekly, against about 75,000 in 1934, and 102,000 weekly in 1933. The shipments are governed by the British import control program, which forms the basis for the Danish hog marketing control plan. The basic bacon hog prices are set in accordance with British bacon prices, and cards are issued periodically to cover the number of hogs eligible to receive the export price. In 1935, cards were issued to cover 4,027,000 hogs, representing 90 percent of the total inspected slaughter of hogs.

Germany

A further increase in German hog market receipts brought the February figure for 14 cities up to 226,000 head, according to cabled in formation from the Berlin office of the Foreign Agricultural Service. Increased hog numbers and regulations designed to confine sales to established channels continue to produce larger marketing figures. For the period October-February 1935-36, however, total receipts were 43 percent below the corresponding 1934-35 total. Hog slaughter at 36 centers also increased in February, with the total for the season to February 29 slightly more than 43 percent below last year's comparable figures.

The larger number of hogs reported as of March 3, 1936, was largely responsible for an increase effective April 6 in the permitted weekly hog slaughter by firms and individuals. The new figure is 80 percent of the average weekly hog slaughter by such firms and individuals in the period

October 1, 1934 - September 28, 1935. The permitted
creased from 60 percent of the base figure as suppli
available and as regulations against direct marketin
tive since late in 1935.

The number of hogs in Germany on March 3, 193
was an increase of 5 percent compared with the numbe
ing to a cable to the Foreign Agricultural Service D
Commissioner H. E. Reed. A further increase in hog
months is indicated by the fact that the number of b.
greater than the number reported in March 1935. You
to 1 year numbered 372,000 on March 3, 1936, an incr
a year ago, whereas bred sows of over 1 year numbere
15 percent.

All classes of hogs increased with the except.
over 1 year, which decreased 36 percent. The number
excluding bred sows and slaughter hogs over 1 year, v
thousands of head with percentage of last year given
pigs under 8 weeks, 5,502 (112); pigs 8 weeks to 6 mc
slaughter hogs 6 months to 1 year, 3,656 (108); brood
594 (108); brood sows over 1 year, 1,401 (113).

Germany: Number of hogs on March 1, 1936, w:

March 1 - 5	:Farrows: under 8 weeks	:Young pigs 8 weeks to 6 months	Hogs 6 months to 1 year Total, excl. sows & boars	Brood sows Total	:In far-row(preg nant)	Hogs Total, excl. sows &: boars
	Thous.	Thous.	Thous.	Thous.	Thous.	Thous.
1931	5,750	10,230	3,176	706	425	291
1932	5,014	9,975	3,256	549	323	298
1933	5,152	9,379	3,392	528	316	294
1934	5,715	10,022	3,831	561	327	334
1935	4,920	9,574	3,593	554	333	444
1936	5,502	9,590	3,656	594	372	385

Compiled from cable received from Commissioner H. E.
official sources for earlier years.

There has been little change in the German fat supply situation. Total imports of lard for February were more than 7,000,000 pounds, the largest imports since l st November and more than 2,000,000 pounds larger than the February 1935 imports. Denmark was the chief supplier in February, sending nearly 2,500,000 pounds, compared with around 1,200,000 pounds from Hungary, usually chief source of supply in recent months. Yugoslavia and Argentina also made important contributions, with only 291,000 pounds credited to the United States. The Netherlands sent only 67,000 pounds. Total lard imports for the period October 1, 1935 to February 29, 1936 were 41.4 percent larger than those of a year earlier, but they were 35.7 percent smaller than the imports in 1933-34, and 64.5 percent below figures for 1932-33.

Bacon imports continue slightly below last year's level, with the Netherlands as the leading supplier. In February, Yugoslavia was in second place, followed by Hungary and Denmark. Total imports for the month amounted to little more than 2,000,000 pounds, with imports for the period October to February being 15.3 percent below those of last season.

Other countries

South American lard exports large in 1935.- Total exports of lard from Brazil and Argentina for the year 1935 amounted to about 49,000,000 pounds, according to estimates based on information supplied by United States Consular Officers. That figure represents an unusually large movement of South American lard into export channels, but it is equivalent to only about 50 percent of the greatly reduced exports from the United States during the same period and less than 10 percent of the usual United States exports. The large exports from South America reflected the shortage of United States lard on European markets and the unusually high prices obtainable there. Most of the South American lard went to the British market.

At 28,000,000 pounds for the period January-November 1935, exports of lard from Brazil exceeded combined shipments from Brazil and Argentina for t e entire year 1934 by 55 percent and comparable 1934 Brazilian exports by 192 percent. Argentine lard exports of nearly 7,500,000 pounds for 1935 also were much above average, showing an increase over 1934 figures of 177 percent and nearly equaling the combined 1934 exports from Brazil and Argentina. It is unlikely that such exports from either Brazil or Argentina will continue after lard from the United States is again available in normal quantities, though indications are for continued relatively large shipments during 1936.

Hogs and pork products: Indices of foreign supplies and demand

Country and item	Unit	1909-10: to 1913-14: average	1924-25: to 1928-29: average	Oct. - Feb. 1932-33	1933-34	1934-35	1935-36
UNITED KINGDOM							
Production							
Supplies, domestic: fresh pork, London	1,000 pounds		30,483	44,266	36,111	38,924	42,555
Imports							
Bacon							
Denmark	"	98,904	207,453	313,809	204,082	180,479	162,203
Irish Free State	"		26,778	10,263	14,276	20,701	23,450
United States .	"	78,471	46,916	1,578	2,313	1,622	799
Canada	"	15,974	33,510	6,951	37,493	46,668	39,732
Others	"	17,010	61,983	164,315	113,490	81,949	74,097
Total	"	210,359	376,640	496,418	371,655	331,420	300,281
Ham, total	"	36,919	49,767	34,679	30,055	27,492	27,116
Lard, total	"	95,585	108,006	114,633	136,483	99,451	66,880
DENMARK							
Exports							
Bacon	"		205,721	317,526	214,458	181,187	
CANADA							
Slaughter							
Hogs, inspected .	1000's	732	1,230	1,174	1,298	1,319	1,309
GERMANY							
Production							
Hog receipts							
14 cities	"		1,334	1,310	1,343	1,436	815
Hog slaughter							
36 centers	"	1,844	1,662	1,784	1,824	1,934	1,087
Imports	1,000						
Bacon, total	pounds	1,305	8,890	17,835	13,953	13,728	11,644
Lard, total	"	85,046	92,334	117,397	64,898	29,713	41,732
UNITED STATES							
Slaughter							
Hogs, inspected .	1000's	14,927	22,070	20,314	20,913	17,221	13,179
Exports							
Bacon	1,000						
United Kingdom	pounds	57,392	28,428	1,275	1,094	927	341
Germany	"	947	4,747	1,045	2,181	0	0
Cuba	"	3,094	8,999	1,688	1,557	2,157	381
Total	"	78,202	61,697	7,955	11,194	4,094	1,111
Ham, shoulders ..	"						
United Kingdom	"	56,747	56,784	20,094	21,577	17,547	14,179
Total	"	65,481	69,046	24,168	25,476	22,046	16,669
Lard							
United Kingdom	"	72,817	93,664	119,202	129,490	71,557	24,913
Germany	"	62,463	79,896	85,926	41,742	2,513	2,205
Cuba	"	14,893	35,047	3,781	4,800	14,863	7,634
Netherlands ...	"	17,255	20,471	19,710	15,333	9	39
Total	"	204,561	313,436	275,250	240,263	96,336	36,147

Hogs and pork products: Foreign and domestic average prices per 100 pounds
for the month indicated, and stocks at the end of each month

Item	1909-1913 average	1925-1929 average	Feb. 1935	Jan. 1936	Feb. 1936
	Dollars	Dollars	Dollars	Dollars	Dollars
PRICES					
Hogs, Chicago, basis packers' and shippers' quotations	7.43	10.68	8.35	9.85	10.37
Corn, Chicago, No. 3 Yellow	1.02	1.64	1.57	1.08	1.09
Hogs, heavy, Berlin, live weight	11.39	14.32	15.78	17.70	17.70
Potatoes, Breslau feeding ..	.39	.54	.86		
Barley, Leipzig	1.76	2.35	3.07	3.23	3.29
Lard -					
Chicago	10.18	14.31	14.44	12.15	12.06
Liverpool	11.60	15.03	13.43	13.48	12.99
Hamburg	13.91	15.40		13.14	12.83
Cured pork -					
Liverpool					
American short cut green: hams	13.00	22.04	19.10	19.23	18.71
American green bellies		20.23	15.11	15.19	15.27
Danish Wiltshire sides	14.20	21.96	18.82	19.43	20.58
Canadian green sides ..	13.49	20.92	15.22	16.45	17.82
	1,000 pounds	1,000 pounds	1,000 pounds	1,000 pounds	1,000 pounds
STOCKS					
United States					
Processed pork 1/		795,507	671,315	436,042	451,800
Lard in cold storage		120,024	110,508	75,669	78,879

1/ Dry salt cured and in process of cure; pickled, cured, and in process of cure;
and frozen.

- - - - O - - - -

.

UNITED STATES DEPARTMENT OF AGRICULTURE
Bureau of Agricultural Economics
Division of Statistical and Historical Research
Washington

HP-78

WORLD HOG AND PORK PROSPECTS

May 28, 1936

Quarterly Summary

Increases in the numbers of hogs on hand in the spring of 1936 were reported in Germany, Denmark and the Netherlands. In all three of these countries the number of bred sows in early 1936 was larger than a year earlier, indicating that a further increase in numbers in the remainder of 1936 is probable. Also in the United States and Canada an increase in the 1936 spring pig crop is expected. The expansion in hog numbers above noted doubtless will result in an increase in hog slaughter in the various countries later this year. Changes in hog slaughter in the last half of the present year as well as further changes in hog numbers, however, will depend to a considerable extent upon the production of feed crops in 1936. In the last year the relationship between hog prices and feed prices in most important producing countries has been favorable for increased hog production.

Imports of hog products into Germany have increased considerably in the last 6 months. Practically all of the German imports, however, are now being secured from other continental European countries including Poland, Denmark, Netherlands and the Danube countries and such imports have been made possible largely by barter agreements between the various countries and Germany. Imports of American hog products into Germany have been very small in recent months chiefly because of foreign exchange conditions in Germany and relatively short supplies of such products in the United States for export.

Imports of bacon and hams into the United Kingdom in the last 6 months have been somewhat smaller than a year earlier as a result of the restrictions on imports to that country. Although total imports were reduced, shipments from Empire countries including Canada and the Irish

ed a much larger proportion of the total than usual.

applied solely to imports from non-Empire countries.

Britain in the last 6 months were about 33 percent sm

Although the United States continued to be the leadin

imports, imports from other countries in 1935-36 repr

proportion of the total than usual.

Domestic hog prices declined during late April

slaughter increased. Slaughter supplies in the United

continue to increase through June with some decrease e

summer. In view of the high hog-corn price ratio in t

is likely that the 1936 spring pig crop is materially

1935. Such an increase will be reflected in larger su

domestic slaughter after next September.

Hog Numbers

Estimates of hog numbers in the spring of this y
indications of increased hog production in important pi
1936, with further expansion probable as a result of th
hog-feed price ratio in most countries.

Already increases in total hog numbers are evide
estimates of Denmark, Netherlands and Germany as compan
The Danube Basin exporting countries appear to have a s
of hogs on hand as a further increase is reported in th
in 1936. In the United States and Canada, breeding int
indicate increases in the number of sows to be bred dur
1936 as compared with a year ago.

In Denmark and the Netherlands, the most importa
countries, latest estimates show increases of 13 and 9
above the small numbers reported in the spring of 1935.
important deficit country, there was an increase of 4 1
as of March 3, 1936 as compared with the number in Marc
this spring also was larger than in March 1932 or 1933
than in March 1934. Estimates for the spring of 1936 s
for other European countries.

Further expansion in hog numbers in 1936 is indicated by the fact that bred sows showed an increase in number this spring as compared with last in all countries reporting. There was an increase of 13 percent to 289,000 in the total number bred in Denmark and an increase of 9 percent to 158,000 in the Netherlands. The greater increase in Denmark was in the younger sows which increased 31 percent to 117,000. In Germany, the March 1936 estimate of the total number of bred sows showed an increase of 14 percent to 1,207,000 as compared with March 1935. Contrary to the situation in Denmark the greater increase in Germany was in older bred sows of 1 year and over which numbered 835,000, a 15 percent increase over March 1935. There was also an important increase in young and suckling pigs and hogs of slaughter age in these three countries.

There will be an increase of about 24 percent to 6,220,000 in the number of sows to farrow in the United States during the months December 1935 to June 1936, if breeding intention reports are borne out. In Canada present indications are for an increase of 28 percent to 593,000 in the number to farrow this spring.

Summing up the situation, the total number of hogs in Denmark the Netherlands and Germany this spring was 26,001,000, 6 percent above the number on hand in the spring of 1935 but 3 and 5 percent less than in the years 1933 and 1934, respectively. The number of bred sows in the same three European countries numbered 1,654,000 this spring, an increase of 14 percent over a year earlier. The number of sows to be bred in the United States and Canada combined this spring is 6,813,000 or 24 percent more than a year ago but less than in 1932-33 and 1933-34.

At the beginning of 1936 the number of hogs in nine surplus and deficit countries was 86,360,000, 4 percent above the low point reached in 1935. The number of hogs in the five important surplus producing countries was 52,576,000, an increase of 8 percent over 1935 when the number was unusually small. The number in the four deficit countries showed a reduction of 2 percent to 33,784,000. The total number in these nine countries which are important in international trade is only about 30 percent of the estimated world total, taking the latest estimate for the individual countries.

The number in the United States and Canada at the beginning of 1936 shows an increase of 9 percent over the same date of the preceding year, but was still 25 percent below the number reported in 1934. There was an increase of 3 percent to 6,085,000 in 1936 in three European exporting countries reporting, Denmark, Netherlands and Lithuania, but the level of the 3 years, 1932 to 1934, has not been reached in these countries.

There has been a material increase in the number of hogs in Russia between January 1, 1934 and January 1, 1936, the number having increased from 11,500,000 to 25,900,000 according to official estimates. However, Russia does not play an important role in the international trade of hogs and pork products at present, and is not likely to be on an export basis for some time.

Hogs: Numbers in specified surplus and deficit hog and
producing countries, 1932-1936.

Country	Date of estimate	1932	1933	1934
		Thou-sands	Thou-sands	Thou-sands
SURPLUS COUNTRIES -				
United States .. ..:	Jan. 1	59,301	62,127	58,621
Canada ....:	Jan. 1 1/	4,263	4,125	3,588
Australia ....:	Jan. 1 1/	1,168	1,162	1,162
New Zealand ....:	Jan. 31	513	592	660
Total 2 countries reporting to 1936......:		63,564	66,252	62,209
European countries				
Irish Free State ....:	Jan. 1	---	---	799
Denmark.................:	Jan.	5,457	2/4,543	3,474
Netherlands .. ..:	Jan. 1 1/	3/2,382	3/2,300	4/2,484
Lithuania ....:	Jan. 1 1/	1,338	1,234	1,235
Rumania ....:	Jan. 1 1/	3,221	2,965	---
Yugoslavia ....:	Jan. 1 1/	3,133	2,863	2,656
Total 3 European countries reporting to 1936................:		9,177	8,077	7,193
Total 5 surplus countries reporting to 1936......:		72,741	74,329	69,402
DEFICIT COUNTRIES -				
England and Wales... .. ..:	Feb.	2,153	5/2,823	---
Northern Ireland ....:	Jan. 1	6/ 212	---	295
Germany ....:	Jan. 1 1/	23,808	22,859	23,890
France ....:	Jan. 1	6,398	6,488	6,769
Belgium ....:	Jan. 1	1,235	1,246	1,353
Czechoslovakia ....:	Jan. 1	2,576	2,621	3,430
Total 4 deficit countries reporting to 1936......:		34,017	33,214	35,442
Total 9 surplus and deficit countries reporting to 1936..... :		106,758	107,543	104,844
Total 12 surplus and deficit countries reporting to 1935......:		111,572	112,160	109,322
Soviet Russia..... ......:	Jan. 1	---	---	8/11,575

Compiled from reports of United States Agricultural Commissioner
sources, and the International Institute of Agriculture.
1/ Any estimates reported in December have been considered as of
following year.   2/January 23.   3/Unofficial estimate
centage change as furnished by Assistant Agricultural Attache' D.
pared with Census of June 1930.   4/Estimates for November of
are the nearest estimates available to the first of the year.   5
6/1931.   7/Including the Saar, the number was 22,824,000.
8/ Calculated by using official estimates.

Denmark: Official 1936 spring estimate of hog numbers compared
with earlier years

Date	Boars: 4 months and over	Brood sows			Other hogs (new classification)				
		In farrow	Not in farrow	Total	132 pounds and over	77 to 132 pounds	Under 77 pounds	Suckling pigs	Total
	Thousands	Thousands	Thousands	Thousands	Thousands	Thousands	Thousands	Thousands	Thousands
July 15, 1933	25	280	164	444	827	997	1,068	1,029	4,390
Oct. 14, 1933	24	244	161	405	825	951	1,075	916	4,169
Dec. 15, 1933	23	212	150	362	740	892	974	733	3,724
Jan. 16, 1934	21	210	141	351	669	817	890	726	3,474
Mar. 1, 1934	22	237	110	347	649	743	792	631	3,184
Apr. 14, 1934	22	238	110	348	639	694	719	659	3,081
June 1, 1934	22	284	115	363	595	664	672	711	3,027
July 15, 1934	21	231	124	355	523	647	737	774	3,057
Oct. 15, 1934	20	216	117	333	590	711	734	720	3,108
Dec. 1, 1934	20	238	106	344	621	646	745	653	3,029
Jan. 15, 1935	19	253	105	358	451	667	762	668	2,925
Mar. 1, 1935	20	255	114	369	508	637	738	695	2,967
Apr. 13, 1935	20	241	132	373	463	629	740	813	3,038
May 25, 1935	20	255	125	380	500	635	797	724	3,056
June 20, 1935									3,056
July 16, 1935	20	275	114	389	456	729	761	760	3,025
Aug. 24, 1935	21	259	124	383	545	693	742	782	3,166
Oct. 5, 1935	21	264	141	405	534	683	792	860	3,295
Nov. 16, 1935	21	278	132	410	565	674	882	766	3,318
Dec. 28, 1935	21	278	127	405	450	723	885	732	3,216
Feb. 8, 1936	21	270	137	407	518	722	816	779	3,263
Mar. 21, 1936	22	289	140	429	558	700	826	819	3,354

Compiled from Statistiske Efterretninger published by the Statistical Department
of Denmark, and reports from Agricultural Commissioner H. E. Reed, United States
Department of Agriculture.

herlands: Official 1936 spring estimate of number
classes, compared with earlier years

:e	: Sows : in :farrow	: Pigs : under : 6 : weeks	: Hogs. : up to : 132 : pounds	: Hogs : 132 to : 200 : pounds
	: Thousands	Thousands	Thousands	Thousands
June 1910 :	130	279	----	980
June 1921 :	147	371	---	1,148
June 1930 :	242	472	940	263
1/ :				
1930	254	420	1,072	337
1931 :	232	571	1,053	4
1931 :	210	557	1,250	321
1931	196	571	1,278	358
1931	213	434	1,241	355
1932	196	562	1,109	331
1932	179	458	1,213	266
.1932 2/ :	265	535	1,012	624
1933 :	235	544	769	367
1933	240	437	982	399
1934	157	453	707	366
1934	153	321	817	391
1934	146	296	572	470
1934	142	329	448	355
1935 :	145	271	445	310
1935	146	306	635	188
1935	153	397	544	335
1935	146	331	574	272
1936	158	320	497	312

rom Verslag oven den Landbouw in Nederland 1928 - (
Wickel, January 16, 1931 and International Institu
arch 1933. Later estimates from Agricultural Comm
eign Agricultural Service.

ial estimates based on percentage change from June
by Berlin Office of Foreign Agricultural Service a
an Wickel.
es of Varkenscentrale - not strictly comparable wi
 The number for September 1, 1932 adjusted from th
 estimated at 2,600,000 compared with 2,622,000 on

Germany, excluding the Saar: Official 1936 spring estimate of hogs,
by classes, compared with earlier years

Mar. 1 - 5	Farrows under 8 weeks	Young pigs 8 weeks to 3 months	Hogs 6 months to 1 year			Hogs over 1 year			Grand total
			Total excl. sows & boars	Brood sows		Total excl. sows & boars	Brood sows		
			:Total:	In farrow (pregnant)		:Total:	In farrow (pregnant)		
	Thou-sands	Thou-sands	Thou-sands	Thou-sands	Thou-sands	Thou-sands	Thou-sands	Thou-sands	Thou-sands
1931	5,750	10,230	3,176	706	425	291	1,517	927	21,790
1932	5,014	9,975	3,256	549	323	298	1,425	875	20,633
1933	5,152	9,379	3,392	528	316	294	1,381	832	20,238
1934	5,715	10,022	3,831	561	327	334	1,433	841	22,010
1935	4,920	9,574	3,393	554	333	444	1,236	724	20,225
1936	5,502	9,590	3,656	594	372	285	1,401	835	21,138

Compiled from cable received from Commissioner H. E. Reed, and original
official sources for earlier years.

United States

The seasonal decline in hog prices which began in late April probably
will continue through June, although a considerable part of the anticipated
decrease already has occurred. In the late summer, however, prices are likely
to advance, as is usual for that time of year. These probable price changes
will occur primarily as a result of changes in the slaughter supplies of hogs.
Marketings of hogs began to increase in the last half of April as the movement
of fall-farrowed pigs got under way in fairly large volume. The peak of the
summer supply of hogs will probably be reached in late June or early July,
after which marketings are expected to decline. In view of the very high hog-
corn price ratio in the last 6 months it is probable that the 1936 spring pig
crop is materially larger than the spring crop of 1935. Such an increase
will be reflected in materially larger hog marketings after next September.

After advancing almost steadily through March and the first half of
April hog prices declined fairly sharply in late April and early May as
supplies of hogs were seasonally increased. Prices of heavy weight butcher
hogs and packing sows have weakened somewhat more than the prices of light
and medium weight hogs since mid-April. Only a part of the March and early
April price advance was lost in late April and consequently the hog prices
for April averaged higher than in March. The average price of hogs at Chicago
in April was $10.47 per 100 pounds compared with $10.24 in March and $8.94 in
the corresponding month last year. The average price in April of this year
was the highest monthly average since last September and was the highest
average for the month since 1929.

Hog slaughter under Federal inspection in A
head was slightly smaller than in March but was 17.
unusually small April slaughter last year. Slaught
April was somewhat larger than in the preceding weel
feeding conditions in April somewhat improved over
of hogs marketed also improved. The average weight
leading markets was 241 pounds compared with 240 poi
pounds in April last year. Inspected hog slaughter
season October 1935 to April 1936 amounted to 18,35
a decrease of about 16 percent in the slaughter in 1
Nearly all of this decrease occurred in the 3 month
Thus, in the present hog marketing year hog slaught
relative to slaughter a year earlier since December,
decreased considerably compared with a year earlier
increase in slaughter in recent months compared with
reflects in part a later movement of spring pigs to
since hogs marketed in recent months have been finis
weights than a year earlier. The more favorable hog
greater feed supplies available this year than last
responsible for the increase in weights.

Although hog prices averaged higher in April
also advanced, and the hog-corn price ratio did not
to April. Based on farm prices for the 15th of the
ratio in the Corn Belt States in April was 19.2 comp
and 10.1 in April a year earlier. Although the rati
lower than that of February, it was the highest for

Wholesale prices of fresh pork advanced sharp
April following a sharp decline for 1 week at the be
Such prices, however, declined rather rapidly in ear
in slaughter supplies in hogs. Prices of most cured
during April but averaged higher than in March. The
price of hog products in New York in April was $20.9
with $20.75 in March and $20.62 in April 1935.

Exports of both pork and lard in March increa
small exports in February. Exports of lard were gre
month during the present marketing year and exceeded
corresponding month a year earlier for the first tim
hog marketing year. In the first half of the presen
exports of pork totaled only 29,800,000 pounds compa
in the first half of the 1934-35 marketing year. Th
to the United Kingdom were largely responsible for t
exports in the first half of the current year. The
was relatively greater than those of pork during the
present marketing year, the total being about 55 per
lard shipped abroad during the same period in 1934-3

Exports of hams and shoulders, the principal
March compared with the preceding month, but such ex
percent smaller than in March 1935. Most of the inc
cuts from February to March was in the shipments to
the first half of the 1935-36 marketing year exports
totaled about 19,000,000 pounds, a decrease of about
with the same period in 1934-35.

Lard exports in March totaled 11,566,000 pounds and were the largest for any month since February 1935. The March exports of lard, however, were relatively small compared with monthly shipments in years prior to 1935. Nearly all of the leading lard importing countries took increased quantities of lard from the United States in March compared with earlier months of the marketing year, but the increase was greatest in the shipments of this product to the United Kingdom.

A detailed statistical summary of the domestic situation for hogs and hog products for the first half of the 1935-36 marketing year appears on page 10. It will be noted that the number of hogs slaughtered under Federal inspection in this period was about 20 percent smaller than that of the same period in 1934-35, but the total dressed weight of hogs slaughtered under Federal inspection was only 13 percent less than a year earlier. The difference in these rates of decrease is accounted for by the increase of about 7 percent in the average dressed weight of hogs slaughtered under Federal inspection in the first half of the current marketing year. Exports of pork and lard in the October - March period, 1935-36, were only about one-half as large as in 1934-35, but imports were several times larger than last year. Despite this increase imports were much smaller than the exports, and were very small in relation to the domestic production. Storage holdings of pork products increased somewhat from the beginning of October 1935 to the end of March 1936, as is usual for this season of the year but such stocks were at a relatively low level throughout the winter. The apparent domestic disappearance of federally inspected hog products in the first half of the current hog marketing year was about 15 percent smaller than that of a year earlier and about 30 percent smaller than the 5-year average. Lard production under Federal inspection thus far in 1935-36 has been about 17 percent smaller than that of 1934-35 and about 46 percent less than the 5-year average. The yield of lard per 100 pounds of hogs slaughtered under Federal inspection was only slightly less than last year but it was about 20 percent less than the 5-year average yield for the first half of the marketing year.

Canada.- Larger supplies of hogs for slaughter are in prospect for the first half of 1936 as compared with a year ago according to the Canadian Government Hog Survey. The average price of bacon hogs at Toronto for the first 4 months of 1936 was $8.47 per 100 pounds weighed off cars, compared with $8.49 for the same period a year earlier. The price for the 4 weeks ended April 30, 1936 was $8.32 per 100 pounds compared with $8.49 in March and $8.70 for April 1935. Canadian exports of pork products and live hogs converted to a meat basis showed an increase of 10 percent during the first 3 months of 1936 as compared with a year earlier. The bulk went to the United Kingdom as usual, but exports to that country showed a slight decrease whereas there was an increase in the exports to the United States.

Hogs and pork products: United State
with comparisons, specif

Item	Unit	5-year average 1930-31 to 1934-35	19;
Hogs -			
Inspected slaughter:	number	23,876,265	19,(
Carcasses condemned:	"	67,527	
Average live weight:	pound	223.42	
Average dressed " :	"	168.50	
Total dressed weight:			
(excl. condemned)	1000 lbs	4,011,820	3,(
Storage Oct. 1 be-			
ginning of market-			
ing year -			
Fresh pork.. .. .:	" "	102,239	1
Cured pork........:	" "	412,806	;
Lard ....:	" "	103,960	1
Total. ....:		619,005	(
Imports -			
Fresh pork........:	" "	423	
Pork, pickled, and			
preserved... . .:	" "	1,600	
Total... ..		2,023	
Available for			
consumption 1/....:	" "	4,632,848	3,7
Exports -			
Pork.............:	" "	68,129	
Lard ....:	" "	272,920	1
Total.....:		341,049	1
Storage Apr. 1, end			
of period -			
Fresh pork ....:	" "	208,504	2
Cured pork ... .:	" "	497,631	4
Lard ....:	" "	104,853	1
Total... . :		810,988	7
Apparent consumption 2/		3,480,811	2,8
Lard -			
Production			
Per 100 lbs. live			
weight..........:	pound	14.49	
Total......:	1000lbs.	772,684	5
Apparent consumption 3/	" "	498,871	4
Hogs - Average cost			
for slaughter. ....:	dollars	5.10	

1/ Total dressed weight plus imports plus sto
2/ Available for consumption - (exports plus
3/ Production plus storage October 1, beginni
end of period).

Canada: Number of sows to farrow December to May and prospective
marketings, 1932-33 to 1935-36

Provinces	Sows to farrow Dec. to May				Hogs for market and for farms and local slaughter Dec. to May			
	1932-33	1933-34	1934-35	1935-36	1932-33	1933-34	1934-35	1935-36
	Thou-sands	Thou-sands	Thou-sands	Thou-sands	Thou-sands	Thou-sands	Thou-sands	Thou-sands
Principal Eastern Provinces -								
Ontario	128	129	137	172	801	750	714	814
Quebec	94	107	115	137	252	204	311	365
Total..	222	236	252	309	1.053	954	1,025	1,179
Three Prairie Provinces								
Manitoba	25	24	20	29	145	93	104	87
Saskatchewan	64	75	67	92	380	309	281	276
Alberta	78	93	95	131	427	498	534	492
Total..	167	192	182	252	952	900	919	855
Total, 5 Provinces	389	428	434	561	2,005	1,854	1,944	2,034
Others	24	25	29	32	112	96	105	119
Grand total	413	453	463	593	2,117	1,950	2,049	2,153

Compiled from Monthly Bulletin of Agricultural Statistics of Canada, February 1936.

Canada: Number of hogs on farms by provinces, December 1, 1933 - 1935

Provinces	1933	Percentage of total	1934	Percentage of total	1935	Percentage of total
	Thou-sands	Per-cent	Thou-sands	Per-cent	Thou-sands	Per-cent
Principal Eastern Provinces						
Ontario	1,061	30	1,152	32	1,460	37
Quebec	484	14	590	16	666	17
Total.	1,545	44	1,742	48	2,126	54
Three Prairie Provinces:						
Manitoba	214	6	222	6	194	5
Saskatchewan	648	18	630	17	607	15
Alberta	904	25	869	24	815	21
Total	1,766	49	1,721	47	1,616	41
Total 5 Provinces.	3,311	93	3,463	95	3,742	95
Others 1/	277	7	186	5	208	5
Grand total	3,588	100	3,649	100	3,950	100

Compiled from Monthly Bulletin of Agricultural Statistics of Canada, February 1936.

Canada: Hog survey, December 1, 1932-1935

Provinces	Sows farrowed June to Nov.				Pigs born June to Nov.			
	1932	1933	1934	1935	1932	1933	1934	1935
	Thou-sands	Thou-sands	Thou-sands	Thou-sands	Thou-sands	Thou-sands	Thou-sands	Thou-sands
Principal eastern provinces								
Ontario ....:	141	130	130	154	1,351	1,283	1,302	1,574
Quebec ....:	66	54	62	74	593	506	592	699
Total ....:	207	184	192	228	1,944	1,789	1,894	2,273
Three prairie provinces								
Manitoba ....:	29	17	18	17	240	154	162	152
Saskatchewan ...:	76	63	60	55	602	518	503	468
Alberta ....:	74	70	70	89	621	623	640	827
Total ....:	179	150	148	161	1,463	1,295	1,305	1,447
Total 5 provinces	386	334	340	389	3,407	3,084	3,199	3,720
Other ....:	23	18	19	23	206	185	193	218
Grand total ......:	409	352	359	412	3,613	3,269	3,392	3,938
	Pigs saved June-Nov.				Pigs saved per litter			
	1932	1933	1934	1935	1932	1933	1934	1935
	Thou-sands	Thou-sands	Theu-sands	Thou-sands	Number	Number	Numbor	Number
Principal eastern provinces								
Ontario ....:	1,080	991	1,042	1,219	7.7	7.6	8.0	7.9
Quebec ....:	478	408	474	574	7.2	7.5	7.6	7.7
Total ....:	1,558	1,399	1,516	1,793				
Three prairie provinces								
Manitoba ....:	183	118	126	112	6.3	6.8	6.9	6.8
Saskatchewan ...:	466	400	396	365	6.1	6.4	6.6	6.9
Alberta ....:	484	496	521	642	6.5	7.1	7.5	6.5
Total ....:	1,133	1,014	1,043	1,119				
Total 5 provinces	2,691	2,413	2,559	2,912				
Other ....:	160	145	151	172				
Grand total ......:	2,851	2,558	2,710	3,084	7.3	7.0	7.6	7.5

Compiled from Monthly Bulletin of Agricultural Statistics of Canada,
    February 1936.

Despite the forecast of an increase of 5 percent in the number of hogs for slaughter for the period December 1935 to May 1936 to 2,153,000 head, gradings of live and dead hogs during the first 4 months of the year were approximately the same as in the corresponding period of 1935. April gradings of hogs, however, amounted to 261,000 head, an increase of 6 percent over the same period last year. The indicated increase in Canadian hog numbers as shown by the December Hog Survey points to larger supplies during the next 3 months.

The number of sows to be bred in the period December 1935 to May 1936 is estimated at 593,000 or 28 percent more than in 1934-35. An increase of 22 percent is indicated for the two most important eastern provinces, Ontario and Quebec, and an increase of 38 percent in the three Prairie Provinces.

On December 1, 1935 the number of hogs on farms in Canada was estimated at 3,950,000, an increase of 8 percent over 1934 and 10 percent over 1933. The two important eastern provinces of Ontario and Quebec showed an increase of 22 percent, whereas there was a decrease of 6 percent in the three Prairie Provinces.

Although exports of Canadian pork products and live hog converted to a meat basis reached 50,000,000 pounds in the first 3 months of 1936, an increase of 10 percent compared with a year ago, exports of bacon to the British market were 14 percent smaller and amounted to only 36,000,000 pounds. Monthly exports to that country averaged only 12,000,000 pounds in the first quarter of 1936 compared with 14,000,000 pounds in the same period of 1935. There was an increase in pork exports to the United States during the same period from 494,000 pounds last year to 2,591,000 pounds this year. Lard exports, principally to the United Kingdom, reached 6,680,000 pounds compared with 2,111,000 pounds in the first 3 months of 1935.

United Kingdom and Irish Free State

A revision of the British import quota figures covering the period May 1 - August 31, 1936, places the total cured pork to be imported into the United Kingdom at 1,813,458 hundredweight (203,107,000 pounds), according to information supplied by Agricultural Attaché C. C. Taylor at London. This figure represents an increase from the quota tentatively announced early in April of approximately 1,640,000 pounds. The revised monthly quota rate is about 3 percent under that prevailing during the comparable 4 months of 1935, but is 7 percent above that of the January-April 1936 period. The United States share remains 8.1 percent of the total, plus adjustments for seasonal trade, previous undershipments, and extra quota allowances.

om: Total cured-pork allocations, May 1-August 31,
o the United States, October 1, 1935-August 31,1936

otal allocation May 1- :			:	Allocation to Uni	
Aug. 31, 1936 :		Month	:	States, Oct. 1-	
Allocations :			:	Aug. 31, 1936	
			:	:Allocation 1/:Impor	
cent :	Cwt.	:1,000lbs:	:	1,000 lbs.	:1,000
:	:	:	:	:	
63.50:1,151,546:	128,973:Oct. .....:		3,794	:	2,4
9.50: 172,278:	19,295:Nov. .....:		3,794	:	2,9
7.95: 144,170:	16,147:Dec. .....:		3,794	:	4,6
4.70: 85,232:	9,546:Jan. .....:		3,877	:	2,3
2.95: 53,497:	5,992:Feb. .....:		3,642	:	2,1
.75: 13,600:	1,523:Mar. .....:		3,990	:	2,5
.40: 7,254:	812:Apr. .....:		3,862	:	
.70: 12,695:	1,422:May .....:		4,113	:	
.85: 15,414:	1,726:June ....:		4,113	:	
.70: 12,695:	1,422:July ....:		4,113	:	
8.00: 145,077:	16,249:Aug. ....:		4,113	:	
:	:	:	:	:	
00.00:1,813,458:	203,107:			:	

upersede those appearing on page 7 of HP-77, dated Apr
been adjusted to include the 0.1 percent of the total
States on account of exports of American pork through
show allowances for seasonal United States ham trade,
bate given American shippers during the period January
al 1,644 cwt. granted the United States as share in t
period January-March, nor the redeemable United Stat
e January 1.
t.

s of cured pork from quota countries, at nearly 297,0
t half of the season, exceeded the basic allocation f
14,000,000 pounds. Imports from the United States
,000 pounds, whereas the basic allocation for the peri
0 pounds. The United States, therefore, has undershi
5 percent and, instead of supplying 8.1 percent of to
countries, has furnished but 5.76 percent. Imports f
however, for the first 6 months of each year are cons
location for the period, even in such years as 1933-3
mports from the United States considerably exceeded t
ossible that attractive prices and the usual seasonal
hams during the summer will bring imports from the U
re 1935-36 season up to quota figures.

ured pork into the United Kingdom from all sources du
he current season, October 1935-March 1936, continued
he past 5 years, reflecting the restriction on import
gn suppliers. Though total imports for this period w
rresponding 1931-32 figures, exporters of bacon and h

in Empire countries have found the British market an increasingly attractive
and important outlet. In the first half of the 1931-32 season, cured pork
from Empire countries represented 4.71 percent of total imports. In the
current season, the amount of such imports, 90,587,000 pounds, is nearly
three times 1931-32 figures and represents 22.9 percent of the total.

Canada has increased her share of total imports of cured pork into
the United Kingdom from 2 percent during October-March 1931-32 to 15.5
percent in 1935-36. The absolute increase in shipments, 46,593,000 pounds,
represents a gain of over 312 percent. The Irish Free State has also
benefited from the quota system, though to a lesser extent. Imports
from that country have increased 61 percent since 1931-32, or from 2.5
percent of total imports to 7.3 percent. Canadian shipments of cured
pork to British markets have declined during the last 6 months from the
high levels of last season, but those from the Irish Free State have
continued their steady rise, and indications are for a further increase
in this trade. Effective February 18, 1936, Great Britain increased the
Irish Free State cured-pork quota by 10 percent, and a number of obstacles
to the trade between the two countries were removed. Unlike Canadian hog
numbers, which have decreased 7 percent since 1933 and by 25 percent
since 1931, hog numbers in the Irish Free State have increased 17 percent
during the last 3 years.

The increase in Empire supplies of cured pork in the British market
has been accompanied by progressive declines in receipts from the principal
foreign sources, or quota countries. This latter group, which in the first
6 months of the 1931-32 season furnished 95.5 percent of the total
703,436,000 pounds of cured pork imported into the United Kingdom, in the
like period of 1935-36 supplied but 75 percent of the greatly reduced
total, 395,603,000 pounds.

Denmark alone shipped 65 percent of the 1931-32 cured-pork imports.
By 1935-36 her share had declined to 49 percent. Total imports from
Denmark for October-March 1935-36 amounted to 195,500,000 pounds as against
comparable 1934-35 figures of 216,300,000 pounds, a decrease of over 10
percent. Though the percentage share in total imports from all quota
countries has not been drastically reduced, as has Denmark's, since the
inauguration of the quota system the reduction in absolute amounts furnished by the Netherlands, Sweden, and Poland has been correspondingly great:
65, 44, and 68 percent, respectively. Lithuanian imports in 1935-36 at
less than 11,000,000 pounds, represent a decline from 1931-32 levels of
approximately 70 percent. In comparison, imports from minor quota
countries and from the United States have not declined so much, the
reduction from the base year 1931-32 in the case of the United States
amounting to only 38 percent.

United Kingdom: Arrivals of Wiltshire sides in Grea
continental countries, by weeks, 1935-36 and compa
1934-35 and 1935-36 1/

Week ended	: Danish : at all : ports		At London			
		: Danish	: Swedish	: Dutch	: Polish	:Li :ai
Season 1935-36	: Bales :	Bales	Bales	Bales	Bales	I
Oct. 4....:	38,389	19,814	1,348	2,326	3,635	
11 ...:	32,332	16,271	1,223	2,014	3,225	
18 ...:	32,306	16,493	1,309	1,180	3,539	
25 ...:	32,759	17,028	1,154	1,806	2,791	
Nov. 1 ...:	33,482	17,423	1,262	1,857	3,076	
8 ...:	31,766	16,504	1,200	2,231	2,327	
15 ...:	32,221	17,368	1,328	2,276	2,639	
22 ...:	31,285	16,327	1,371	2,229	2,024	
29 ...:	31,095	15,927	1,445	3,116	2,529	
Dec. 6 ...:	31,321	16,187	1,441	2,024	2,167	
13 ...:	33,283	17,505	1,430	2,660	2,740	
20 ...:	37,590	19,096	1,465	3,320	2,628	
27 ...:	26,543	13,189	710	1,784	2,308	
Jan. 3 ...:	29,554	14,916	1,386	1,599	2,216	
10 ...:	30,174	15,650	1,153	1,745	2,866	
17 ...:	31,790	15,929	1,429	1,929	2,210	
24 ...:	31,944	16,022	1,288	1,754	2,582	
31 ...:	31,187	15,359	1,397	1,814	3,042	
Feb. 7 ...:	31,057	15,170	1,027	2,043	2,895	
14 ...:	32,932	15,734	1,221	1,850	2,427	
21 ...:	33,760	16,501	1,415	2,129	2,845	
28 ...:	30,150	15,314	1,661	2,298	2,289	
Mar. 6 ...:	32,044	15,755	1,167	2,301	2,927	
13 ...:	31,759	16,682	1,523	2,674	2,485	
20 ...:	31,060	16,303	1,084	2,743	2,532	
27 ...:	32,389	16,162	1,335	2,525	2,652	
Apr. 3 ...:	33,476	16,942	1,122	2,693	3,039	
10 ...:	32,692	17,022	1,576	1,668	3,260	
17 ...:	31,624	16,501	1,275	2,349	2,960	
24 ...:	30,285	15,383	1,283	2,450	2,795	
Totals to date:						
1935-36 ..:	962,249	490,477	39,028	65,387	81,650	5
1934-35 ..:	1,054,048	554,805	46,091	72,253	77,161	4

1/ London Provision Exchange.   Sides are packed 4 to 6 to
to weight of sides.   The most popular bale is that carryi
total weight ranging 220-260 pounds.

United Kingdom: Bacon and ham imports, October-March, 1931-36

Country	1931-32		1932-33		1933-34		1934-35		1935-36	
	Amount: 1,000 pounds	Per- cent of total	Amount: 1,000 pounds	Per- cent of total	Amount: 1,000 pounds	Per- cent of total	Amount: 1,000 pounds	Per- cent of total	Amount: 1,000 pounds	Per- cent of total
Empire countries										
Canada	14,914	2.12	17,180	2.72	56,878	11.82	65,861	15.41	61,507	15.55
Irish Fr.S.	18,022	2.56	12,981	2.05	18,050	3.75	25,405	5.94	29,076	7.35
Others	164	.03	11	---	7	---	125	.03	4	---
Total Empire ..	33,100	4.71	30,172	4.77	74,935	15.57	91,391	21.38	90,587	22.90
Quota countries										
Denmark ...	457,718	65.07	372,401	58.90	244,210	50.74	216,303	50.61	195,539	49.43
Netherlands	1/28,506	4.05	72,367	11.45	36,991	7.69	29,407	6.88	25,845	6.53
Sweden	24,858	3.53	19,603	3.10	18,114	3.76	15,584	3.65	13,894	3.51
Poland	77,057	10.95	61,475	9.72	33,933	7.05	24,330	5.69	24,291	6.14
Lithuania .	37,014	5.26	32,035	5.07	19,882	4.13	8,333	1.95	10,714	2.71
Estonia 2/.	4,077	.58	4,059	.64	3,336	.69	2,633	.61	2,621	.66
Finland 2/.	2,058	.29	2,491	.39	2,099	.44	1,296	.30	3/1,158	.39
Latvia 2/ .	1,389	.20	1,819	.29	2,148	.45	1,870	.44	2,023	.51
USSR 2/ ...	2,006	.29	2,431	.38	2,601	.54	2,600	.61	3/2,389	.61
Argentina4/	2,719	.39	2,867	.45	1,042	.22	1,067	.25	1,418	.36
U. S.	27,443	3.90	25,201	3.99	25,905	5.38	21,184	4.96	17,091	4.32
Total quota ...	664,845	95.51	596,749	94.38	390,261	81.09	324,607	75.95	296,983	75.07
Minor suppliers..	5,491	.78	5,359	.85	16,073	3.34	11,415	2.67	8,033	2.03
Total	703,436	100	632,280	100	481,269	100	427,413	100	395,603	100

1/ An unusually low annual figure. 2/ Approximation based on annual statistics.
3/ March figure, preliminary. 4/ Ham imports only; bacon figures not available.

Liverpool bacon quotations during April declined steadily from the high level maintained during February and March. Danish Wiltshire sides, at $20.46 per 100 pounds, averaged 10 cents less than during the previous month, and Canadian green sides made an average of $17.70 per 100 pounds against $17.87 in March. These prices, however, were the highest April averages in 5 years. American green bellies were offered in too small quantities for price quotations. April quotations on American short cut green hams reached an average of $20.88 per 100 pounds, which was $1.23 above the March and April 1935 averages. It was not only the highest monthly average since last October, but the highest April average since 1930.

The outstanding feature of the March h
imports of hams from Canada were larger than
Imports from the United States, however, were
than in the preceding month, and, in response
present obtainable on the British market, may
At 16,126,000 pounds for the first half of th
reduction from corresponding 1934-35 figures
year 1929-30 of 61 percent. United States ha
56 percent of the total ham imports into the
62 percent. Imports from the United States i
than 50 percent of the total. On the other h
creased from 16 to 37 percent during the same
October 1 to March 31, 1935-36 furnished over
compared with less than 19 percent in 1931-32

United Kingdom: Ham imports, C

Country	1931-32		1932-33		1933-
	Amount	Per-cent of total	Amount	Per-cent of total	Amount
	1,000 pounds	Per-cent	1,000 pounds	Per-cent	1,000 pounds
Empire countries:					
Canada	6,397	16.13	7,732	18.99	9,841:2
Irish Fr.S.	1,081	2.73	1,216	2.99	985
Total Empire ..	7,478	18.86	8,948	21.98	10,826:2
Principal quota suppliers:					
U.S.	22,327	56.32	23,248	57.11	23,113:6
Poland	6,607	16.67	5,468	13.43	2,324
Argentina .	2,719	6.86	2,867	7.04	1,042
Total 3 countries.	31,653	79.85	31,583	77.58	26,479:7
Others	510	1.29	179	.44	38
Total	39,641	100	40,710	100	37,343

Liverpool lard quotations for April ave
the highest April average in the past 8 years
since last September. Imports for the season
below corresponding 1934-35 imports and repres
from those of 1933-34. The United States cont
of lard to the British market, furnishing, how
total this season as against 77 percent a year
Brazil, Canada, and Hungary have supplied the
imports originating outside the United States.

Domestic supplies.- The number of pigs contracted for delivery in 1936 is approximately 2,000,000 head compared with 1,854,513 in 1935. According to the contracts, the distribution of deliveries by 5-month periods will be approximately the same as last year, when 32 percent of the pigs were contracted for delivery during the first 4 months.

During 1935 special bonuses were paid for maximum deliveries during the 4 months January-April. The Class A bonus was paid on contracts where 33-1/3 percent and over of the annual total was contracted for, delivered, and accepted during these months. Class B bonus was paid on the range of 30 percent to 33-1/3 percent, and Class C bonus for 25 percent up to 30 percent. In November, preliminary bonus payments of 6, 4, and 2 pence per score (around 62, 41, and 21 cents per 100 pounds), were paid on these three classes. The final payments in March brought the three bonus payments up to 8.7, 5.8, and 2.9 pence per score (about 91, 61, and 30 cents per 100 pounds), respectively, and brought the total bonus distribution up to £ 121,500.

The bonus scheme, together with the requirement that at least 25 percent of the total number of pigs contracted for should be in the first 4 months and not more than 45 percent in the last 4 months, resulted in a somewhat more even distribution of deliveries than in the previous years. Contracts from January to April were 32.03 percent, May to August 30.69 percent, and September to December 37.28 percent of the total. However, actual deliveries were smaller in the first period and larger thereafter.

In 1936 a Class A bonus will be paid for deliveries of at least 33-1/3 percent during the first 4 months and a Class B bonus, one-third as large, for 25 but less than 33-1/3 percent. In addition a special bonus is paid to those qualifying for Class A or Class B bonus on the lowest accepted deliveries (weight basis) during any one of the first 4 months, thus encouraging more equal deliveries during each of these months.

Government aid in the Irish Free State.- Pigs and Bacon Marketing Boards were established in the Irish Free State in September 1935, and became operative on October 1. Prices by classes and grades of pigs sold to bacon curers were fixed by the Pigs Marketing Board. Internal production of bacon with quotas for each factory was fixed by the Bacon Marketing Board. Up to the end of September 1935, there was levied an excise tax of 5s. per carcass (about $1.25), or portion thereof, used for production of bacon.

Export bounties have been paid on hog products since September 1932, and on live pigs since October 1932. The payment of these bounties followed the imposition of British special duties on live pigs and pig products from the Irish Free State in July 1932. Exports to the United Kingdom of any form of bacon and ham and live pigs and pig carcasses intended for conversion into bacon have been subject to quota since September 1933. The export of live pigs has been prohibited except under license since August 1934.

The effect of the Government aid to pig producers has been decidedly stimulating. The number of fat pigs purchased for curing increased from 851,681 in 1933 to 1,062,253 in 1935. Similarly, the number of fat pigs exported from the Irish Free State increased from 54,080 to 108,886 during this period. Exports of bacon and hams increased even more rapidly from 25,979,000 pounds in 1933 to 56,126,000 pounds in 1935. On the other hand, the exports of fresh pork declined from 21,697,000 pounds in 1933 to 15,748,000 pounds in 1935.

Countries Important in British Market Supplies

Denmark.- Monthly statistics relative to slaughter at export slaughterhouses show slaughter in 1935 to be smaller than for any year since 1926, according to Agricultural Commissioner H. E. Reed at Berlin. Other data show the average weekly slaughter in 1935 to be 83,107 head compared with 92,128 in 1934 and 122,270 in 1933. In 1935, hogs with cards made up a greater proportion of total slaughter than in the 2 previous years and accounted for 4,026,662 of the total slaughter of 4,341,673. Hogs without cards and hogs outside the scope of control measures accounted for 37,640 and 117,371, respectively in 1935. An increase in marketings and slaughter in 1936 is indicated by production trends and present market possibilities.

Exports of bacon during the first 3 months of 1936 totaled 103,427,000 pounds compared with 111,588,000 pounds during the same period of 1935, increased exports to Germany failing to offset the reduction in the quantity sent to England. Lard exports during January-February 1936 were smaller than for the same period in 1935, although February exports of lard exceeded those of February 1934 and 1935. Live hog exports for the period January 1-March 29 totaled 24,927 head compared with 537 during January-March 1935. Germany was the sole outlet for live hogs and the increase in numbers exported, together with the heavy weights of hogs which are sent to Germany, probably has about offset the reduction in bacon and lard exports.

A continuation of the tendency for Danish hog production to increase was to be expected from the favorable marketing situation which was obtained in Denmark during the last few months. Supplementary quotas granted by England and increased exports of live hogs to Germany - all of which are included in the card issue - have materially reduced the number of hogs marketed without cards. Prices of hogs without cards have been greatly reduced during the early months of 1936 when compared with the high prices which obtained for hogs without cards in December 1935; but, while the bacon-feed ratio for hogs without cards has been decidedly unfavorable (averaging about 6:1 during the first 3 months of 1936), usually it has applied to an insignificant part of total marketings. Prices for hogs with cards have been very favorable throughout the first quarter of 1936, the bacon-feed ratio for such hogs fluctuating between 12.6:1 and 13.5:1. Feeder pig prices have also advanced sharply and steadily during the first quarter of 1936.

In view of a possible increase in the British quota, which may accompany the adoption of an earmarked tariff for subsidizing British hog producers, and the possibilities of continued exports to Germany on a barter basis, the increase in Danish hog production to date does not appear to be greatly in excess of probable market outlets. Nor is it likely that production will get out of hand and a surplus ensue. Just as soon as marketings exceed profitable outlets, the influence of the low and

unremunerative prices for hogs without cards will again become effective
and act as a check on the upward trend in production. The Danish control
measures so far have been effective in bringing production to, and maintain-
ing it at about the level dictated by remunerative market outlets, and it
appears that they will so continue. Long-time planning by the control
authorities, however, is impossible until they have a better idea as to
the policy which Great Britain will adopt with respect to import restrictions.

Netherlands.- In the Netherlands, total hog slaughter in 1935 was
the lowest for any year since 1923, Mr. Reed reports. The proportion of
total slaughter represented by export slaughter also declined and was
lower than for any other year for which data are available. Increased
slaughter during 1936 is indicated by the increase in production of pigs
which occurred in 1935.

Netherlands: Annual hog slaughter, 1930-1935

Year	Total slaughter	Home slaughter			Export slaughter	Percent- age home is of total	Percent- age export is of total
		Inspected	Non- inspected	Total			
	Head	Head	Head	Head	Head	Percent	Percent
1930	2,752,235	1,257,829	291,046	1,548,875	1,203,360	56.28	43.72
1931	3,666,594	1,771,971	395,426	2,167,397	1,499,197	59.11	40.89
1932	3,554,982	1,830,938	395,631	2,226,569	1,328,413	62.63	37.37
1933	2,775,939	1,408,325	259,145	1,667,470	1,108,469	60.07	39.93
1934	2,545,968	1,412,491	303,023	1,715,514	830,454	67.39	32.61
1935	2,015,893	1,166,413	269,453	1,435,866	580,027	71.20	28.80

The upturn in production, which was in evidence throughout 1935,
continued into 1936. The February 1936 census, while showing a seasonal
decline from November 1935 numbers, shows a marked increase compared with
February 1935 numbers, with substantial increases in all important categories,
the most important increases being shown in numbers of sows, suckling pigs,
and other pigs up to 132 pounds. Only slight increases occurred in the
heavier weight classes.

A total of 2,239,793 earmarks, from the allocation of 2,321,000
for the fourth period (1935) were issued. During the first quarter of
1936, 263,143 earmarks were used from the total allocation of 2,245,616
for the fifth period (1936). While production in the Netherlands is increasing, the earmark system is expected to prevent the occurrence of any
great annual surplus. Seasonal production, however, has not as yet been
entirely brought into line with seasonal demand.

Hog marketings and slaughter increased during the first quarter of 1936 as compared with the first and last quarter of 1935. With the increase in supplies, prices have shown an easier tendency, but the support extended by the control agency has prevented any great decline. Export prices paid by the Centrale were adjusted downward in early February to conform to domestic prices. Feed prices have advanced and with the decline in hog prices producers were not making a "reasonable profit" at the end of March. Consequently, the Centrale increased the price for export fatbacks at the beginning of April.

Poland.- Marketings during the first quarter of 1936 at Posen, which presumably are representative of conditions in the Polish Corridor, were smaller than in the same period of 1935. This decrease, however, has doubtless been offset to some extent by an increase in direct marketings under contracts between hog producers and bacon factories. It is reported that total marketings from bacon-hog areas in Poland during the first quarter of 1936 were practically as large as in the first quarter of 1935. Production and marketings for the remainder of the year 1936 are not clear. Hog and feed price movements during the latter half of 1935 point to an upturn in production and the Polish Government is continuing its efforts to increase the production and export of livestock and livestock products in an effort to improve the economic and cultural level of the rural population.

Despite the reduction of approximately 5 percent in total numbers shown by the June 1935 hog census, slaughter of hogs at 32 principal markets in Poland was larger in every month of 1935 than in the corresponding months of 1934. If the census figures are correct, the maintenance of slaughter at the higher level is probably due to the improvement which has taken place in total hog and pork exports.

The decline in hog prices from the high point reached in September 1935 continued into 1936. Prices at Posen declined in January, improved in February, and declined further in March. Between the beginning and close of the first quarter of 1935, the decline in prices at Posen amounted to about 10 percent, but prices averaged approximately one-third higher than in the first quarter of 1935. Advancing feed prices and the lower hog prices combined during the first quarter of 1936 to reduce the favorable hog-feed price ratio which Poland had enjoyed since August 1935.

The improvement in Poland's export trade in hogs and pork products noted in 1935 continued into 1936. Exports for January and February 1936 exceeded those of the previous year. A sharp increase in bacon exports to England in February has been due to an increase in export business with other countries conducted through British ports. The increase in ham exports may be accounted for by increased trade in Polish tinned hams. The increase in lard exports was to be expected in view of Poland's policy of exporting lard under a subsidy in order to prevent accumulated lard stocks from depressing domestic hog prices.

The German-Polish trade arrangement and Czechoslovakia's reduced hog numbers are responsible for the improvement in live hog and fresh pork exports compared with last year. Exports of live hogs and pork to Germany in February and March, however, were less than in December 1935 and January 1936 because

of Poland's inability to absorb the German goods offered in payment for the
hogs. Poland's hog quota for export to Germany in January was reduced to
60 percent of the December quota. The February quota was reduced to 20
percent and the March quota to 26.6 percent. It is reported that an improvement in Polish purchases of German goods has permitted an increase in the
April quota to 40 percent of the December quota.

Central European Importing Countries

Germany.- Increased domestic hog production and slaughter, imports
of hogs and butter, and increased imports of cattle and beef have combined
to bring about a more favorable meat and fat supply situation in Germany,
for the present at least, according to Mr. Reed. The improvement has been
developed despite declining cattle numbers and an enforced reduction in
cattle slaughter. The increase in domestic hog production has been the most
important factor in the situation. Hog numbers as of March 1936 exceeded
those of the same time in 1935, and feed supplies, which show considerable
reduction compared with last year, loom as the limiting factor in the pork
and fat situation until the time when the new feed crop becomes available.
Maintained imports of hogs and butter under existing trade agreements along
with some reduction in the present margarine output are to be expected.

The gradual increase in weekly receipts of hogs at German markets,
which began in late October 1935, continued into 1936 and, by late March,
weekly marketings at 39 important centers exceeded those of corresponding
weeks in 1935. The seasonal decline which occurred in inspected slaughter
between December 1934 and February 1935 was probably accentuated by the
regulation prohibiting slaughter of hogs under 180 pounds, live weight,
with the result that inspected slaughter during January and February 1936
was the lowest for any comparable period since 1930. March and April receipts
at 39 markets, however, indicate that inspected slaughter for those months
will at least approximate, and likely exceed, inspected slaughter for the
same months of 1935. The regulation limiting weekly slaughter by individuals
and firms to 60 percent of their average weekly slaughter during October
1934 was altered to allow 80 percent of their average weekly slaughter during
the period October 1, 1934 to September 28, 1935, and the allowance was raised
to 90 percent as of May 11. In view of the pork and fat situation which
obtained during the latter part of 1935, it is reasonably to assume that
home slaughter has increased, and certainly it was an important factor in
alleviating the fat shortage during December 1935 and the first quarter of
1936. A continuation of the increased slaughter allowances is indicated
by the March hog census.

The average hog slaughter weight, reported by large slaughterhouses,
increased from 216 pounds in November 1935 to 220 pounds in December 1935,
was maintained at that figure in January 1936, and declined slightly to 218
pounds in February. While an increase in slaughter weight in those months
is usually expected from seasonal influences, the unusually heavy weights
attained this year in the face of increasing hog numbers and declining feed
supplies may be attributed to the regulations which fixed minimum slaughter
weights and those which reestablished and increased price spreads between
hog classes. Receipts by weight classes at 12 markets show that a relatively
high percentage of hogs in the heavy weight classes was reached in December
1935 and maintained during the first quarter of 1936.

Germany: Total inspected slaughter of hogs, and marketings
at 36 important markets, 1934-1936

Period	1934	1935	1936
	Head	Head	Head
Slaughter			
Jan.	1,812,736	1,825,816	1,582,464
Feb.	1,619,682	1,627,719	1,535,043
Mar.	1,741,106	1,619,117	
Dec.	2,061,722	1,878,206	
Marketings			
Jan.	477,696	473,974	318,092
Feb.	444,437	427,152	339,307
Mar.	475,525	464,849	
Dec.	436,283	312,066	

Imports of cattle have shown a marked increase in 1936, but monthly
hog imports during the first quarter, although larger than in the corresponding period of 1935, were smaller than during November and December 1935.
Denmark was the principal source of live cattle imports and Denmark, Poland,
Hungary, and Yugoslavia were the principal suppliers of hogs and pork products.
Meat imports increased, due to shipments of frozen beef from South America
and hog carcasses from Poland and Hungary. Monthly lard imports for the
period November 1935-February 1936 have fluctuated within relatively narrow
limits, Denmark and Hungary being the principal suppliers. A small increase
in imports of American lard has occurred recently. Most of the imports of
cattle, hogs, meats, and fats are the result of trade arrangements with neigh-
boring and South American countries, and the periods for which those arrangements have been made indicate that imports for the remainder of 1936 will
be larger than during 1934 and 1935, provided the exporting countries are
able to take the German goods offered in exchange and the clearings are
satisfactory.

Fixed prices, which obtain in Germany for hogs, cattle, and edible
fats, do not, of course, reflect supply and demand conditions. Price changes
occurring in the period under review have been largely due to adjustments
which were made to correct certain difficulties arising from previous price-
fixing measures. While hog prices have been stable, grain and potato prices
have advanced, and the hog-feed price ratio has tended to become unfavorable.
However, the present feed situation in Germany is such that without fixed
feed prices the ratio would undoubtedly be even more unfavorable.

Serious fat shortages have not been in evidence during the first
quarter of 1936, with the exception of a short period during February. In
fact, domestic lard production has increased to such an extent that practically all lard imports since the beginning of the year have been placed
in storage. The improved situation has also resulted in some relaxing of
the numerous regulations affecting the sale of fats in Germany.

In spite of the improvement, the long-time fat problem has not been solved. It is now generally recognized that Germany is and will continue to be a deficit fat area, dependent on imports. Earnest efforts to reduce the quantity which must be imported are being continued, but ideas about self-sufficiency in fats have apparently been abandoned. The financial and economic situations demand that imported fat supplies come, as far as possible, from those countries with which Germany has clearing or other trade arrangements, and that foreign exchange be used for fat imports only to the extent which necessity demands. As with pork supplies, future domestic fat supplies depend largely on the 1936 feed crops.

Czechoslovakia.- Reduced domestic hog supplies and increased hog imports were the features of Czech hog markets in 1935. Hog imports (195,812 head) although more than double those of the previous year (82,776) did not offset the decline in domestic receipts. Taxed slaughter for 1935 totaled 3,998,661 head compared with 4,386,300 in 1934 (the year of heaviest slaughter) and 3,561,737 in 1933. As a result of reduced slaughter, total pork and fat consumption declined.

Preliminary census data as of January 1, 1936 show a continuation of the decline in Czechoslovakian hog numbers which began in 1934. Total numbers have been reduced approximately 10 percent since January 1, 1935, although sow numbers show a decline of only about 6 percent. The 1935 reduction in numbers was not so large as the reduction in 1934, when the drought and Government measures brought about liquidation. Favorable hog prices in Czechoslovakia offer little if any stimulus to production because they have been more than offset by high feed prices. Hog prices were steady through January and February but declined in March. March prices, while showing about 10 percent reduction from the high prices of October and November 1935, are much higher than during March of last year. High feed prices, which have resulted from operations of the State Grain Monopoly, made for an unfavorable hog-feed ratio, and hog production is reported to be unprofitable.

The policy of securing needed pork and fat supplies from Danubian countries and Poland in exchange for industrial and other goods is being continued. Hog imports in 1936 have increased sufficiently to cause marketings at Prague during the first quarter of the year to exceed greatly comparable marketings for 1935.

Imports of lard and fatbacks during the first quarter of 1936 were much larger than during the same period of 1935 but were seasonally smaller

Czechoslovakia: Hog slaughter, 1933-1935

Period	1933	1934	1935
	Head	Head	Head
Jan.-Oct. ..... :	2,638,701	3,271,606	3,104,861
Nov. .... :	287,359	376,780	267,366
Dec. .... :	655,677	737,914	626,434
Total ...... :	3,561,737	4,386,300	3,998,661

than in the last quarter of 1935. The reduced duty rates, amounting to about 2.26 cents per pound for rendered lard and about 1.51 cents per pound for raw fat and fatback imports, expired February 10, 1936 but were extended until June 9, 1936. The bulk of lard and fatback imports continues to come from the Danube Basin, particularly Hungary. Hungary is reported to have been successful in covering corn requirements through bilateral agreements with Yugoslavia and Rumania, and the Czechs are confident that Hungary will be able to deliver lard, fatbacks, and hogs in quantities equal to past shipments.

Danube Basin Exporting Countries

The Danube Basin lard exports for the first quarter of 1936 are now placed at about 22,000,000 pounds compared with about 20,000,000 pounds in the corresponding 1935 period, according to the Belgrade office of the Foreign Agricultural Service. Exports for April are estimated to be about 7,500,000 pounds against 3,977,000 pounds a year earlier. Of the April 1936 figure, Hungary's share is only about 58 percent compared with over 83 percent of the exports for the year 1935. The declining Hungarian share of an increasing 1936 total was the result of expanding shipments from Yugoslavia and Bulgaria while the Hungarian movement remained fairly constant.

About 50 percent of the 4,409,000 pounds of Hungarian lard exported in April went to Germany, 30 percent to Czechoslovakia, and 20 percent to Great Britain. Germany is reported to have paid the equivalent of 14.7 cents per pound for Hungarian lard in April. April prices are also being paid for the May quotas of 2,745,000 pounds of melted Hungarian lard and 430,000 pounds of unrendered fat sides.

Adjustment of German-Yugoslav exchange problems resulted in the German absorption of most of the estimated 1,764,000 pounds of Yugoslav lard exported in April. In Bulgaria, this season's lard exports are reported as nearing completion, after having amounted to about 3,204,000 pounds from January 1 to April 30, 1936. Most of the Bulgarian lard went to Germany, with some going also to Czechoslovakia and Great Britain.

Danubian live hog exports for the first 4 months of 1936 totaled about 204,000 head against 124,000 head in the corresponding 1935 period. More than half of this year's live hog exports have come from Yugoslavia. Last year, Hungary was the chief exporter of the group. Danube Basin exports of hog carcasses and fresh pork totaled about 35,167,000 pounds for the first quarter of 1936. Of this total, about 65 percent originated in Hungary, 27 percent in Yugoslavia, and 8 percent in Bulgaria. Exports declined sharply in April to only a few thousand pounds, largely because of the advance in Hungarian hog and pork prices. Since March 21, the price situation has prevented exports from Hungary to Germany. The April exports were largely from Yugoslavia to Austria.

High pork prices and lower feed prices resulted in expanded feeding operations in Hungary during March and April. A new trade agreement with Rumania involving corn has improved the Hungarian feed situation materially. At this year's annual livestock show, 71 percent of the breeding hogs on exhibition were purchased, compared with only 50 percent at last year's show.

Lard: Exports from the Danube Basin, by months, 1935-36

Year and month	Hungary	Yugoslavia	Total
	1,000 pounds	1,000 pounds	1,000 pounds
1935			
Jan. .... :	4,648	801	5,449
Feb. .... :	5,149	1,066	1/ 6,237
Mar. .... :	7,343	816	8,159
First quarter :	17,140	2,683	1/ 19,845
Apr. .... :	3,421	556	3,977
May .... :	4,207	662	4,869
June .... :	4,520	154	4,674
Second quarter:	12,148	1,372	13,520
July .... :	5,325	491	5,816
Aug. .... :	3,567	973	4,540
Sept. .... :	2,302	721	3,023
Third quarter :	11,194	2,185	13,379
Oct. .... :	4,657	1,242	5,899
Nov. .... :	4,149	1,518	5,667
Dec. .... :	3,914	1,433	2/ 5,371
Fourth quarter:	12,720	4,193	2/ 16,937
Total 1935 :	53,202	10,433	3/ 63,681
1936			
Jan. .... :	4,824	2,249	7,073
Feb. .... :	6,260	543	4/ 7,046
Mar. .... :	4,017	2,219	5/ 7,984
First quarter :	15,101	5,011	6/ 22,103
Apr. .... :	4,409	1,764	7/ 7,540

1/ Includes 22,000 pounds from Bulgaria.   2/ Includes 24,000 pounds from
Rumania.   3/ Includes 22,000 pounds from Bulgaria and 24,000 pounds from
Rumania.   4/ Includes 243,000 pounds from Bulgaria.   5/ Includes
110,000 pounds from Rumania and 1,638,000 pounds from Bulgaria.
6/ Includes 110,000 pounds from Rumania and 1,881,000 pounds from Bulgaria.
7/ Includes 1,323,000 pounds from Bulgaria and 44,000 pounds from Rumania.

The assurance of important export outlets for Danubian hogs and pork
products in 1936 is embodied in the series of quotas granted by importing
countries, notably Germany, Czechoslovakia, and Austria. The quotas announced
to date suggest a volume of exports for 1936 somewhat larger than the exports
reported for 1935. Live and dressed hogs and lard are the leading items
covered by the quotas. All four exporting countries also have secured small
quotas for bacon from Great Britain.

Danube Basin: Quotas on hogs, pork, and lard granted by principal markets,
1936

Exporting countries and countries granting import quotas	Live hogs	Dressed hogs	Fresh pork	Lard and fat sides
	Head	Head	1,000 pounds	1,000 pounds
Hungary				
Germany		1/ 200,000		38,029
Czechoslovakia ..	43,655			17,064
Austria	2/ 150,000			
Total	193,655	200,000		55,093
Yugoslavia				
Germany		40,000	8,818	6,614
Czechoslovakia ..	42,200			8,267
Austria	3/ 125,000		4/ 3,969	
Total	167,200	40,000	12,787	14,881
Rumania				
Germany		20,000		
Czechoslovakia ..	60,000			5/
Austria	60,000			
Total	120,000	20,000	---	---
Bulgaria 6/				
Turkey	7/ 2,000			
Total	2,000	---	---	---
Total Basin .	482,855	260,000	12,787	69,974

1/ 80,000 head regular annual quota, plus 120,000 head extra quota for first
half year.
2/ Between 120,000 and 150,000 head.
3/ Includes 21,000 meat-type and 104,000 lard-type hogs.
4/ Consisting of 1,323,000 pounds of meat from lard-type hogs and 2,646,000
pounds from meat-type hogs.
5/ Czechoslovakia in 1933 granted a substantial lard quota to Rumania but
practically no use has been made of it.
6/ Bulgaria has been granted dressed-hog and lard quotas by Germany and a lard
quota by Czechoslovakia but has made little use of them to date.
7/ To be shipped between June 11, 1935, and June 10, 1936. Almost none was
shipped in 1935.

Hogs and pork products: Measures of foreign supplies and demand,
specified years

Country and item	Unit	1909-10 to 1913-14 average	1924-25 to 1928-29 average	Oct. - Mar. 1932-33	1933-34	1934-35	1935-36
UNITED KINGDOM							
Production							
Supplies, domestic fresh pork, London ..	:1,000 pounds		35,279	51,463	42,201	45,577	50,205
Imports							
Bacon							
Denmark	"	120,293	250,889	372,401	244,210	216,303	195,539
Irish Free State	"		30,160	11,765	17,065	24,422	27,428
United States	"	95,790	57,716	1,953	2,792	1,757	965
Canada	"	19,889	39,767	9,448	47,037	55,727	49,394
Others	"	20,376	75,024	196,001	132,820	96,090	89,705
Total	"	256,348	453,556	591,570	443,926	394,298	363,031
Lard, total	"	115,615	132,506	145,902	160,051	119,176	79,569
Ham, total	"	44,415	60,079	40,660	37,343	33,115	32,572
DENMARK							
Exports							
Bacon			250,965	381,089	254,813	219,455	202,248
CANADA							
Slaughter							
Hogs, inspected	:1,000s	874	1,461	1,424	1,537	1,562	1,572
GERMANY							
Production							
Hog receipts 14 cities	"		1,636	1,561	1,641	1,740	1,107
Hog slaughter 36 centers	"	2,237	2,038	2,131	2,224	2,331	1,479
Imports	:1,000						
Bacon, total ...	:pounds	1,475	10,106	18,961	16,786	15,031	13,937
Lard, total	"	105,362	113,311	124,312	74,430	32,257	52,613
UNITED STATES							
Slaughter							
Hogs, inspected	:1,000s	17,416	25,967	23,916	23,952	19,379	18,355
Exports							
Bacon	:1,000						
United Kingdom	:pounds	68,346	35,407	1,393	1,319	1,042	372
Germany	"	1,045	6,099	1,159	2,390	0	0
Cuba	"	3,801	10,869	2,078	2,226	2,486	494
Total	"	92,954	75,371	9,233	12,977	4,684	1,328
Hams, shoulders							
United Kingdom	"	68,594	70,441	24,934	26,239	21,537	16,510
Total	"	79,265	85,024	29,875	30,866	26,855	19,440
Lard							
United Kingdom	"	89,430	114,898	145,902	155,566	79,445	32,500
Germany	"	76,146	99,125	93,701	45,602	2,513	3,031
Cuba	"	18,216	41,883	4,667	6,628	16,631	10,310
Netherlands	"	21,218	23,674	22,005	16,250	9	39
Total	"	250,009	379,652	322,941	279,756	106,971	47,608

Hogs and pork products: Foreign and domestic
for the month indicated, and stocks a

Item	1909-1913 average	1925-1 avera
	: Dollars	Dolla
PRICES	:	
Hogs, Chicago, basis		
packers' and shippers'		
quotations .... :	8.02	11.
Corn, Chicago, No. 3 Yellow :	1.04	1.
Hogs, heavy, Berlin, live :		
weight .... :	11.35	14.
Barley, Leipzig .... :	1.75	2.
Lard		
Chicago .... :	10.60	14.
Liverpool .... :	11.80	15.
Hamburg .... :	13.89	15.
Cured pork		
Liverpool :		
American short cut green:		
hams .... :	13.80	22.
American green bellies :		20.
Danish Wiltshire sides :	14.70	23.
Canadian green sides .. :	14.14	1/22.
	: 1,000	1,00
STOCKS	: pounds	poun
United States	:	
Processed pork 2/ ...... :		822,8
Lard in cold storage .... :		135,8

1/ Three-year average only.
2/ Dry salt cured and in process of cure; pickl
and frozen.

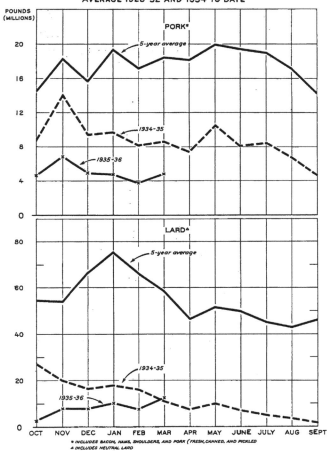

PORK AND LARD' EXPORTS FROM UNITED STATES,
AVERAGE 1928-32 AND 1934 TO DATE

POUNDS
(MILLIONS)

PORK*

5-year average

1934-35

1935-36

LARD*

5-year average

1934-35

1935-36

OCT   NOV   DEC   JAN   FEB   MAR   APR   MAY   JUNE   JULY   AUG   SEPT

* INCLUDES BACON, HAMS, SHOULDERS, AND PORK (FRESH, CANNED, AND PICKLED
* INCLUDES NEUTRAL LARD

U.S. DEPARTMENT OF AGRICULTURE   NEG 29226   BUREAU OF AGRICULTURAL ECONOMICS

FIGURE 1.- EXPORTS OF BOTH PORK AND LARD IN 1934-35
WERE SMALLER THAN FOR MANY YEARS. AS COMPARED WITH
1933-34 THE DECREASE IN EXPORTS WAS PRIMARILY THE RE-
SULT OF THE MARKED DECLINE IN DOMESTIC HOG PRODUCTION.
BUT AS COMPARED WITH EARLIER POST-WAR YEARS THE DECREASE
WAS DUE CHIEFLY TO INCREASED EUROPEAN HOG PRODUCTION AND
RESTRICTIONS ON IMPORTS IN SEVERAL COUNTRIES. HOG
SLAUGHTER IN THIS COUNTRY HAS INCREASED IN RECENT
MONTHS AND EXPORTS HAVE ALSO TENDED TO INCREASE.

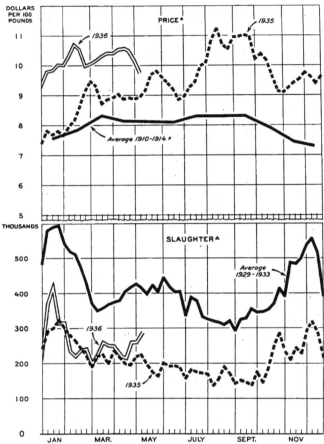

HOGS' AVERAGE PRICE AT CHICAGO, AND FEDERALLY INSPECTED SLAUGHTER

U.S. DEPARTMENT OF AGRICULTURE   NEG. 26215   BUREAU OF AGRICULTURAL ECONOMICS

FIGURE 2.– HOG PRICES ADVANCED FROM JANUARY TO MID-
APRIL 1936 AND THE LEVEL OF PRICES WAS SOMEWHAT HIGHER
DURING THIS PERIOD THAN A YEAR EARLIER. IN LATE APRIL
AND EARLY MAY, SLAUGHTER SUPPLIES OF HOGS INCREASED
SEASONALLY AND PRICES DECLINED SHARPLY. SLAUGHTER
SUPPLIES DURING THE FIRST FOUR MONTHS OF 1936 WERE
SOMEWHAT LARGER THAN IN EARLY 1935, AND IT IS PROBABLE
THAT HOG SLAUGHTER WILL BE CONSIDERABLY LARGER DURING
THE REMAINDER OF 1936 THAN DURING THE SAME PERIOD LAST
YEAR.

UNITED STATES DEPARTMENT OF AGRICULTURE
Bureau of Agricultural Economics
Division of Statistical and Historical Research
Washington

HP-79   June 24, 1936

WORLD HOG AND PORK PROSPECTS

Summary

Slaughter supplies of hogs in the United States will continue well
above the levels of a year earlier in the remainder of the 1935-36 hog
marketing year ending September 30, 1936. The movement of hogs to market
in May and early June apparently was delayed somewhat by the feeding of
hogs to heavier weights. However, in view of the apparent large increase in
the 1935 fall pig crop it is expected that a larger than usual proportion of
the summer (May - September) slaughter supply will be marketed after mid-June.

The relationship between hog prices and corn prices in the last 6
months has been very favorable for a further expansion in hog production in
this country. Although definite information as to the size of the 1936
spring pig crop will not be available until the release of the June 1936
Pig Crop Report it seems probable that there was a material increase in the
spring crop this year. The high hog-corn price ratio of recent months also
indicates some increase in the 1936 fall pig crop, but fall farrowing will
be affected to a considerable extent by the outturn of the 1936 corn crop.

Hog slaughter in Germany and Denmark, the two leading European
hog-producing countries, will probably increase somewhat in the remainder of
1936. In Germany, however, slaughter has been curtailed considerably in
the last 6 months, and in Denmark, despite the expected increase, slaughter
for the entire year 1936 will probably be smaller than in other recent
years except 1935. A substantial increase in hog marketings in the Danube
Basin in the last half of 1936 is also indicated. In the last year exports

of hog products, chiefly lard, from the Danube Basin have increased greatly, with most of such exports going to Germany.

International trade in hog products thus far in 1936 has continued near the low levels of 1935. The reduction in exports and imports in the last 18 months has resulted from the continuation of restrictions to imports in Great Britain, the leading importing country, the decrease in hog production in the United States, and foreign exchange difficulties in several countries, notably Germany. In the last 3 months, however, exports of lard from the United States have increased somewhat as domestic hog slaughter has increased from the low level of a year earlier. It is also probable that the existing restrictions to imports of cured pork into Great Britain will be modified to some extent by early 1937.

United States

Slaughter supplies of hogs will continue well above the levels of a year earlier in the remainder of the 1935-36 marketing year and probably in most of 1936-37. The hog-corn price ratio has been relatively high thus far this year, and with an average corn crop in 1936, the ratio between hog prices and corn prices will probably be favorable for a further expansion in hog production. The outturn of the corn crop in the present year is, of course, very uncertain this early in the season. The movement of hogs to market in recent weeks has apparently been delayed somewhat by feeding to heavier weights, but in view of the apparent large increase in the 1935 fall pig crop, it is expected that a larger than usual proportion of the summer (May - September) slaughter supply will be marketed after mid-June.

Although definite information as to the size of the 1936 spring pig crop will not be available until the release of the June 1936 Pig Crop Report, it is now apparent that the severe weather in the late winter and early spring reduced materially the average number of pigs saved per litter in several sections of the Corn Belt. This decrease in the number of pigs saved per litter will partially offset the probable large increase in the number of sows farrowed. It seems probable, however, that the 1936 spring pig crop was materially larger than the very small spring crop of 1935.

Hog prices advanced in the last half of May, after having declined rather sharply from late April to mid-May. Increased hog marketings and relatively large slaughter supplies of cattle were probably the chief factors responsible for the drop in prices in the first half of May. In the third week of May the decline in prices was checked and toward the end of the month an upturn in prices began. By early June a considerable part of the decline occurring in the first half of May had been regained. The advance in prices was fairly uniform among the several weight classes of hogs. The average price of hogs at Chicago in May was $9.58 compared with $10.47 in April and $9.31 in May 1935. Although the May average was nearly $1.00 less than the April average, it was the highest average price at Chicago for May since 1930.

Hog slaughter under Federal inspection in May totaled about 2,579,000 head, which was only slightly larger than in April, but it was 19 percent greater than the very small slaughter for the corresponding month a year earlier. Except for May last year, inspected slaughter in that month in 1936 was the smallest for May since 1914. The usual summer seasonal increase in the proportion of packing sows included in the marketings of hogs apparently started in late May. For the most part, however, the bulk of the slaughter supply in recent weeks consisted of medium and heavy weight butcher hogs, with those weighing under 200 pounds being comparatively scarce. Although May was the fourth month since last December in which Federally inspected hog slaughter was larger than the corresponding month a year earlier, total slaughter in the first 8 months of the current marketing season, October to May, was about 13 percent smaller than that for the same period in 1934-35. Because of the increase in average weights, however, the total dressed weight of inspected hog slaughter for the marketing year thus far was only about 6 percent less than that of a year earlier. The average weight of hogs at the seven principal markets was 242 pounds in May compared with 241 pounds in April and 235 pounds in May 1935.

Corn prices declined fairly steadily through May, but because prices advanced during April, the average price of No. 3 Yellow corn in May of 63.2 cents per bushel was the same as the April average price. In May last year the average price of this grade of corn was 87.6 cents. In the first half of May the drop in hog prices exceeded that in corn prices and the hog-corn price ratio declined. This decline in the ratio, however, was checked in late May as hog prices advanced. Based on farm prices for the 15th of the month, the hog-corn price ratio in the North Central States in May was 16.3 compared with 19.2 in April and 10.3 in May last year. Although lower than in April, the hog-corn price ratio in May was the highest for the month since 1926.

In the first 2 weeks of May wholesale prices of fresh pork continued the decline started in late April, but all of this drop was recovered in the last half of the month. In late May prices of some fresh cuts advanced to the highest levels reached thus far in 1936. Wholesale prices of cured pork also showed some weakness in early May, but were steady to higher at the end of the month. Similarly, lard prices declined fairly sharply in the first half of May, but rose later in the month as prices of other hog products advanced. The composite wholesale price of hog products in New York in May was $20.57 per 100 pounds compared with $20.99 in April and $21.26 in May 1935.

Exports of both pork and lard in April were below March levels, but lard exports in April were larger than the small shipments of a year earlier. Total lard exports for the October - April period, 1935-36, however, were about 50 percent smaller than the exports for the same months in 1934-35. Exports of pork in April were 5 percent less than in March and they were 38 percent smaller than in April last year. The decrease in pork exports from the preceding month is accounted for by the reduction in shipments of fresh and canned pork, since exports of cured pork were larger than in March. Shipments of both pork and lard from the principal ports in May were smaller than those of a year earlier, but the shipments of pork were slightly larger than those of April.

Exports of hams and shoulders from the United States in April were larger than for any month since January, but were somewhat smaller than in April 1935. Most of this increase was in the shipments to the United Kingdom, the most important foreign outlet for these products. Bacon exports in April also were larger than in March, but they were equal to only about half of the relatively small bacon exports in April last year. Exports of fresh pork, which were of considerable importance in 1934, were lower in April than for any month in several years.

Lard exports in April, totaling 9,535,000 pounds, were about 2,000,000 pounds less than the exports for March, but were over 2,000,000 pounds greater than the quantity exported in April 1935, when domestic hog slaughter was greatly reduced. Although shipments of lard to the United Kingdom and Cuba in April showed a substantial decrease from a month earlier, lard exports to Germany, amounting to 1,320,000 pounds, were the largest since July 1934. This quantity, however, is equal to only a small fraction of the average monthly exports of lard to Germany in the post-war years prior to 1934.

Canada

Marketings of hogs at Canadian stockyards and packing plants during the first 5 months of 1936 have been about 3 percent larger than in the same period of 1935. This is in line with the forecast of the Canadian Government Hog Survey that slaughter supplies during the first half of 1936 would exceed those of a year ago.

In the first 2 months of the year gradings of live hogs at Canadian stockyards and packing plants were smaller than in the same months of 1935 but in March, April, and May they have exceeded slaughter in the same months, of 1935 considerably. The price of bacon hogs at Toronto was

$8.14 per 100 pounds American currency for the 4-week period ended May 28, compared with $8.33 for the month of April, and $9.38 in May 1935.

The number of hogs and hog carcasses graded in Canada this year in the 4-week period ended May 28 was 272,000 compared with only 229,000 head a year ago. The total number graded from the beginning of this year up to May 28 was 1,385,000 head, an increase of 3 percent above the same period of 1935. The distribution of hogs by principal grades and the percentage each grade represents of the total number graded has been as follows so far this year, with same information for last year given in parentheses: Select bacon hogs, 319,000 head, 25 percent (287,000 head, 22 percent), bacon hogs, 554,000 head, 43 percent (549,000, 42 percent); butcher hogs, 232,000, 18 percent (291,000, 22 percent). The bulk of bacon for export comes from the bacon and select grades of hogs which weigh from 180 to 230 pounds and are the type producing bacon suitable for the British market.

Live hog exports to the United States from Canada in the first 4 months of 1936 numbered 22,639 head compared with only 156 head during the same period of 1935. Bacon and ham exports from Canada during the first 4 months of this year amounted to 46,322,000 pounds compared with 50,466,000 pounds in the same period of 1935. This year 98 percent of the total went to the United Kingdom compared with practically 100 percent for the same period last year. The United States took 507,000 pounds of bacon and hams this year compared with only 115,000 pounds in the same 4 months of 1935. Pork exports from Canada reached 4,879,000 pounds for the first 4 months of 1936, 3,240,000 pounds of which came to the United States. Live hogs and pork formed the bulk of the exports to the United States - exports of bacon to this country being relatively small.

Although bacon exports to the United Kingdom during the first four months of 1936 amounting to 45,581,000 pounds were smaller by 9 percent than a year ago, there was an increase in lard exports of 170 percent to 8,416,000 pounds. Exports of all hog products from Canada to the United Kingdom amounted to 54,497,000 pounds in the first 4 months of 1936, an increase of 2 percent above the corresponding period of 1935.

United Kingdom and Irish Free State

On June 20, 1936, the Anglo-Danish trade agreement expired. This treaty provided, among other things, that cured pork should be admitted into the United Kingdom free of duty, and that Denmark's share in the total quota allotted foreign suppliers should be at least 62 percent. According to recent official information, the extension of the agreement with Denmark continues the present system of duty-free quotas until the end of 1936. It is understood, however, that the British Government probably will impose an import duty on cured pork, effective on or after January 1, 1937, and that cured pork quotas will be continued, probably with modifications.

Liverpool bacon quotations for May continued the steady decline of the past 4 months. Danish Wiltshire sides averaged $20.09 per 100 pounds, 37 cents under the April average and 7 cents below that for May 1935. Canadian green sides at $17.55 per 100 pounds averaged 15 cents less than during the previous month and 36 cents below the May 1935 figure. American green bellies were not quoted.

Total bacon receipts in the United Kingdom for the month of April at about 61,000,000 pounds were some 5,300,000 below April 1935 imports. Total imports for the period October 1 to the end of April, at 424,400,000 pounds, represented a decline of 8 percent from the quantity imported during the first 7 months of last season and of 45 percent from the corresponding imports in the peak season 1931-32.

Imports into the United Kingdom from Denmark amounted to approximately 228,000,000 pounds for the period October 1935-April 1936. Last year to the same date Denmark had shipped over 252,000,000 pounds and from October 1, 1931 by April 30, 1932, nearly 534,000,000 pounds. Imports of bacon from the Irish Free State for the month of April at 4,413,000 pounds were 13 percent above imports for April 1935, 196 percent above those of April 1932, and 35 percent higher than the imports for the corresponding period of the peak year for Irish bacon imports, 1928-29. The total for the season October-April, at about 32,000,000 pounds, however, is still over 20 percent smaller than comparable 1928-29 imports. Canadian imports for the current season, though some five times as large as those of the comparable period of 1931-32, are not so large as record receipts of last year. At 58,000,000 pounds for the season to the end of April, they showed a decline from October-April 1934-35 figures of 11 percent. Imports of bacon into the United Kingdom from the United States reached a record low for the month of April at 44,000 pounds. The total for the current season to April 30 amounted to little over 1,000,000 pounds.

Liverpool quotations on American short cut green hams continued their seasonal rise, averaging for the month of May $21.28 per 100 pounds. This is the highest May average since 1929 and represents an increase of 60 cents over April figures and $1.72 over those of May 1935.

British imports of ham for the 7 months October to April, amounted to 37,400,000 pounds, a decline of 7 percent from last season's comparable imports. The United States share, at approximately 18,000,000 pounds, represented 49 percent of the total, whereas October-April 1934-35 imports from the United States at nearly 24,000,000 pounds represented 59 percent of the total imports. In the same months of the 1929-30 season, the United States shipped to the British market over 50,000,000 pounds of ham, or 84 percent of total receipts in that market. Imports of Canadian ham declined somewhat during April, yielding the lead again to the United States product. The Canadian share in total imports for the season to April 30 amounted to only a little less than that of the United States and represented 38 percent of the total from all sources. Last year they represented but 31 percent, and in 1931-32 less than 16 percent. Imports of ham from the Irish Free State at less than 1,900,000 pounds for the period represented a slight increase over imports for comparable periods of the several years preceding and amounted to nearly 5 percent of total imports.

The price of refined lard on the British market as indicated by Liverpool quotations was materially reduced during May, making an average for the month of $12.25 per 100 pounds compared with $13.85 in April and $13.01 a year ago. The American product was again offered in considerable quantity, almost 9,000,000 pounds being imported in April, probably accounting in part for the price decline. April imports of lard from the United States were the highest in more than a year, although still less than half the size of usual monthly imports before January 1935. The figure for total American lard imports into the United Kingdom to the end of April was a record low at slightly over 35,000,000 pounds, representing a decline of 64 percent and 79 percent, respectively, from comparable 1934-35 and 1933-34 imports. Imports of lard from the United States during the current season made up only 36 percent of the total, whereas last season the American product represented 74 percent and during October-April 1933-34, 91 percent of lard imports into the United Kingdom.

Supplies of British and Irish pork at London Central Markets during April were rather high for that month, bringing the total for the season to around 57,000,000 pounds. This amount was 10 percent above the comparable one for 1934-35 and the highest in the last 4 years.

The United States has been allotted a frozen pork quota of 25,309 hundredweight (2,834,608 pounds) for the third quarter of 1936. This allocation is the same as that granted the United States in 1935.

Denmark

Average weekly hog slaughter in Denmark for the period May 1-February 25, 1936-37, is expected to exceed the 1935 weekly average, according to estimates reported by Vice Consul L. W. Taylor at Copenhagen. The semi-official Danish Agricultural Council estimates that, on the basis of the increases in most age groups in the hog census of May 2, 1936, the average weekly slaughter for the 1936-37 period indicated should reach 95,000 head, against an average of 83,000 head for the calendar year 1935. The Council estimates the average litter at 5.5 pigs. It is observed, however, that since about 41 percent of the piggy sows as of May 2 were pregnant for the first time, that figure probably is too high, and that, therefore, the weekly killings will be somewhat under the present estimate. It is evident, however, that Danish hog numbers have increased sufficiently to increase the 1936 rate of killing over that of 1935. See following table.

Danish exports of bacon in April remained at the reduced level of recent months. The current figure of 32,521,000 pounds also continued the general level of reduction below last season's exports. For the period October-April 1935-36, exports of bacon were 7.8 percent under comparable 1934-35 figures, and were below exports of other recent seasons to a considerably greater degree. In the first 4 months of the calendar year 1936, exports of Danish lard also were slightly under last year's figures, the current total standing at 8,423,000 pounds. Exports of live hogs, however, reached nearly 39,000 head in the 1936 period against less than 600 in 1935. All of the hogs exported were taken by Germany.

Denmark: Number of hogs, May census, 1935 ar

Classification	May 25,1
	Thousand
Boars aged 4 years or over ....:	20
Sows in farrow:	
Young ....:	83
Other ....:	172
Total sows in farrow ....:.....:	255
Other sows:	
With litters ....:	88
Barren ....:	25
Condemned ....:	12
Total other sows ....:..:	125
Total sows ....:	380
Hogs other than breeding stock:	
Suckling pigs ....:	724
Hogs under 77 pounds ....:	797
Hogs 77 to 132 pounds ....:	635
Hogs 132 pounds and over ....:	500
Total non-breeding stock ....:	2,656
Total all classes ....:	3,056

Compiled from Statistiske Efterretninger for May 20,

Germany

The larger numbers of marketable hogs in Germa
reflected in increased marketings and slaughter. Mon
still under those of a year ago, but April figures fo
295,000 head, were the largest for any month since Ap
receipts at those markets for the period from October
31.9 percent under the comparable 1934-35 figures. S
also tended to increase, but the April figures were a
March returns and well under those of a year ago.

The considerable increase in imports of lard i
earlier months of this year was continued during Apri
10,000,000 pounds were received. That figure was nea
than the April 1935 imports, and was the largest Apri
The April figures brought total imports for the peric
to a quantity nearly double that of the corresponding
and Denmark continue to supply most of the lard now i
slavia, Argentina, and Brazil all rank ahead of the U
For the first 4 months of 1936, lard imports from the
990,000 pounds, were 41.7 percent smaller than the co
1935.

German imports of bacon in April, at 1,454,000 pounds, were smaller than for any month since last June. Total bacon imports for the first 4 months of 1936, however, were about 33 percent larger than imports for the corresponding 1935 months. So far this year the Netherlands continues to be the leading supplier. For the 1935-36 season, October 1 to April 30, total bacon imports were 8.9 percent below the 1934-35 level.

Danube Basin

Farmers' intentions reports for Hungary as of April 1, 1936, indicate an increase of 37 percent over 1935 in the numbers of lard hogs to be finished for market in the period April-September 1936. The Belgrade office of the Foreign Agricultural Service reports also that the number of meat-type hogs on feed in the same period is expected to show an increase of 9 percent in the same period. The intentions reports suggest a substantial increase in marketings during the fall and winter of 1936-37 over comparable 1935-36 figures. For the period April-September, however, the decline in the monthly rate of marketings anticipated by the Belgrade office appears to be materializing, following the unusually large sales made in the period January-March 1936. Hungary is the Basin's leading lard and pork exporting country.

Lard exports from the Danube Basin in the 2 months April-May 1936 were maintained at a monthly rate below that of the 3 preceding months. Total exports for the 2 recent months, at about 13,000.000 pounds, however, were about 53 percent larger than in the corresponding months of 1935. For the first 5 months of 1936, total lard exports from the Basin reached about 34,800,000 pounds, an increase of 24 percent over the comparable 1935 figures. So far this year, Hungary has accounted for 68.4 percent of the total exports against 85 percent last year. Exports from Hungary were about the same this year as last, all of the current increase in total exports being accounted for by larger exports from the other three Basin countries, notably Yugoslavia and Bulgaria.

The downward movement of lard prices in Great Britain during May apparently resulted in a sharp decline in exports of Danube lard to that market. Hungarian shipments to Great Britain stopped about May 10, and were continued that long only because of the export premium paid on lard. As a result, the May exports were concentrated largely in the movement to Germany, with Czechoslovakia as the second important outlet. The German quota of 3,175,000 pounds granted to Hungary for May was exhausted before the end of the month. The trade anticipated late in May that the June quota would be about the same size as the May quota.

The exports of Danubian live hogs in April and May were somewhat smaller than in earlier months of this year, but continued larger than in 1935. Seasonal considerations reduced marketings to the extent of leaving unfilled the May quotas granted to Hungary and Yugoslavia by Austria and Czechoslovakia, despite the maintenance of March and April price levels in the consuming countries. Also exports of hog carcasses declined during May, largely because of lower prices ruling in Germany. The small Austrian quotas held by Yugoslavia and Hungary are the only outlets now available to exports of hog carcasses from the Danube Basin.

Switzerland

The importation of 110,321 kilograms (243,214 pounds) of lard into Switzerland has been authorized since February 15, 1936, the effective date of the trade agreement between the United States and Switzerland, according to the American Consul at Bern. Of the amount authorized, all had been admitted by May 28, and all of the imports were of American origin. United States shippers were guaranteed by the trade agreement at least 90 percent of the authorized amount of imports. That provision, however, was not to become effective until May 15, or 3 months after the agreement became effective. The Consul reports that it is the policy of the Swiss Government to allow as large an importation of lard from the United States as is possible, taking into consideration the domestic situation. So far there are no indications as to how large future imports may be.

Under the terms of the agreement, the Swiss Government agreed to lift its virtual embargo on imported lard by May 15. According to official monthly import figures, however, it appears that Switzerland has been allowing the importation of lard at least since February 15, since 220,901 pounds are recorded as having been imported in the months February-April. This suggests that, of the total of 243,214 pounds received to May 28, 22,113 pounds were received during May. The Swiss import duty on lard was reduced 50 percent by the agreement, the present rate being about 3 cents per pound.

Hogs and pork products: Indices of foreign supplies and demand

Country and item	Unit	Oct. - Apr.					
		1909-10 to 1913-14 average	1924-25 to 1928-29 average	1932-33	1933-34	1934-35	1935-36
UNITED KINGDOM:							
Production-							
Supplies, domestic							
fresh pork,	:1,000						
London ....:	pounds		39,277	56,724	47,211	52,140	57,274
Imports-							
Bacon-							
Denmark ....:	"	140,624	292,492	423,424	285,744	252,234	228,285
Irish Free State.:	"		33,417	13,209	19,558	28,322	31,841
United States ...:	"	111,875	66,293	2,446	3,228	2,020	1,009
Canada ....:	"	23,571	45,364	13,317	57,422	65,263	58,055
Others ....:	"	23,978	89,129	224,345	153,647	113,111	105,234
Total ....:	"	300,048	526,695	676,743	519,601	460,949	424,423
Ham, total ....:	"	52,215	70,379	48,534	44,885	40,234	37,405
Lard, total ....:	"	131,658	156,855	168,690	183,035	133,684	97,327
DENMARK:							
Exports-							
Bacon ....:	"	..	291,558	435,181	301,890	255,452	234,769
CANADA:							
Slaughter-							
Hogs, inspected ..:	1000's	1,010	1,674	1,656	1,809	1,818	1,839
GERMANY:							
Production-							
Hog receipts							
14 cities ....:	"		1,916	1,811	1,976	2,059	1,402
Hog slaughter							
36 centers ......:	"	2,612	2,366	2,470	2,639	2,757	1,866
Imports-	:1,000						
Bacon, total .....:	pounds	1,669	11,146	19,764	17,454	16,907	15,391
Lard, total ......:	"	123,290	134,571	134,004	81.177	34,811	62,565
UNITED STATES:							
Slaughter-							
Hogs, inspected ..:	1000's	19,732	29,303	27,763	27,363	21,556	18,355
Exports-							
Bacon-	:1,000						
United Kingdom ..:	pounds	78,385	40,387	1,661	1,584	1,148	390
Germany ....:	"	1,145	6,862	1,170	2,400	0	13
Cuba ....:	"	4,406	12,297	2,542	2,679	2,761	604
Total ....:	"	106,958	85,390	10,212	14,192	5,187	1,584
Hams, shoulders-							
United Kingdom ..:	"	80,219	82,848	31,882	30,590	25,737	19,234
Total ....:	"	92,762	99,490	37,591	35,910	31,672	22,551
Lard-							
United Kingdom ..:	"	102,520	136,501	165,123	177,215	83,939	37,996
Germany ....:	"	86,057	112,673	102,297	48,737	2,513	4,351
Cuba ....:	"	21,065	48,198	6,880	8,455	18,683	12,293
Netherlands .....:	"	23,377	26,510	25,927	16,699	9	40
Total ....:	"	285,333	437,782	361,682	319,106	114,164	57,097

Hogs and pork products: Foreign and domestic average prices per
100 pounds for the month indicated, and stocks at the
end of each month

	1909-1913 average	1925-1929 average	Apr. 1935	Mar. 1936	Apr. 1936
	Dollars	Dollars	Dollars	Dollars	Dollars
Prices -					
Hogs, Chicago, basis packers' and shippers' quotations ....:	8.04	12.05	8.94	10.24	10.47
Corn, Chicago, No. 3 yellow	1.11	1.65	1.56	1.09	1.13
Hogs, heavy, Berlin live weight ....:	11.18	13.78	15.27	17.70	17.70
Barley, Leipzig ....:	1.77	2.37	1/ 2.94	3.31	3.33
Lard -					
Chicago ....:	10.33	14.78	14.66	11.88	11.90
Liverpool ... .' ..:	11.70	15.02	13.55	13.00	13.85
Hamburg ....'..:	12.90	15.43	----	12.53	12.78
Cured pork -					
Liverpool -					
American short cut green hams ....:	14.10	23.72	19.24	19.65	20.88
American green bellies ....:		20.56	14.57	Nominal	Nominal
Danish Wiltshire sides ....:	15.00	24.55	18.60	20.56	20.46
Canadian green sides.:	14.16	2/ 21.55	16.46	17.87	17.70
	1,000 pounds	1,000 pounds	1,000 pounds	1,000 pounds	1,000 pounds
Stocks -					
United States -					
Processed pork 3/....:		814,486	565,699	450,149	457,402
Lard in cold storage...:		141,462	100,920	76,814	83,615

1/ Breslau market. Leipzig quotation not available.

2/ Four-year average only.

3/ Dry salt cured and in process of cure; pickled, cured, and in process
of cure, and frozen.

-0-

HP-80   July 30, 1936

WORLD HOG AND PORK PROSPECTS

Summary

Larger marketings of hogs in the United States next fall and winter appear probable in view of the marked increase in the spring pig crop of 1936 over 1935. Because of this increase in supplies it is expected that prices for hogs will decline seasonally in the fall months of this year. The further improvement in consumer demand in prospect, however, will offset in part the effect of the increase in supplies upon hog prices.

The June Pig Crop Report recently released indicated that there would be an increase of about 14 percent in the number of sows to farrow in the fall of 1936. This indication, however, was based upon breeding intentions reported by farmers on about June 1. Since early June severe drought conditions have developed in the Corn Belt, which is the principal hog producing area. These conditions have reduced the 1936 corn crop prospects materially, and it is probable that there will be little if any increase in the 1936 fall pig crop. The outturn of the corn crop is still very uncertain, but if corn production this year is curtailed considerably by drought, as now appears probable, some liquidation of sows and spring pigs will occur in the next few months. A small corn crop this year would cause corn prices to rise relative to hog prices, and the hog-corn price ratio would be much less favorable for increases in hog production than it has been in the last year. If this ratio is reduced materially it is also probable that average weights of hogs marketed in 1936-37 will be much lighter than the heavier-than-average weights this year.

A further increase in the number of hogs in Germany was reported in early June, and slaughter supplies of hogs in that country continue to increase.

Although United States exports of lard to Germar
months they are still at a very low level. Rest
countries generally have tended to fix an upper
of this country cannot increase. Because of the
this country, exports of pork and lard in 1935-3
this upper level. With an increase in hog slaug
half of the 1936-37 marketing year, it is probat
ports will occur. Whether this increase continu
depend chiefly upon the trend in domestic hog pr
be governed largely by the effect of the present
crop.

Domestic Situation

In view of the large increase in the 1936
of hogs slaughtered in the fall and winter (Octo
probably will be considerably larger than a year
indicated in the June Pig Crop Report in the num
fall of 1936 is realized there will also be an i
the summer of 1937 compared with the present sum
drought conditions prevailing in the Corn Belt s
does not seem probable that the indicated incree
farrow this fall will materialize.

Although the number of hogs on farms over
was estimated to be only 7 percent larger than a
probable that hog slaughter in August and Septen
than in those months last year. In view of the
that some liquidation of sows and spring pigs wi
will represent an addition to the number of hogs
in these months if there had been no drought. S
and September, however, will be smaller than in
probable that hog prices will advance seasonally
of the large increase in the 1936 spring pig cro
hog slaughter in the coming fall and early winte
and a decline in hog prices is probable after Se
improvement in consumer demand in prospect and a
for hog products this winter likely, the drop in
to the end of 1936 may not be greater than the u
this period.

The 1936 spring pig crop was estimated to
than that of 1935, according to the June 1936 pi
of Agricultural Economics. Despite this large i
produced in the spring of 1936 was the smallest

except 1935, when the spring crop was very sharply curtailed because of the 1934 drought. As indicated in the table on page 5 showing the estimates of the spring pig crop by regions, increases in pig production were reported in all areas, with the greatest increases occurring in the Corn Belt and in the Western States. In the North Central States (Corn Belt) the number of pigs produced in the spring of 1936 was 32.5 percent larger than the number produced in the spring of 1935. Last year the greatest decrease in the spring pig crop occurred in the North Central States, where drought conditions in 1934 were very severe.

It was also indicated in the June Pig Crop Report that the number of sows to farrow in the fall of 1936 will be about 14 percent larger than the number farrowing in the fall of 1935. This indication was based upon interpretations of breeding intentions reported by farmers on or about June 1. Since June 1, however, severe drought conditions have developed in the Corn Belt and corn crop prospects for 1936 have declined greatly. Hence it seems unlikely that the increase in the number of sows to farrow this fall, which was indicated on the basis of reports on June 1, will be realized.

The number of hogs over 6 months of age on farms on June 1, 1936 was estimated to be about 7 percent larger than a year earlier for the United States as a whole, and about 11 percent larger for the North Central States (Corn Belt). The number of hogs on farms over 6 months of age on June 1 includes mostly hogs that will be marketed in the following 4 months and sows bred or to be bred for fall farrow. In past years there has been a fairly close relationship between changes in number of hogs over 6 months of age in the Corn Belt and changes in inspected hog slaughter from June to September. The change in the number of hogs on farms on June 1, after making allowance for the increase in hog slaughter in June compared with a year earlier and for the estimated increase in the number of sows to farrow this fall, would indicate that inspected hog slaughter in the period from July to September 1936 would be little if any larger than that of a year earlier. This indication of slaughter in the summer months, however, is somewhat at variance with the large increase in summer slaughter supplies indicated by the estimated increase of over 30 percent in the 1935 fall pig crop. It should be noted that the indication of summer slaughter supplies of hogs given in the June issue of this Report was based entirely upon the increase in the 1935 fall pig crop, since the estimate of the number of hogs on farms over 6 months of age on June 1, 1936 was not then available. Regardless of which of these indications is correct, slaughter supplies of hogs in July, August, and September probably will be larger than otherwise and larger than last year because of drought conditions which have recently developed.

Hog prices advanced somewhat in late May and early June and advanced further in late June and early July. Since slaughter supplies of all species of livestock increased from May to June, the advance in hog prices in recent weeks reflects an improvement in consumer demand for meats considerably greater than was anticipated several months ago. The average price of hogs at Chicago for the last week of June was $9.99, the highest weekly average since late April. For the entire month of June the average price of hogs at Chicago was $9.88 per 100 pounds compared with $9.58 in May and $9.27 in June last year. The advance in prices in recent weeks was somewhat greater for light and medium weight butcher hogs than for heavy weight butcher hogs and packing sows.

Slaughter supplies of hogs in June were somewhat larger
but the increase was less than average for this period. Hog sl
Federal inspection in June, totaling about 2,759,000 head, was
percent larger than in June last year. With the exception of J
however, inspected slaughter in June this year was the smallest
since 1917. The proportion of packing sows included in the man
of hogs increased materially during June, as is usual for this
Average weights of all hogs in June continued heavier than a ye
The average weight of hogs at the seven leading markets for the
253 pounds, compared with 242 pounds in May and 244 pounds in .

Corn prices advanced moderately during the first 3 week;
advanced sharply in late June and early July as crop condition;
Belt became unfavorable. The average price of No. 3 Yellow co;
in June was 64 cents compared with 63 cents in May and 85 cent;
year. The advance in corn prices in June and early July was so
than the rise in hog prices, and as a result the hog-corn price
during this period, but it continued to be higher than average
than last year. Based on Chicago prices, the hog-corn price re
week ended July 3 was 14.8 compared with 16.0 in early June and
earlier. The ratio has been above average since August 1935 an
much above average since last November. The high hog prices in
corn prices in the last year were an importatn factor in causin
in the number of pigs produced in the fall of 1935 and in the
and they also have been the chief reason for the increase in a
of hogs marketed during the current hog marketing year. If the
crop is sharply curtailed by drought, it is probable that corn
rise relative to hog prices in the coming year, and as a result
for further increases in hog production will be considerably l

Prices of fresh pork declined in early June but were fa
during the remainder of the month. Prices of most cuts of cur
during June, while lard prices were about steady. The composi
price of hog products at New York averaged $20.99 per 100 poun
compared with $20.57 in May and $21.96 in the corresponding mo
earlier.

Exports of pork in May were materially larger than in A
were considerably smaller than in May last year. A large part
from April to May was accounted for by the larger shipments of
shoulders, most of which are consigned to the United Kingdom.
8 months of the 1935-36 hog marketing year exports of pork wer
percent smaller than in the corresponding month of 1934-35.

Exports of lard in May, totaling nearly 11,000,000 poun
than in April 1936 and in May last year. Except for May 1935,
exports in May this year were the smallest for the month in th
Lard exports both to Great Britain and Cuba in May were larger
and shipments to Cuba were larger than in the corresponding mo
earlier. Exports to Germany in May were almost negligible, wh
they amounted to about 1,000,000 pounds. In the first 8 month
lard exports of about 68,000,000 pounds were 45 percent less t
and more than 80 percent smaller than in 1933-34.

United States: Spring pig crop, by geographic divisions,
1935 and 1936

Geographic division	Spring pigs saved (Dec. 1 to June 1)			Spring pigs saved per litter		Sows farrowed in spring (Dec. 1 to June 1)		Sows to be farrowed in the fall of 1936 compared with the fall of 1935 (June 1 to Dec. 1)		
	1935	1936 1/ Total	Percentage of 1935	1935	1936	1935	1936	1935	1936 2/ Total	Percentage of 1935
	Thousands	Thousands	Percent	Number	Number	Thousands	Thousands	Thousands	Thousands	Percent
North Atlantic	614	724	118	6.04	6.01	102	120	104	122	117
East North Central	8,880	10,579	119	6.41	6.15	1,385	1,720	1,020	1,231	121
West North Central	14,539	20,462	141	6.03	6.01	2,411	3,403	1,336	1,414	106
Total North Central	23,419	31,041	132	6.17	6.06	3,796	5,123	2,356	2,645	112
South Atlantic	2,651	2,900	109	5.76	5.58	460	520	399	462	116
South Central	4,644	5,764	124	5.50	5.66	845	1,018	747	895	120
Mountain and Pacific (West)	1,052	1,455	138	5.77	5.89	182	247	160	185	115
United States	32,380	41,884	129	6.01	5.96	5,385	7,028	3,766	4,310	114

Compiled from the Pig Crop Report of June 1, 1936.

1/ Preliminary.
2/ Number indicated to farrow from breeding intention reports.

Canada

Marketings of hogs in Canada in the first half of 1936 were about
6.5 percent larger than in the same period of 1935. Despite this increase
in marketings, hog prices thus far this year have averaged only slightly
lower than a year earlier. Bacon exports, which are largely consigned to
the United Kingdom, have been slightly smaller thus far in 1936/ than in 1935,
but exports of other kinds of pork have increased this year. Total exports of hogs and
hog products combined in the first 5 months of 1936 were slightly larger
than in the corresponding months last year.

Hog prices in Canada advanced somewhat during June. The average
price of bacon hogs at Toronto for the 4 weeks ended June 25 was about
$8.80 (United States currency) compared with $8.16 in the month of May and

$9.91 in the month of June last year. The number of hogs
graded at public stockyards and packing plants in Canada
ended June 25 totaled 259,000 head, which was a decrease
compared with the gradings in May but was an increase of
with those of the corresponding period in 1935. The incr
hog marketings in 1936 compared with a year earlier has o
in the last 4 months, since marketings in January and Feb
than in 1935.

Foreign Situation

United Kingdom and Irish Free State

On June 19, 1936, a supplementary agreement betwee
Danish Governments was signed, continuing in force the An
ment of June 20, 1933, according to information received
Attache C. C. Taylor at London. The agreement is subject
notice of renunciation by either party. Minor changes we
of the provisions, but that affecting bacon importations
Kingdom, contrary to expectations, was not altered.

Liverpool bacon quotations for the month of June h
than during the previous month, Danish Wiltshire sides ma
of $20.33 per 100 pounds and Canadian green sides, $18.08
sides averaged 24 cents above the May figure but 82 cents
1935 average. The June average for Canadian green sides
the comparable May figure, though 67 cents under that of

Total imports of bacon for the first 8 months of t
amounted to over 484,000,000 pounds as against 528,000,0C
months of the 1934-35 season and 861,000,000 during the O
of the peak 1931-32 season. This represents a decline of
the past 4 years. Danish imports into the United Kingdom
period show an even greater decline, amounting for the 4
Imports from Denmark for the 1935-36 season to the end of
260,000,000 pounds as against over 582,000,000 pounds in

Imports of bacon from the Irish Free State continu
totaling nearly 36,000,000 pounds in the period October t
compared with 32,000,000 pounds last year and less than 1
during the same months of 1932-33, the year of lowest bac
the United Kingdom from that source. Imports thus far th
the highest for any 8-month period since the 1928-29 seas
reached a little over 40,000,000 pounds. Canadian shipme
the United Kingdom during the period October to May 1935-
below those of a year ago and slightly under those of the
Such imports amounted to about 68,000,000 pounds, which r
of 9 percent from the comparable period of a year earlier
some 30 times larger than imports from Canada during the
period.

Imports of United States bacon into the United Kin
small, amounting for the month of May to but 78,000 pound
season to the end of May to slightly over 1,000,000 pouhc
months of 1929-30, British imports of bacon from the Unit
46,700,000 pounds.

American short cut green hams were quoted on the Liverpool market at an average for the month of June at $21.95, or 67 cents above the May average. This is the highest June average since 1929, amounting to $2.12 more than the comparable 1935 figure.

Total ham imports into the United Kingdom have been fairly well maintained during the first 8 months of the season, reaching nearly 45,000,000 pounds as against about 48,000,000 for comparable months of the 1934-35 period. They represent, however, a decline of 25 percent from October-May imports of the 1932-33 season, and of 38 percent from those of 1929-30. Imports of hams from the United States increased somewhat during May, amounting, however, to less than 4,000,000 pounds. The total imports into the United Kingdom from the United States for the current season of 22,000,000 pounds represent decreases from those of comparable months of the 1934-35, 1933-34, and 1932-33 seasons of 22 percent, 31 percent, and 37 percent, respectively. The United States so far this season has furnished 50 percent of total imports into the United Kingdom, whereas in the 1929-30 period it supplied 85 percent. During October-May 1935-36, receipts of Canadian ham in the British market amounted to about 38 percent of the total imports.

Liverpool average quotations on refined lard for the month of June fell to $11.83, 42 cents below the previous month's average and $1.81 under the average price in June last year. Aside from the June 1935 average, this was the highest for the month since 1929. Lard imports into the United Kingdom for the current season, October 1 to May 31, reached a total of less than 110,000,000 pounds. This figure represents a decline of 37 percent from 1934-35 comparable imports and of 50 percent from those of 2 years ago. The United States thus far this season has supplied only 36 percent of this greatly reduced total compared with 70 percent in the same period of last year and 92 percent in 1933-34. British lard imports from the United States have declined over 80 percent during the last 2 years.

Germany

The increase in German hog numbers noted in recent months has been reflected in an increase in receipts and slaughter of hogs in May, when slaughter was larger than for any month since early 1935. For the first 8 months of the 1935-36 season, however, hog receipts were still about 27 percent smaller than in the corresponding 1934-35 period, according to figures covering 14 points transmitted by the Berlin office of the Foreign Agricultural Service. Slaughter at 36 centers for the period October to May 1935-36 was about 28 percent below comparable 1934-35 figures. The number of young stock and breeding sows appearing in the June 1936 hog census indicates a continuance of the increase in marketable hogs. Total hog numbers in June this year were placed at 22,200,000 head, or 11 percent larger than a year earlier. Marketable hogs aged 6 months to 1 year were up 7 percent last month over a year earlier, while brood sows in the same age group increased 18 percent. The number of all young pigs under 6 months old in June this year was 12 percent larger than in 1935.

Germany continues to import somewhat larger quantities of hog products this year than last, but imports in May were smaller than in other recent months. The general level of imports, however, continues relatively low.

Imports of lard in May of 5,489,000 pounds were the smallest since August
1935. The United States was the chief supplier of the reduced total,
accounting for nearly 2,000,000 pounds, or about 36 percent. Brazil was
next, with slightly more than 1,000,000 pounds. At least nine other
countries supplied lard to Germany during May, of which Hungary was the
most important. For the period January-May, however, the United States
supplied less than 3,000,000 pounds, or only about 7 percent of a total of
40,322,000 pounds. For the first 8 months of the 1935-36 season, Germany
imported about 80 percent more lard than in the corresponding period of
1934-35. Bacon imports in May, nearly all of which came from the Netherlands, were smaller than in either the preceding month or in the corresponding month a year earlier, reaching only 1,100,000 pounds. Total bacon
imports into Germany in the period October-May 1935-36 were about 12 percent
smaller than those of a year earlier.

Hogs and pork products: Indices of foreign supplies and demand

Country and item	Unit	Oct.-May					
		1909-10 to 1913-14 average	1924-25 to 1928-29 average	1932-33	1933-34	1934-35	1935-36
UNITED KII'GDOM:							
Supplies,							
domestic fresh	1,000						
pork, London ..	pounds		42,025	60,597	50,976	57,494	62,106
Imports-							
Bacon-							
Denmark ......:	"	162,459	333,487	482,619	329,339	289,230	260,012
Irish F.State.:	"		36,682	14,539	22,359	32,345	35,797
United States.:	"	124,784	74,637	3,183	3,543	2,221	1,087
Canada ....:	"	27,289	50,282	18,883	67,984	74,810	67,767
Others ....:	"	27,954	105,553	250,321	175,462	129,450	119,801
Total ......:	"	342,486	600,691	769,547	598,690	528,105	484,463
Ham, total ...:	"	60,729	81,403	59,271	52,119	47,612	44,607
Lard, total ..:	"	148,270	181,212	192,995	217,370	149,693	109,588
DENMARK:							
Exports-							
Bacon ....:	"		332,285	492,205	345,854	292,231	
CANADA:							
Slaughter-							
Hogs,inspected:	1000's	1,154	1,880	1,935	2,076	2,063	2,119
GERMANY:							
Production-							
Hog receipts							
14 cities ...:	"		2,198	2,119	2,308	2,348	1,708
Hog slaughter :							
36 centers ..:	"	3,000	2,731	2,873	3,064	3,145	2,262
Imports-	1,000						
Bacon, total .:	pounds	1,855	12,065	21,713	18,551	18,757	16,497
Lard, total ..:	"	138,404	150,588	168,456	89,897	37,986	68,054
UNITED STATES:							
Slaughter-							
Hogs,inspected:	1000's	22,467	32,856	32,049	31,581	24,015	20,934
Exports-							
Bacon-	1,000						
United Kingdom:	pounds	87,643	45,404	1,815	1,937	1,274	423
Germany ......:	"	1,204	7,931	1,189	2,447	0	29
Cuba ....:	"	5,114	14,027	2,918	3,342	3,156	775
Total ......:	"	119,927	96,436	11,123	16,128	5,805	1,884
Hams,shoulders-:							
United Kingdom:	"	92,422	95,006	37,779	35,420	31,831	23,739
Total ......:	"	107,272	113,979	44,099	41,660	38,454	25,780
Lard-							
United Kingdom:	"	118,283	155,919	187,483	216,681	90,973	44,606
Germany ......:	"	98,123	130,674	114,406	53,953	2,513	4,441
Cuba ....:	"	24,895	54,772	7,848	10,282	20,730	15,212
Netherlands ..:	"	26,136	29,392	30,125	19,022	9	40
Total ......:		326,974	500,470	407,720	385,273	123,904	67,934

Hogs and pork products: Foreign and domestic average prices per 100
pounds for the month indicated, and stocks at the end of each month

Item	1909-1913 average	1925-1929 average	May 1935	April 1936	May 1936
	Dollars	Dollars	Dollars	Dollars	Dollars
Prices-					
Hogs, Chicago, basis packers' and shippers' quotations ....:	7.81	11.13	9.31	10.47	9.58
Corn, Chicago, No. 3 Yellow ....:	1.16	1.71	1.52	1.13	1.13
Hogs, heavy, Berlin live weight ....:	10.96	13.89	15.69	17.70	17.70
Barley, Leipzig ....:	1.75	2.44	3.14	3.33	3.37
Lard-					
Chicago ....:	10.68	14.74	14.65	11.90	11.12
Liverpool ....:	11.80	15.16	13.01	13.85	12.25
Hamburg ....:	12.65	15.67	----	12.78	11.83
Cured pork-					
Liverpool-					
American short cut green hams ......:	14.80	24.39	19.56	20.88	21.28
American green bellies ....:		21.19	14.25	Nominal	Nominal
Danish Wiltshire sides ....:	15.60	25.16	20.16	20.46	20.09
Canadian green sides ....:	14.64	22.76	17.91	17.70	17.55
	1,000 pounds	1,000 pounds	1,000 pounds	1,000 pounds	1,000 pounds
Stocks-					
United States-					
Processed pork 1/ ...:		780,179	503,413	457,402	440,618
Lard in cold storage ....:		145,332	89,986	83,615	99,656

1/ Dry salt cured and in process of cure; pickled, cured, and in process
of cure, and frozen.

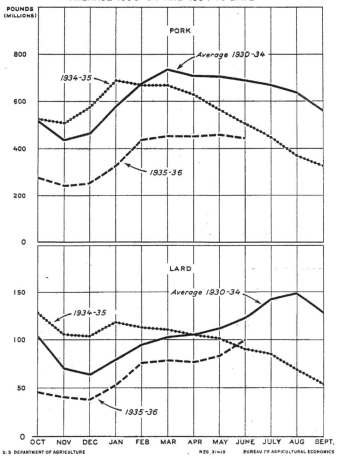

STORAGE HOLDINGS OF PORK AND LARD ON FIRST OF EACH MONTH,
AVERAGE 1930-34 AND 1934 TO DATE

POUNDS
(MILLIONS)

PORK

800

Average 1930-34

1934-35

600

400

1935-36

200

0

LARD

150

Average 1930-34

1934-35

100

50

1935-36

0

OCT   NOV   DEC   JAN   FEB   MAR   APR   MAY   JUNE   JULY   AUG   SEPT.

U. S DEPARTMENT OF AGRICULTURE   NEG. 31410   BUREAU OF AGRICULTURAL ECONOMICS

FIGURE I.— STORAGE HOLDINGS OF PORK USUALLY INCREASE
FROM EARLY NOVEMBER UNTIL FEBRUARY OR MARCH AND THEN DE-
CLINE DURING THE REMAINDER OF THE HOG MARKETING YEAR.
STOCKS OF PORK THIS YEAR HAVE BEEN MUCH BELOW AVERAGE,
BUT THEY HAVE ONLY RECENTLY BEGUN TO DECLINE. STOCKS OF
LARD USUALLY INCREASE FROM DECEMBER TO AUGUST AND THEN
DECLINE FROM SEPTEMBER TO NOVEMBER. ALTHOUGH LARD STOCKS
THIS YEAR ARE BELOW AVERAGE, THE USUAL SEASONAL INCREASE
HAS OCCURRED SINCE LAST DECEMBER.

SPRING PIG CROP, AND FEDERALLY INSPECTED HOG SLAUGHTER DURING FOLLOWING OCT.-APR., UNITED STATES, 1924 TO DATE

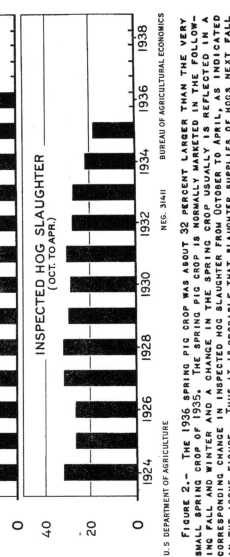

U.S DEPARTMENT OF AGRICULTURE

NEG. 31411   BUREAU OF AGRICULTURAL ECONOMICS

FIGURE 2.— THE 1936 SPRING PIG CROP WAS ABOUT 32 PERCENT LARGER THAN THE VERY SMALL SPRING CROP OF 1935. THE SPRING PIG CROP IS NORMALLY MARKETED IN THE FOLLOW- ING FALL AND WINTER AND A CHANGE IN THE SPRING CROP USUALLY IS REFLECTED IN A CORRESPONDING CHANGE IN INSPECTED HOG SLAUGHTER FROM OCTOBER TO APRIL, AS INDICATED IN THE ABOVE FIGURE. THUS IT IS PROBABLE THAT SLAUGHTER SUPPLIES OF HOGS NEXT FALL

UNITED STATES DEPARTMENT OF AGRICULTURE
Bureau of Agricultural Economics
Division of Statistical and Historical Research
Washington

HP-81

WORLD HOG AND PORK PROSPECTS

Quarterly Summary

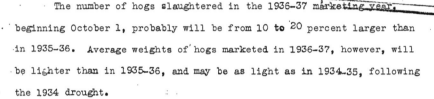

The number of hogs slaughtered in the 1936-37 marketing year, beginning October 1, probably will be from 10 to 20 percent larger than in 1935-36. Average weights of hogs marketed in 1936-37, however, will be lighter than in 1935-36, and may be as light as in 1934-35, following the 1934 drought.

Hog prices in 1936-37 probably will average about as high as in 1935-36, since the probable increase in slaughter supplies will be about offset by the further improvement in consumer demand now in prospect. Hog slaughter in the period from October to December 1936 is expected to be much larger than that of the corresponding period a year earlier, and a decline in hog prices is likely to occur during these months. As slaughter supplies are reduced in the late winter and spring, however, prices are likely to advance.

It is probable that producers have reduced materially the number of sows to be farrowed in the fall of 1936 from the number indicated by the June Pig Crop Report, in view of the very unfavorable feed crop prospects which have since developed. The 1936 fall pig crop, therefore, probably will be no larger, and may be smaller, than that of 1935. It is also probable that the 1937 spring pig crop will be smaller than that of 1936.

Exports of hog products are likely to increase somewhat in the first half of the 1936-37 hog-marketing year, in view of the larger domestic slaughter supplies of hogs in prospect. In the last half of the probable smaller domestic hog slaughter is lik

exports no greater than in the last half of the pr

The current volume of exports is smaller than that

. by foreign markets under present policies limiting

increasing indications of larger British import quo

January 1, 1937. The increase, however, undoubtedl,

the application of import duties, the revenue to b

ting British hog production. Meanwhile, hog number

larger than a year ago. Increases also are appare

other countries interested in supplying the British

the only important pork-importing country of conti

a current upward movement in hog numbers. In virtu

l European importing countries there is a definite

og production to the numbers for which domestically

. This development suggests some increase in the f.

luding lard. At present most of the lard imports a

arter or exchange arrangements, largely with Europe.

es.

ading practices indicate that there may be difficul

antial share of the continental European lard marke

uct becomes available in more usual quantities. Th

with respect to the formerly important German mark

virtually closed to American lard unless German coi

lly changed. It may be difficult also to overcome

ze fats other than lard which has developed during

American lard production following the drought of .

noticeable in Great Britain, the leading foreign ma

for American lard, as well as in central European areas deficient in lard.
Concessions secured from foreign countries in the reciprocal trade agreements, on the other hand, will tend to encourage exports of hog products,
especially lard, as domestic hog production is increased.

Hog Numbers in Principal Countries

Hog numbers in mid-summer 1936, in commercially important hog producing countries were about 15 percent above the low point reached on the
same date of 1935. The 1936 United States spring pig crop increased 29
percent to 41,884,000 head. In six 1/ European countries, for which mid-
summer estimates are available for 1936, hog numbers increased 6 percent
to 33,256,000, compared with mid-summer 1935. A further increase in these
countries appears to be in prospect, as the number of brood sows in June
1936 was about 15 percent larger than in June 1935. These six countries
support about two-fifths of the total hog numbers in Europe, exclusive of
the Union of Soviet Socialist Republics. The number of hogs in the Soviet
Union at the beginning of 1936 was 26,200,000 compared with 17,100,000 in
1935 and only 11,500,000 in 1934.

Hog numbers in Germany increased 11 percent to 22,200,000 between
June 1935 and June 1936. The number of hogs is now only 0.8 percent smaller
than in the summer of 1934 and 1.5 percent smaller than in the record year
1931. There has been a 20 percent increase in young bred sows and an 11
percent increase in older bred sows, this June as compared with last. Young
pigs up to 6 months showed an increase of 12 percent to 15,752,000 as compared with June a year ago. The June 1936 estimate of the number of
slaughter hogs and those being fed for slaughter was 4,164,000, which was
6 percent more than in June of last year but 7 percent less than in June
1934.

In Great Britain (England, Wales, and Scotland), the number of
hogs reported on land on June 1, 1936 was 4,037,000 and was 1 percent smaller
than at the same date a year ago, when it was unusually large. There were also
3% fewer brood sows than there were a year ago. The number of hogs in
Irish Free State, which exports live hogs and bacon to Great Britain in
relatively large quantities, was 1,010,000 on June 1, 1936, 9 percent below
the number on the same date of 1935.

The June 13, 1936 hog estimate for Denmark was 3,374,000. While there
is no strictly comparable estimate for last year, the number reported on May
25, 1935 was only 3,056,000 and the number on July 15, 1935 was 3,034,000.
Bred sows were reported at 314,000 on June 13 this year, which was at least
15 percent more than in 1935 when the number on May 25 was only 255,000. The
number on July 15 of the same year was 271,000. A further expansion in hog
numbers this year is expected in the Netherlands where the early spring
estimate showed an increase of 8 percent above February 1935 in total numbers,
and 9 percent in bred sows. (See table of hog numbers in specified countries
in mid-summer 1936 and detailed table for Germany, Denmark, and Great Britain,
and Irish Free State.)

1/ Germany, Denmark, England and Wales, Scotland, Irish Free State, and Hungary.

Hogs: Numbers in specified surplus and deficit countries i
mid-summer 1936, with comparisons

Country	Date of estimate	1931	1932	1933	1934	19
		Thou-sands	Thou-sands	Thou-sands	Thou-sands	Th sa
RPLUS COUNTRIES						
iropean:						
ed States 1/	June 1				39,698	32
la	"	4,717	3,639	3,801	3,654	3
ean:						
1 Free State	"	1,227	1,108	931	968	1
ark, in rural						
mmunities	June 1-20	5,453	4,886	4,407	3,027	2/3
erlands	May-June	2,434	2,244	(2,100)3/	2,022	4/1
1d	June	7,321	5,844	5,753	7,053	6
ary	July	2,715	2,361	1,899	2,502	3
1a	June	712	582	586	686	
1ia	Summer	323	303	277	282	
1ania	June 30	1,569	1,390	1,306	1,288	1
al 3 surplus						
opean countries						
orting to 1936		9,395	8,355	7,237	6,497	7
DEFICIT COUNTRIES						
1d and Wales	June 1	2,783	3,185	3,069	3,320	3
1nd	"	162	165	167	206	
ern Ireland	"	236	220	271	380	
l United Kingdom .		3,181	3,570	3,507	3,906	4
1y	"	22,529	21,289	21,174	22,368	20
oslovakia	July 1	5/3,088	3,082	3,314	3,888	3
7	June	317	304	319	550	
l 3 deficit						
opean countries						
orting to 1936 ...		25,474	24,639	24,410	25,894	24
l 6 surplus and						
leit countries						
orting to 1936 ...		34,869	32,994	31,647	32,391	31
l 15 surplus and						
icit countries						
orting to 1935,						
.United States ..		55,586	50,602	49,374	52,194	49
Russia		14,400	11,600	12,068	17,450	22

ed from reports of United States Department of Agriculture offi
l, official sources and the International Institute of Agricultu
entheses interpolated.
ing pig crop, i.e., number of pigs saved December 1-June 1. Fig
931-33 being revised.
r 25.
August 1934 the number had fallen to 1,875,000.
gust.
sus, May 1930.

According to the 1936 Summer Hog Outlook report recently released
by the Bureau of Agricultural Economics, hog slaughter during the last
2 months of the present marketing year ending September 30 will be somewhat larger than was indicated by the number of hogs on farms over 6
months of age on June 1 as shown by the June Pig Crop report. Because of
the large increase in the 1936 spring pig crop, the number of hogs that
will be slaughtered during the first 6 months (October-March) of the 1936-37
marketing year, is expected to be larger than the slaughter for the same
period in either of the 2 previous years. The number of hogs to be
slaughtered in the entire year 1936-37 probably will be from 10 to 20 percent larger than in 1935-36 and 1934-35, when the totals were the smallest
in many years. With short corn supplies and high corn prices in prospect
as a result of the 1936 drought, average weights of hogs marketed in
1936-37 will be lighter than in 1935-36 and may be about the same as in
1934-35, following the drought of 1934.

As a result of the severe drought conditions prevailing over most
of the Corn Belt in July, the indicated production of corn in that area
on August 1 was smaller than in 1934. In view of these unfavorable feed
prospects, it is probable that producers have reduced materially the number
of sows to be farrowed in the fall of 1936 from the number indicated by
the June Pig Crop report, which was based upon breeding intentions reported
about June 1. The number of sows to be farrowed in the coming fall was
estimated in June to be 14 percent larger than the number of farrowed hogs
in 1935. Because of the development of the severe drought, the number of
sows farrowed in the fall of 1936 will probably be no larger and may be even
smaller than a year earlier. It is also probable that the 1937 spring pig
crop will be smaller than that of 1936.

Hog prices in 1936-37 probably will average about as high as in the
present year, since the probable increase in the aggregate live weight of
hogs slaughtered will be offset by the further improvement in consumer
demand now in prospect. Prices in the early months (October-December) of
the 1936-37 year, however, are likely to decline because of the anticipated
increase in hog slaughter. The effect of the increased slaughter supplies
in this period upon hog prices will be offset to some extent by the further
improvement in consumer demand in prospect for hog products and a strong
prospective storage demand for these products. However, as slaughter
supplies of hogs are reduced in the late winter and early spring, an advance
in hog prices at that time is probable.

After an advance in late June, hog prices weakened somewhat during
the first half of July, but again advanced toward the end of the month.
In late July and early August the top price of hogs at Chicago reached the
highest level since late September 1935. The July average price at Chicago
was $9.76 per 100 pounds compared with $9.88 in June and $9.49 in July last
year. The advance in hog prices in late July and early August was confined
almost entirely to hogs that were well finished. Prices in hogs lacking
in finish tended to weaken in this period.

Hog slaughter under Federal inspection in July, totaling 2,69 head, was only 2 percent smaller than in June, and was 57 percent la than in July last year, when the total was the smallest in over 30 y Although inspected slaughter for the first 9 months of the 1935-36 n ing year was slightly below the total for the same period in 1934-38 slaughter for the first 3 months of the summer marketing season (May September) amounted to 8,010,000 head compared with 5,712,000 head d the same period last year, when summer slaughter supplies of hogs we lowest in about 25 years. Slaughter supplies of hogs in July includ relatively large proportion of packing sows and hogs lacking in fini This is partly a reflection of the reduced feed supplies and advanci feed prices resulting from the severe drought in the principal hog r areas. It is probable that further liquidation of such hogs will oc the next few months. With corn prices high relative to hog prices i prospect this fall, it is likely that 1936 spring pigs will be marke early and that the proportion of the total hog slaughter for 1936-37 occurring in October, November, and December will be relatively larg

The average weight of hogs at the seven leading markets in Ju 258 pounds compared with 253 pounds in June and 254 pounds in July 1 The increase in average weights in the last 2 months was largely the of the increase in the proportion of packing sows in the supplies, r than the feeding of hogs to heavier weights. Although the average w of hogs in July was heavier than in the preceding month, weights dec somewhat after early July as a result of increased numbers of unfini hogs marketed.

Corn prices rose sharply during the month of July as severe d conditions continued. The average prices of No. 3 Yellow corn at Ch rose from a level slightly above 60 cents a bushel in early July to $1.00 at the end of the month, and in the first week of August reach average of $1.11. Since the average prices of hogs did not change g during this period, the hog-corn price ratio dropped rapidly. Based Chicago prices for hogs and corn, the hog-corn price ratio for the w ended August 8 was 8.9 compared with 16.0 in early June, before drou conditions became severe, and 12.9 a year earlier. The hog-corn pri ratio during the remainder of the present hog marketing year and in first 3 months of the 1936-37 year will probably continue much lower in the first half of the current marketing year.

Wholesale prices of fresh pork declined during the first half July, probably as a result of very high temperatures prevailing over of the country. This decline was recovered, however, in late July a cooler weather served to stimulate the demand for meats. Prices of cured products weakened slightly during the greater part of July, bu advanced near the end of the month. The composite wholesale price o products in New York in July was $21.35 per 100 pounds compared with in June and $22.69 in the corresponding month last year.

Exports of both pork and lard in June showed a slight increas those in May. Lard exports exceeded those of a year earlier for the consecutive month, while the quantity of pork exported was only sli below that of June 1935. Exports of both pork and lard, however, ir this year were considerably below the June average for the years 1930-34. For the first 9 months of the present hog marketing year, total exports of pork, amounting to slightly less than 50,000,000 pounds, were about 41 percent smaller than the shipments for the same period of 1934-35, and were much below those of earlier years. Exports of lard have increased somewhat during 1936, but for the first 9 months of the 1935-36 hog marketing year they were about 40 percent less than in 1934-35. Shipments of pork and lard from principal United States ports in July exceeded those of a year earlier.

With larger slaughter supplies of hogs in prospect in this country in the first half of the 1936-37 marketing year, it is probable that exports of hog products will increase somewhat in this period. In the last half of 1936-37, however, the probable smaller domestic hog slaughter is likely to be accompanied by a level of exports no greater than in the last half of the present marketing year.

Canada

The price of bacon hogs in Canada continued to advance in July, and for the 4-week period ended July 30 the average at Toronto was $9.05 per 100 pounds compared with $8.95 for the 4-week period of June and $9.51 in the 4-week period of July a year ago.

The price of hogs has held up well despite an increase of 8 percent in marketings in the first 7 months of the year. The price of bacon hogs at Toronto during the first 7 months averaged $8.56 per 100 pounds compared with $8.98 a year ago. The increased supplies originated principally in Ontario, Quebec, and Saskatchewan. Marketings of live and dead hogs in the principal provinces so far this year have been as follows, with percentage of the same period last year in parentheses: Ontario, 686,000 (127); Quebec, 229,000 (140); Alberta, 516,000 (96); Manitoba, 280,000 (84); Saskatchewan, 202,000 (109).

It appears from available statistics that domestic consumption of commercially produced pork and pork products in Canada has increased during the first 6 months of 1936 as compared with a year ago. Exports have increased about 19 percent, live hogs being converted to an equivalent dressed meat basis.

There has been a fairly large increase in exports of live hogs and bacon and pork to the United States so far this year. In June, almost 3,000 live hogs were shipped to the United States and over 1,000,000 pounds of pork, bacon, and hams. Exports of live hogs to the United States for the first 6 months of this year, reported at 29,283 head, are almost ten times as large as for the same period last year, and exports of pork, bacon, and ham, reported at 5,974,000 pounds, are more than twice as large. The live hog exports to this country in the first half of 1936 are larger than for any whole year since 1927, when 195,000 head came to this country from Canada. Pork, bacon, and ham exports to the United States so far exceed shipments for any year since 1929, but are very small when total United States production and consumption of pork are considered. Exports of those items from the United States to Canada have also increased.

Bacon exports to the United Kingdom from Canada for
months of this year amounted to 72,000,000 pounds and were
smaller than in the same period of 1935, but a little larg
first 6 months of 1934. Shipments during the past 3 month
those of last year, whereas those for the first 3 months s
Although bacon exports have been smaller during the first
than a year ago, shipments of all pork products, amounting
pounds, have exceeded the same period last year by 9 perce
is due to materially larger exports of lard, which have re
pounds so far this year compared with only 6,168,000 pound
the corresponding period.

United Kingdom and Irish Free Sta

British plans for encouraging the domestic producti
pork include import duties on non-Empire pork products, ac
tural Attache C. C. Taylor at London. It is anticipated
imposition of duties will be accompanied by some relaxatio
pork import quotas, and by a higher scale of fixed prices
British hogs. It appears unlikely, however, that any of t
changes will become effective before January 1, 1937. Sin
1929-31, non-Empire countries have lost about 40 percent o
pork market in Great Britain, partly through replacement b
Empire supplies, and partly through the reduction in total
Further displacement may be more gradual, but there is no
of a reversal of this trend.

The total cured-pork quota for the period September-
has recently been announced by the British Government at 1,
weight (178,156,000 pounds). This figure compares with 1,8
weight (203,107,000 pounds), the quota for the current 4-m
represents a reduction of 12 percent. The average monthly
pounds for the last 4 months of this year compares with 53,
the allowed total in September 1935, and 46,935,000 pounds,
monthly rate for the October-December 1935 period. The qu
the last 3 months of 1936 when compared with the rate for c
of 1935 amounts to only 5 percent. The quota reduction fo
of 1935 also amounted to 12 percent when compared with the
in the immediately preceding months. See table page 10.

The United States share in the September-December to
is again 8 percent, with an additional 0.1 percent allowed
in connection with imports previously made through Canada,
14,431,000 pounds for the 4 months. The monthly rate is, 1
3,608,000 pounds. Monthly shipments from the United States
have averaged 3,058,000 pounds against an average allotment
months of 3,922,000 pounds, leaving a total deficit for the
5,182,000 pounds. Of this amount, 2,800,000 were relinquis
shippers during the early months of the year, leaving a rec
for the first half of the year of 2,382,000 pounds. Since
occurring in the first quota period of the year is to be ma
second (May-August), shipments for July and August should e

pounds. This amount is only slightly higher than the June shipments of 5,031,000 pounds. If British prices for American short cut green hams remain attractice, it would seem that the United States may wipe out the deficit balance which has been accumulating since early in 1935. See table page 10.

Liverpool quotations on American short cut green hams remained steady during July at very close to $22.00 per 100 pounds. The average for the month was the highest since last September and the highest July average since 1930.

Total imports of ham into the United Kingdom amounted to a little over 53,000,000 pounds for the current season, October 1, 1935 to June 30, 1936, a reduction of 5 percent from those of the comparable 1934-35 period and of 36 percent when compared with those of the 1929-30 period. Imports from the United States, at about 27,000,000 pounds, represented 51 percent of the total, and those from Canada, at 20,000,000 pounds, 38 percent. The remaining 11 percent of total imports was furnished almost entirely by the Irish Free State, Poland, and Argentina.

Liverpool bacon quotations during July were well maintained at the high levels of the past few months, Danish Wiltshire sides reaching $20.65 per 100 pounds, the highest monthly average in over a year, and Canadian green sides $18.23, the highest since last October. American green bellies were quoted on the Liverpool market during July for the first time since March, averaging $16.71 per 100 pounds, the highest average in over 2 years.

Total bacon imports into the United Kingdom during the 9 months of the period, October 1, 1935 to June 30, 1936, amounted to 545,000,000 pounds as against 590,000,000 last season and 972,000,000 in the peak year 1931-32. Of the total imported, Denmark supplied about 54 percent, Canada 14 percent, the Irish Free State over 7 percent, and the Netherlands approximately the same. About 18 percent of total imports during this period came from minor suppliers, with the United States sending less than 0.5 percent.

Liverpool lard quotations continue well below those of last year, averaging for July $12.37 per 100 pounds against $14.46 in July 1935. Imports of lard into the United Kingdom, which amounted to about 125,000,000 pounds for the first 9 months of the 1935-36 season, were 23 percent smaller than those of the corresponding period last year, and 52 percent smaller than the record imports of 2 seasons ago. The United States share of imports so far this season has been less than 37 percent, whereas during the same months of last season it was 67 percent and of 1933-34, 93 percent. Canada, since the first of 1936, has supplied more than any other one country, with Brazil, Hungary, and the Balkan countries each sending a considerable amount. A number of other countries also have participated in the trade to an unusual degree.

Fat consumption in the United Kingdom was maintained during 1935 despite a 50-percent decrease in lard imports and a slight decrease in the imports of butter and edible oleo fats. These deficiencies were made up by increased imports of vegetable oils, oil seeds, and whale oil. After allowing for exports and re-exports of oil, the net importation of oil seeds, oils, and fats was 1,278,000 long tons in 1935, which was 2 percent less

than in 1934 but 3 percent more than 2 years ago. Even th[
of 2 percent (26,000 tons) does not indicate any real decre
sumption because during the year butter stocks were reduced
the decrease in net soap exports represented a further savi
4,000 tons of oil. Stocks of whale oil and possibly oil se
during the year, and the domestic output of lard and animal
etc., was increased 5,000 to 10,000 tons.

It appears reasonably certain that there was no appr
tive change in the total oil and fat consumption in the Uni
between the years 1933 and 1935, although the proportionate
of the total was materially altered.: Margarine consumption
nearly 12,000 tons more than in 1934 and the consumption of
and shortenings was probably 25,000 to 35,000 tons higher.

Supplies of British and Irish fresh pork, as reflect
Central Markets, have been larger during the first 9 months
season than in any comparable period since October–June 193
of over 62,000,000 pounds at these markets represented an i
percent over those of October–June 1934–35.

United Kingdom: Total cured pork allocations, Septemb
31, 1936, and to the United States, January 1–Decembe

Country	Total allocation, Sept. 1-Dec. 31			Allocation Jan. 1-I	
	Percentage: share of total	Allocations		Month	Allc
	Percent	Hundred-weight	1,000 pounds	1936	1, pc
Denmark ......:	63.50	1,010,083:	113,129:	Jan. :	
Netherlands ..:	9.50	151,115:	16,925:	Feb. :	
Poland ......:	7.95	126,459:	14,163:	Mar. :	
Sweden ....:	4.70	74,762:	8,373:	Apr. :	
Lithuania ....:	2.95	46,925:	5,256:	May :	
Estonia ......:	.75	11,930:	1,336:	June :	
Finland .. ...:	.40	6,363:	713:	July :	
Latvia ....:	.70	11,135:	1,247:	Aug. :	
USSR ....:	.85	13,521:	1,514:	Sept.:	
Argentina ....:	.70	11,135:	1,247:	Oct. :	
United States.:3/	8.00	3/ 127,255:3/	14,253:.	(Nov. :	
				(Dec. :	
Total .....:	100.00	1,590,683	178,156		4

Division of Foreign Agricultural Service.

1/ Final figures with all adjustments made.
2/ Not adjusted for re-exports.
3/ Plus 0.1 percent of total to allow for adjustments in co
   imports through Canada.

United Kingdom: Total bacon imports, by months, 1928-29 to 1935-36

Month	1928-29	1929-30	1930-31	1931-82	1932-33	1933-34	1934-35	1935-3
	1,000 pounds	1,000 pounds	1,000 pounds	1,000 pounds	1,000 pounds	1,000 pounds	1,000 pounds	1,000 pound
Oct.	82,378	72,402	95,809	109,051	114,310	83,272	65,537	58,17
Nov.	79,297	74,868	86,316	105,372	114,458	81,117	66,325	61,14
Dec.	76,771	85,603	112,267	109,857	92,817	66,612	68,370	64,37
Jan.	88,092	74,801	95,273	101,159	96,602	72,309	70,773	59,62
Feb.	68,612	73,721	99,645	112,538	78,231	68,345	60,415	56,96
Mar.	68,923	84,631	93,406	125,818	95,152	72,271	62,878	62,75
Apr.	73,126	75,096	99,464	108,150	85,173	75,675	66,651	61,39
May	87,845	84,615	108,136	89,052	92,804	79,089	67,156	60,04
June	71,894	83,277	109,080	111,194	91,029	70,351	62,070	60,55
July	80,360	85,457	105,607	102,004	87,203	76,298	68,519	
Aug.	82,290	84,758	106,567	104,395	83,381	70,528	69,308	
Sept.	73,505	88,206	105,978	101,571	83,069	64,943	64,237	

Foreign Agricultural Service Division. Compiled from Trade and Navigation of the United Kingdom.

United Kingdom: Total ham imports, by months, 1928-29 to 1935-36

Month	1928-29	1929-30	1930-31	1931-32	1932-33	1933-34	1934-35	19
	1,000 pounds	1,000 pounds	1,000 pounds	1,000 pounds	1,000 pounds	1,000 pounds	1,000 pounds	1,000 pounds
Oct.	6,484	8,105	5,792	7,217	7,497	6,992	5,419	4,797
Nov.	6,782	8,125	5,755	7,550	7,998	7,932	5,887	5,074
Dec.	7,339	9,347	10,111	8,596	6,578	6,155	5,951	7,395
Jan.	8,788	7,920	7,101	4,602	7,100	4,743	5,012	4,839
Feb.	8,232	7,989	6,507	5,146	5,556	4,233	5,223	5,011
Mar.	6,828	8,601	5,337	6,530	5,981	7,288	5,623	5,456
Apr.	8,981	9,539	7,597	5,764	7,874	7,542	7,119	4,833
May	14,136	12,298	9,204	9,664	10,737	7,234	7,378	7,202
June	10,499	10,983	9,773	8,466	9,207	7,021	8,408	8,745
July	12,042	14,391	11,165	11,661	13,568	11,984	8,586	
Aug.	12,073	12,024	7,429	9,091	8,489	9,357	6,072	
Sept.	8,073	7,236	5,613	6,978	9,267	4,962	5,219	
Total	110 257	116 558	91 384	91 265	99 852	85 443	75 8	

Foreign Agricultural Service Division. Compiled from Trade and Navigation of the United Kingdom.

Kingdom: Arrivals of Wiltshire sides in Great Britain from
nental countries, by weeks, 1935-36 and comparable periods
1934-35 and 1935-36 1/

:	Danish :			At London		
:	at all :		:	:	:	
:	ports	:Danish	: Swedish	: Dutch	:	
:	Bales	Bales	Bales	Bales	Bales	Bales
:						
:	424,372	219,132	16,686	28,823	35 628	23 092
:	29,554	14,916	1,386	1,599	2,216	---
:	30,174	15,650	1,153	1,745	2,866	2,565
:	31,790	15,929	1,429	1,929	2,210	2,075
:	31,944	16,022	1,288	1,754	2,582	2,450
:	31,187	15,359	1,397	1,814	3,042	2,695
:	31,057	15,170	1,027	2,043	2,895	3,217
:	32,932	15,734	1,221	1,850	2,427	1,960
:	33,760	16,501	1,415	2,129	2,845	1,703
:	30,150	15,314	1,661	2,298	2,289	1,916
:	32,044	15,755	1,167	2,301	2,927	1,813
:	31,759	16,682	1,523	2,674	2,485	1,793
:	31,060	16,303	1,084	2,743	2,532	1,705
:	32,389	16,162	1,335	2,525	2,652	1,561
:	33,476	16,942	1,122	2,693	3,039	1,565
:	32,692	17,022	1,575	1,668	3,260	1,551
:	31,624	16,501	1,275	2,349	2,960	1,726
:	30,285	15,383	1,283	2,450	2,795	1,768
:	31,135	15,894	1,348	2,726	2,669	1,797
:	31,507	15,615	1,287	2,315	2,352	1,776
:	31,984	16,314	1,277	2,163	2,072	1,320
:	31,750	15,687	1,371	2,464	2,602	1,518
:	31,337	16,512	1,180	2,217	2,030	1,540
:	31,575	17,209	1,215	2,523	2,437	1,755
:	32,560	17,229	1,172	2,453	2,244	1,749
:	31,635	16,012	1,160	2,498	2,409	1,762
:	32,085	16,575	1,347	2,437	2,466	1,770
:	31,720	16,016	1,308	2,446	2,308	1,827
:	31,699	16,891	1,352	2,293	2,536	1,886
:	31,549	16,718	1,358	2,465	2,561	1,679
:	32,367	17,344	1,348	2,275	2,395	1,728
te:						
:	1,375,452	704,793	55,751	96,662	112,731	77,362	2
:	1,484,102	777,629	61,314	101,229	110,029	60,180	3
:						

by the London, England, Office of the Foreign Agricultural Se
ovision Exchange. Sides are packed 4 to 6 to the bale, accor
sides. The most popular bale is that carrying 4 sides with
ranging 220-260 pounds.

United Kingdom: Total lard imports, by months, 1928-29 to 1935-36

Month	1928-29	1929-30	1930-31	1931-32	1932-33	1933-34	1934-35	1935-36
	1,000 pounds	1,000 pounds	1,000 pounds	1,000 pounds	1,000 pounds	1,000 pounds	1,000 pounds	1,000 pounds
Oct.	18,079	21,844	22,897	17,329	19,799	25,407	26,932	12,161
Nov.	21,551	24,004	27,751	19,234	21,305	23,301	22,582	12,700
Dec.	17,480	27,160	27,270	21,276	17,358	25,855	17,365	10,096
Jan.	35,923	27,559	21,459	28,188	24,391	34,945	15,651	15,621
Feb.	29,752	25,187	32,576	37,323	31,490	26,975	16,921	16,302
Mar.	22,224	24,810	26,608	31,248	31,269	23,568	19,725	12,669
Apr.	21,612	18,218	25,276	11,805	22,788	22,984	14,508	17,758
May	26,479	20,772	23,771	20,565	24,305	34,335	16,009	12,261
June	20,498	21,078	27,586	25,890	25,026	39,395	13,628	15,714
July	25,977	31,801	28,538	22,221	28,673	22,564	16,374	
Aug.	21,204	20,438	25,001	16,477	31,403	24,151	15,526	
Sept.	16,899	12,976	17,022	18,556	29,484	19,200	9,063	
Total:	277,688	275,847	305,755	270,112	307,581	322,980	204,284	

Foreign Agricultural Service Division. Compiled from Trade and Navigation of the United Kingdom.

United Kingdom: Bacon imports from Denmark, by months, 1928-29 to 1935-36

Month	1928-29	1929-30	1930-31	1931-32	1932-33	1933-34	1934-35	1935-36
	1,000 pounds	1,000 pounds	1,000 pounds	1,000 pounds	1,000 pounds	1,000 pounds	1,000 pounds	1,000 pounds
Oct.	50,703	47,486	70,906	71,154	75,730	47,545	37,837	34,403
Nov.	48,063	48,525	61,433	72,521	70,445	44,588	36,158	30,798
Dec.	45,580	53,490	81,294	77,467	59,332	37,159	37,776	34,912
Jan.	48,717	48,406	66,819	73,317	57,307	40,106	36,866	31,951
Feb.	41,508	44,439	67,246	75,213	50,495	34,684	31,842	30,139
Mar.	41,985	51,870	65,505	88,046	59,092	40,128	35,824	33,336
Apr.	44,031	46,204	63,224	76,032	51,023	41,534	35,931	32,746
May	46,758	56,206	67,190	48,717	59,195	43,595	36,996	31,727
June	41,886	54,456	66,161	82,653	55,517	41,006	34,020	32,262
July	46,570	55,213	68,704	72,174	53,125	45,676	38,482	
Aug.	48,121	55,066	68,094	70,019	53,152	43,503	40,379	
Sept.	48,350	59,751	67,893	67,587	48,558	37,384	38,130	
Total:	552,272	621,112	814,469	874,900	692,971	496,908	440,241	

Foreign Agricultural Service Division. Compiled from Trade and Navigation of the United Kingdom.

Countries Important in British Market Supplies

Denmark.- The upward tendency in Danish hog numbers increased the total to 3,374,000 head on June 13, 1936, the largest figure for any census period since January 1934, according to Agricultural Commissioner H. E. Reed at Berlin. The increase in bred sows, under way since late 1934, resulted in current figures for that class being larger than at any time since November 1932, when the first British restrictions on imports became effective. The upturn in numbers is seen as a test of the Danish production control plan, which has proved satisfactory in periods of declining and of fairly stable numbers. Any increase in the British market outlet would be favorable to Danish producers, since that market is the dominant factor in the calculations upon which the determination of "surplus" or low-price hogs is based. By June 20, prices being paid for surplus hogs were resulting in a decidedly unfavorable hog-feed price ratio for such hogs. The production of high-price or nonsurplus hogs was still profitable, but prices of these have shown a downward tendency since last March.

Danish bacon exports for the first 9 months of the 1935-36 season were 8.5 percent smaller than in 1934-35, in line with the British restrictions on imports. The smaller export figure coincided during the first half of 1936 with increased Danish market supplies of hogs. During the same period, the exports of live hogs and lard, mostly to Germany, were not large enough to offset the decline in bacon exports. The present situation is difficult, but Danish authorities hesitate to reduce hog numbers materially in view of the possible enlargement of the British quotas. Danish production policy, therefore, cannot take definite shape until British plans are finally announced. Meanwhile, it appears that Denmark will have a surplus of hogs.

Other supplying countries.- Hog numbers in Sweden have been declining since 1933. Slaughter in the first 5 months of 1936 was smaller than that of a year earlier, despite some increase over last year in figures for March, April, and May. The increase in recent months has forced prices down somewhat. Bacon exports have shown little change from last year's figures, but bacon imports are larger this year than last. Lard exports have been larger than last year, and imports have been smaller. In Norway also there has been a decline in total hog numbers this year, although there has been some increase in the numbers of sows and young pigs. The April 1936 census for that country suggests reduced marketings this summer, with some increase developing late in the year. Slaughter this year has been smaller than in 1935. Lard imports are running smaller for 1936 than in 1935, but imports of fat pork have increased substantially.

Slaughter and exports in Lithuania were larger than last year in the first half of 1936, despite the moderate decline in hog numbers noted in the past few years. A reexport trade via British ports has moved additional volumes of bacon this year, with Great Britain and Russia also taking more lard and live hogs, respectively. Lithuanian hogs are marketed under a fixed-price system. Heretofore the fixed prices have proved so high as to require a subsidy payment for the absorption of losses on much of the pork exported. Additional business on that basis appears to be expected, since improvements in slaughtering establishments are being undertaken.

Denmark: Official 1936 midsummer estimate of hog numbers compared
with earlier years

Date	Boars: 4 months and over	Brood sows			Other hogs (new classification)				
		In farrow	Not in farrow	Total	132 pounds and over	77 to 132 pounds	Under 77 pounds	Suck-ling pigs	Total
	Thou-sands	Thou-sands	Thou-sands	Thou-sands	Thou-sands	Thou-sands	Thou-sands	Thou-sands	Thou-sands
July 15, 1933 :	25	280	164	444	827	997	1,068	1,029	4,290
Oct. 14, 1933 :	24	244	161	405	825	951	1,075	916	4,169
Dec. 15, 1933 :	23	212	150	362	740	892	974	733	3,724
Jan. 16, 1934 :	21	210	141	351	669	817	890	726	3,474
Mar. 1, 1934 :	22	237	110	347	649	743	792	631	3,184
Apr. 14, 1934 :	22	238	110	348	639	694	719	659	3,081
June 1, 1934 :	22	284	115	363	595	664	672	711	3,027
July 15, 1934 :	21	231	124	355	523	647	737	774	3,057
Oct. 15, 1934 :	20	216	117	333	590	711	734	720	3,108
Dec. 1, 1934 :	20	238	106	344	621	646	745	653	3,029
Jan. 15, 1935 :	19	253	105	358	451	667	762	668	2,925
Mar. 1, 1935 :	20	255	114	369	508	637	738	695	2,967
Apr. 13, 1935 :	20	241	132	373	463	629	740	813	3,038
May 25, 1935 :	20	255	125	380	500	635	797	724	3,056
July 13, 1935 :	20	271	112	383	453	733	772	673	3,034
Aug. 24, 1935 :	21	259	124	383	545	693	742	782	3,166
Oct. 5, 1935 :	21	264	141	405	534	683	792	860	3,295
Nov. 16, 1935 :	21	278	132	410	565	674	882	766	3,318
Dec. 28, 1935 :	21	278	127	405	450	723	885	732	3,216
Feb. 8, 1936 :	21	270	137	407	518	722	816	779	3,263
Mar. 21, 1936 :	22	289	140	429	558	700	826	819	3,354
May 2, 1936 :	23	308	132	440	562	686	852	768	3,331
June 13, 1936 :	24	314	141	455	559	700	826	810	3,374

Compiled from Statistiske Efterretninger, published by the Statistical Department of Denmark, and reports from Agricultural Commissioner H. E. Reed, United
States Department of Agriculture.

Poland

Hog prices in Poland have advanced materially this year, and the relatively high prices are regarded as a deterrent to the generally improved
Polish export trade in hogs, pork, and lard developed in 1935 and 1936. The
improvement in export markets prompted the Government to urge an increase
in breeding operations last year. If available production and marketing
data are correct, however, it appears that considerable liquidation has taken
place despite the official admonitions.

There are increasing indications of potential hog shortages relative to the continued expansion of export requirements experienced so far this year. There is a firm demand for feeder pigs, and the hog-feed price ratio May 1936, based largely on hog prices and potato prices, was the most favorable since 1930. Feed prices have been favorable since August 1935, but expansion in production has not been great enough so far to influence hog prices materially. The current situation is causing some apprehension regarding the ability of Poland to compete with other pork-exporting countries where production is definitely increasing. The present large volume of trade with the United States in canned hams is regarded in Poland as only temporary.

Continental European Importing Countries

Germany.- Despite some increase in domestic production, the problem of adequate fat supplies in Germany remains to be solved, Mr. Reed states. Recent reports, however, suggest that current German trade policies contemplate no additions to supplies of fats through imports from the United State June imports of lard from all sources were among the smallest for any month on record, being only slightly in excess of 1,100,000 pounds. Prior to 1933, imports in June averaged about 16,000,000 pounds. Denmark was the leading source of imports in June this year, with 647,000 pounds. The smal remainder was divided among 6 other European countries.

The increase in German hog numbers this year has been the outstandin development in the current German fat situation. The June 1936 hog census (excluding the Saar) showed total hog numbers to be 3.35 percent larger tha the average June numbers in the preceding 5 years. Other percentage increa over the average figures were: slaughter hogs 5.3, young hogs 4.0, bred sows 4.0. The 1936 increases over 1935 figures were considerably larger than the increases over the 5-year average. Difficulties may be encountere however, in carrying the hogs on the relatively small supplies of feed on hand pending the availability of the 1936 crop.

The total June 1 stocks of the leading feeds (rye, barley, potatoes) in first and second hands stood at a figure about 24 percent below that of a Year earlier. While farmers are using many other types of feed, it is apparent that feeding operations have been relatively expensive in recent months. The German policy at present is to confine livestock production largely to the numbers which can be carried on domestic feeds. The current expansion in hog numbers has brought forth official advice to producers to feed no more hogs than they can provide for from their own feed crops.

The increase in marketings which began in October 1935 continued through the first half of 1936. For most of the time since early April, marketings have been larger than those of a year earlier. Slaughter in May and June also exceeded last year's figures, and average weights have been above 1935 figures, principally because of the premiums paid for heavy hogs. In February 1936 about 45 percent of the total hog slaughter include arrivals weighing over 120 kilograms (265 pounds). In June, that weight class accounted for over 51 percent of the total slaughter despite the rela tively high cost of feeds. For the first 9 months of the 1935-36 season, however, total receipts at 14 leading markets were 21.5 percent below the corresponding 1934-35 figure, with slaughter at 36 points showing a decline of 23.1 percent.

Germany, excluding the Saar: Official 1936 June estimate of hogs,
by classes, compared with earlier years

June 1 - 5	Farrow under 8 weeks	Young pigs :8 weeks: to 6 : months	Hogs 6 months to 1 year			Hogs over 1 year			Grand total
			Total excl. sows & boars 1/:	Brood sows		Total excl. sows & boars:	Brood sows		
				:Total:	:In farrow: (preg- : nant)		Total:	:In farrow: (preg- : nant)	
	Thou-sands	Thou-sands	Thou-sands	Thou-sands	Thou-sands	Thou-sands	Thou-sands	Thou-sands	Thou-sands
1931	6,027	10,351	3,425	693	409	246	1,663	1,021	22,529
1932	5,501	9,832	3,456	608	374	240	1,534	938	21,289
1933	5,139	9,752	3,751	652	422	250	1,511	978	21,174
1934	5,283	10,436	4,196	547	338	272	1,519	949	22,368
1935	4,556	9,523	3,659	554	355	277	1,361	866	20,042
1936	5,370	10,382	3,928	632	425	236	1,522	958	22,200

Division of Statistical and Historical Research, compiled from cable received
from Commissioner H. E. Reed, and original official sources for earlier years.
1/ Boars under 6 months to 1 year in June were as follows in thousands: 1931,
54; 1932, 46; 1933, 46; 1934, 44; 1935, 46; 1936, 47. Boars of 1 year and
over in June were as follows in thousands: 1931, 71; 1932, 73; 1933, 72;
1934, 71; 1935, 66; 1936, 63.

Imports of bacon in June, at 1,500,000 pounds, were slightly larger
than in other recent months, with Netherlands in the leading position as
a source. Total pork supplies in June were not large as those of a year
earlier, but the quantity available moved into consumption slowly, and a
fair proportion of current slaughter went into storage. The German level
of all meat prices is relatively high, with reduced beef supplies seen
as an important contributing factor. Unfavorably warm weather has hindered
the substitution of pork for the relatively more expensive beef. Increased
imports of beef have not been sufficiently large to offset reduced domestic
supplies.

Czechoslovakia and Austria

In Czechoslovakia and Austria there is a pronounced tendency to confine
hog production to the carrying capacity of domestic feed supplies. This
policy indicates the definite encouragement of exchanging industrial exports
for live hogs and pork products produced in Hungary, Yugoslavia, Poland,
and other European pork-exporting regions.

Czech regulations limiting hog production and feed imports reduced
hog numbers by 23 percent in 2 years, the January 1, 1936, total being
2,735,000 head. In view of present policies, no increase is expected in
the near future. A more liberal attitude toward American lard has been
developed. The earlier policy of making imports of American lard contingent

on imports received from other countries has been abolished. In the first
4 months of 1936, 1,184,000 pounds of American lard were imported against
only 77,000 pounds in the corresponding 1935 period. By June 1936, the
price of American lard at the Czech frontier was lower than the price of
either Hungarian or Yugoslav lard, but quotas and export aids offset the
price advantage considerably. The superior keeping quality of American
lard, however, has prompted the Czech authorities to purchase such lard
for storage in preference to European lard.

The increased Czech interest in imported pork supplies resulted in
imports of live hogs in excess of 80,000 head in the period January-April
1936 against about 40,000 head in those months last year and only 15,000
head in the 1934 period. Despite the larger imports of hogs, lard, and
bacon this year, per capita consumption of pork in the form of meat was
smaller in the first 4 months of 1936 than a year earlier. Because of
the imports, however, there was an increase over last year in the consumption
of pork fat.

In Austria, hog numbers are now at about the level which can be sup-
ported on home-produced feeds, according to Mr. Reed. In general, the
policy of exchanging industrial goods for pork and lard has been fairly
satisfactory, with European exporting countries supplying the Austrian
requirement for imported products. The Austrian commercial commitments,
however, include no allowance for imports of American lard, nor are they
likely to, so long as present arrangements prove tolerably satisfactory.
Arrivals of foreign hogs at Vienna markets in the first half of 1936 were
larger than in 1935, but not large enough to offset the smaller marketings
of domestic hogs. Prices of both pork and lard have moved upward in recent
months.

Switzerland and Belgium

Switzerland is another country wherein steps have been taken to
confine hog production to the number for which domestic feed is available.
This policy resulted in hog numbers as of April 21, 1936 being 20 percent
below the 1935 figures. With imports of hogs also being curtailed, prices
advanced fairly steadily during the first half of this year, the May level
being about 40 percent higher than that of a year ago. There has been
some tendency toward larger imports of American lard.

In Belgium, however, lard imports from both the United States and
Netherlands have declined and imports from France have increased. Hog
slaughter in Belgium this year has been smaller than in 1935, despite some
apparent increase in hog numbers as of January 1, 1936. There were also
some imports of fresh pork this year, whereas there were none in the corresponding months of 1935. Such imports came from Poland, Lithuania, and
Netherlands.

Hogs and pork products: Indices of foreign supplies and demand

Country and item	Unit	1909-10 to 1913-14 average	1924-25 to 1928-29 average	1932-33	1933-34	1934-35	1935-36
UNITED KINGDOM:							
Supplies,							
domestic,fresh	1,000						
pork, London...	pounds		44,567	63,177	53,850	60,959	65,721
Imports-							
Bacon-							
Denmark	"	183,450	376,447	538,136	370,345	323,250	292,274
Irish F.State.	"		40,280	15,597	24,826	35,834	39,834
United States.	"	137,269	81,579	3,888	3,943	2,395	1,214
Canada	"	30,934	57,200	25,225	77,103	83,732	77,185
Others	"	31,879	121,150	277,728	192,822	144,964	134,512
Total	"	383,532	676,656	860,576	669,041	590,175	545,018
Ham, total	"	69,952	93,143	68,478	59,140	56,020	53,352
Lard, total ...	"	165,613	204,650	218,021	257,065	163,321	125,302
DENMARK:							
Exports-							
Bacon	"		375,286	553,233	390,095	328,612	300,624
CANADA:							
Slaughter-							
Hogs,inspected.	1000's	1,303	2,078	2,170	2,299	2,258	2,388
GERMANY:							
Production-							
Hog receipts							
14 cities	"		2,448	2,364	2,651	2,610	2,047
Hog slaughter							
36 centers ...	"	3,361	3,047	3,202	3,474	3,505	2,692
Imports-	1,000						
Bacon, total ..	pounds	2,002	13,140	23,269	20,308	19,676	17,998
Lard, total ...	"	153,048	167,285	176,443	98,351	41,360	69,173
UNITED STATES:							
Slaughter-							
Hogs,inspected.	1000's	25,445	36,706	36,675	35,344	25,556	23,673
Exports-							
Bacon-	1,000						
United Kingdom	pounds	97,094	50,224	2,054	2,203	1,354	598
Germany	"	1,267	9,163	1,213	2,471	0	29
Cuba	"	5,707	15,802	3,236	3,582	3,436	983
Total	"	132,490	107,458	12,285	17,465	6,299	2,433
Hams,shoulders-							
United Kingdom	"	104,711	108,516	46,549	41,453	37,365	28,723
Total	"	121,737	129,627	53,718	48,446	44,598	31,162
Lard-							
United Kingdom	"	133,246	176,592	210,691	244,390	94,735	50,466
Germany	"	108,850	147,661	118,782	55,784	2,513	6,127
Cuba	"	27,801	61,670	8,866	12,447	23,297	17,965
Netherlands ..	"	28,209	32,346	31,575	19,573	10	40
Total	"	363,895	561,145	445,661	426,281	130,781	79,024

Hogs and pork products: Foreign and domestic average pr
pounds for the month indicated, and stocks at the end o

Item	1909-13 average	1925-29 average	June 1935	May 193
	Dollars	Dollars	Dollars	Dolla
Prices:				
Hogs, Chicago, basis packers' and shippers' quotations ....:	7.90	11.22	9.27	9.5
Corn, Chicago, No. 3 Yellow .....:	1.16	1.70	1.52	1.1
Hogs, heavy, Berlin live weight ......:	10.87	15.17	16.08	17.7
Potatoes, Breslau feeding ....:	.37	.60	.86	3.3
Barley, Leipzig ...:	1.73	2.47	3.15	
Lard-				
Chicago ....:	10.77	15.26	15.19	11.1
Liverpool ....:	11.86	15.71	13.64	12.2
Hamburg ....:	14.05	16.18		11.8
Cured pork- Liverpool-				
American short cut green hams .:	15.40	25.24	19.83	21.2
American green bellies ....:		21.73	13.89	Nomin
Danish Wiltshire sides ....:	15.84	24.96	21.15	20.0
Canadian green sides ....:	15.01	23.16	18.75	17.5
	1,000 pounds	1,000 pounds	1,000 pounds	1,000 pound
Stocks:				
United States- Processed pork 3/ :		788,481	445,307	440,6
Lard in cold storage ....:		165,588	84,680	99,6

1/ Three weeks.
2/ Two weeks.
3/ Dry salt cured and in process of cure; pickled, cured, a
    cure, and frozen.

- - - 0 - - -

UNITED STATES DEPARTMENT OF AGRICULTURE
Bureau of Agricultural Economics

Washington

HP-82

September 29, 1936

WORLD HOG AND PORK PROSPECTS

Summary

The United States fall and spring pig crops of 1936-37 are expected
to be considerably smaller than those of 1935-36 as a result of high corn
prices and unusually heavy marketings of breeding stock in July, August
and early September. Hog slaughter during the first half of the 1936-37
year is not expected to show any considerable reduction from this cause,
however, and the number of hogs to be slaughtered in the 1936-37 marketing
year, beginning October 1, is still expected to be larger than in 1935-36.

Current high costs of feed will probably result in early marketings
of the pig crop farrowed last spring, and slaughter supplies from October to
December are expected to be proportionately larger than usual in relation
to those from January to March. A decline in hog prices is in prospect
for the fall and early winter months. Prices in the late winter and early
spring of 1937, however, are likely to advance rather sharply, and relatively
high prices will probably prevail during most of 1937.

Exports of hog products are expected to increase somewhat in the
first half of the 1936-37 marketing year as a result of the prospects for
larger domestic slaughter supplies. Exports in the last half of 1936-37,
however, probably will be no greater than the relatively low level of
exports in the last half of the present marketing year.

A slight increase in the British cured pork import quota applicable
to the September-December period of 1936 was announced by the British Board
of Trade on August 17. The increase was apportioned among the quota countries according to the usual percentages, and resulted principally from

reduction in the estimates of Empire cured pork available for shipment in the last 4 months of the year. The revised quota for the United States is approximately 14,534,000 pounds. Only 152,000 pounds remains as redeemable deficit caused by short shipments earlier in the year. Most of the deficit was made up in June and July when exports to the United Kingdom totaled over 5,000,000 and 6,000,000 pounds, respectively, compared with an average of less than 3,000,000 pounds for the 5 preceding months.

A considerable increase is anticipated in Danish hog slaughter for the period from July 1936 to May 1937 on the basis of the July 18 hog census, which indicated that there were 3,503,000 head of hogs on farms in Denmark on that date, the largest number since July 1933. Smaller hog numbers in the Danube Basin, on the other hand, now indicate some decline in exports of hog products from this area in the second half of 1936 and the first half of 1937.

Lard imports into the United Kingdom continued at unusually low levels in July. Imports from the United States amounted to only 37 percent of the total imported for the season from October 1935 through July 1936 compared with 63 percent for the corresponding period a year earlier. Supplies of fat continue to remain limited in Germany. Decreases in German hog slaughter have tended to hold 1935-36 supplies of domestic lard below the 1934-35 level, and imports of lard, although larger in the first 10 months of the 1935-36 season than in the same period a year earlier, since May have been considerably smaller than those of the corresponding period of 1934-35.

United States

Corn prices rose relatively more than hog prices during July and August, causing the hog-corn price ratio to decline to levels unfavorable for hog production. Marketings of packing sows during the 10 weeks ended September 5 were unusually large in relation to the total number of hogs marketed, the percentage of packing sows marketed averaging 40 percent of total packer and shipper purchases at the seven leading markets compared with

28 percent a year earlier. This relatively large proportion of packing sows marketed, many of which were piggy, resulted in a considerable reduction in breeding stock on farms. Both the fall pig crop of this year and the spring pig crop of next year are likely to be smaller than those of 1935-36, notwithstanding that in early June farmers reported they were planning an increase of 14 percent in fall farrowings over the previous year.

The current high cost of feed is expected to cause the pig crop farrowed last spring to be marketed unusually early, thereby making slaughter supplies from October to December proportionately larger than usual in relation to those from January to March. The effect of the large marketings on hog prices, which ordinarily decline seasonally during this quarter may be no greater than usual, since consumer demand is apparently increasing and demand from packers for storage purposes is expected to be stronger than that of a year earlier. Because of the relatively small supplies in prospect for the late winter and early spring of 1937, the price movement during that period is likely to be sharply upward.

The seasonal up-trend in hog prices which started in May apparently ended in late August, as prices have since been declining moderately. The amount of the summer advance varied considerably as between hogs of different weights and grades. Prices of the better grades of medium weight butcher hogs rose slightly more than $2.00 per 100 pounds, whereas the advances in light weight butchers ranged from $1.20 to $1.90. The smallest advances were in the prices of the extreme light weights and the lowest grades. Price declines occurring since late August have been greatest for the extremely light hogs. Prices of packing sows, however, have continued to show an upward tendency because of decreasing numbers of such hogs in the present market supply. The average price per 100 pounds of packers and shippers at Chicago was $10.06 in August compared with $9.76 in July and $10.78 in August 1935.

Market receipts of hogs in August were the smallest since October 1935. Slaughter under Federal inspection totaled 2,254,000 head, 16 percent below July but 35 percent larger than the unusually small slaughter of August last year. The increase over a year earlier was not so great as that recorded in June, however. Total hog slaughter for the current marketing year, which ends September 30, is expected to be about the same as in the previous year, when the total slaughtered under Federal inspection amounted to 30,700,000 head. Marketings in July and August this year included the largest proportion of packing sows recorded in several years and was comprised of relatively large numbers of unfinished light butcher hogs, and of feeder and slaughter pigs. Storage holdings of pork and lard declined less than in other recent years during August, and have recently exceeded the quantities of both products held in storage a year earlier.

The average weight of hogs in the seven leading markets dropped sharply toward the end of August. Heavy liquidation of large packing sows early in the month caused a later-than usual peak in average weights. Late in August there was a sharp decrease both in number and average weights of packing sows, although the percentage of packing sows was still considerably greater than a year earlier. This, together with the relatively large number of pigs and unfinished butcher hogs, caused a sharp decrease in average weights, and in early September the average was less than a year earlier. Average weights in the seven markets were 256 pounds in August compared with 258 in July and 251 pounds in August of last year.

The sharp rise in corn prices, which started early in July, continued during most of August, but reacted slightly toward the end of the month. Prices during the first week in September were about the same as in early August. The average price of No. 3 Yellow corn at Chicago was 113.5 cents per bushel in August compared with 85.8 cents in July and 80.6 cents in August last year. Based on farm prices on the 15th of the month, the hog-corn price ratio in the North Central States was 9.5 in August, compared with 12.0 in July 1936 and 14.1 in August 1935. The hog-corn ratio in the next few months will probably continue below that of corresponding months of last year.

Wholesale prices of fresh pork rose sharply during the last half of August to the highest levels of this year, but in general were slightly below the peak prices recorded in the late summer of 1935. Prices of lard advanced in the first 3 weeks of August and then reacted slightly. Prices of most cured products were steady to lower. The composite wholesale price of the principal hog products at New York was $21.94 per 100 pounds in August compared with $21.35 in July and $25.77 in August last year.

Total pork exports in July were nearly 20 percent larger than in June and exceeded corresponding monthly exports of a year earlier for the first time this season. The increase in shipments of cured pork accounted for almost the entire gain in pork exports, with hams and shoulders, the principal cured item, accounting for about 80 percent of the entire increase. Hams and shoulders exported totaled 6,557,000 pounds in July. Exports of this item to the United Kingdom, the leading market, accounted for nearly all of the increase since June. Bacon exports totaled 627,000 pounds in July and showed some increase over the amount shipped in June, but were less than the total for July 1935, and the smallest for the month on record.

Exports of lard from the United States in July, amounting to 7,555,000 pounds, were about 32 percent smaller than those for June, but were over 50 percent greater than the extremely low total for July of last year. Exports of lard to the United Kingdom were the smallest since October 1935. The decrease in lard shipments to Germany from June, when the total was relatively high, to July may have been due in part to the increasing difficulties of making satisfactory arrangements for payment with German buyers. Exports of hams and bacon to Cuba showed some increase during July, while shipments of lard to that country showed a relatively small decrease. Total exports of both pork and lard for the first 10 months of the 1935-36 season, however, were far below those of any recent year preceding the 1934-35 marketing season, and were somewhat below those of that year.

Canada

Hog prices averaged higher at Toronto in August than in July, although prices tended to weaken somewhat in the last week of the month. Bacon hogs at Toronto averaged $9.29 per 100 pounds, United States currency, compared with $9.05 for the month of July, and $9.90 in August of last year.

Marketings of hogs were heavier in August than in July and in August 1935. In the 4-week period ended August 27 the number graded at stockyards and packing plants in Canada reached 230,000 head compared with 223,000 head in the 4-week period ended July 30, and only 173,000 head in the corresponding period of August 1935. The increase in hog marketings so far this year as compared with the same period of 1935 amounts to about 200,000 head or 11 percent.

It is anticipated by Canadian marketing officials that the present scarcity and prospective high price of feed may result in over-liquidation of sows and unfinished hogs. Heavy marketing of sows at this time, unless checked, is likely to cause a falling off in fall litters and thus bring about a shortage in pig supplies for next spring and summer. Spring farrowings this year showed an increase of 28 percent above 1935.

Canadian trade statistics show that exports of pork products to the United Kingdom in July amounted to 15,693,000 pounds. Bacon exports, which comprised 83 percent of the total, increased 10 percent above June and 24 percent above July 1935, whereas there was a decrease in lard exports of 14 percent as compared with June, but an increase of 166 percent as compared with July 1935. Total exports of pork products from Canada to the United Kingdom during the first 10 months of the current hog marketing year, October 1 to July 31, amounted to 133,000,000 pounds, an increase of 13 percent above the same period of 1934-35.

United Kingdom and Irish Free State

On August 17, the British Board of Trade announced an upward revision in the cured-pork quota for the last 4 months of 1936, the total to equal 1,602,138 hundredweight (179,439,000 pounds) instead of the 1,590,683 hundredweight (178,156,000 pounds) previously announced. See table, page 6. Larger importations will be allowed from foreign countries because of reductions in the estimates of Empire cured pork available for shipment during the last 4 months of the year. In addition to this slight increase in the September-December allocation, 1,295 hundredweight (145,000 pounds) were apportioned according to the usual percentages among the quota countries. The adjustment was made because of the failure of Yugoslavia to use this amount of the quota granted as compensation for loss of the principal Yugoslav market for cured pork when sanctions against Italy were first applied. The new quota figure represents an increase of less than 1 percent over that announced earlier, leaving the reduction from the May-August 1936 period still 12 percent, but only 4.4 percent from the average monthly rate for October-December 1935.

The United States share in the revised September-December total British cured-pork quota is approximately 14,534,000 pounds, representing a monthly rate of nearly 3,634,000 pounds. Monthly imports of American cured pork into the United Kingdom for the first 7 months of 1936 averaged 3,532,000 pounds. July imports, however, were up to nearly 6,400,000 pounds, bringing the redeemable deficit caused by short shipments earlier in the year down to a negligible quantity (152,000 pounds). See table, page 6.

The seasonal decline in the price of American short cut green hams as reflected by quotations on the Liverpool market began a month earlier than usual this year, the average for August amounting to $20.58 per 100 pounds as against $21.97 for July and $23.29 for August 1935. Total ham imports into the United Kingdom during July amounted to 9,463,000 pounds, an increase of more than 700,000 pounds over June imports and of nearly 900,000 pounds over comparable 1935 figures. Imports from the United States accounted for all of this increase, shipments from Canada, the second/and almost only other important supplier, being considerably lower in July than in June.

Liverpool bacon quotations, unlike those for ham, rose steadily during August, Danish Wiltshire sides at $22.26 per 100 pounds, making the highest average since April 1930 and Canadian green sides at $20.31 the highest since June 1930. American green bellies also shared in the upward price tendency, averaging $17.03 during August against $16.71 in July. Total supplies of bacon reached unusually low levels in British markets during August. Imports of bacon into the United Kingdom in July were 3,446,000 pounds higher than in June. Total imports for the season, however, at 609,000,000 pounds were nearly 8.5 percent below comparable 1934-35 figures. Though imports from Denmark were over 1,600,000 pounds higher in July then in June, total imports from that country for the season to the end of July were 10 percent below those of a year ago.

United Kingdom: Revised total cured pork allocations, September 1-
December 31, 1936, and to the United States, January 1-December
31, 1936

Country	Total allocation, Sept. 1-Dec. 31 Percentage share of total			Allocations to United States Jan. 1-Dec. 31, 1936		
		Allocations		Month	Allocation 1/	Imports 2/
	Percent	Hundred-weight	1,000 pounds	1936	1,000 pounds	1,000 pounds
Denmark ......:	63.50	1,017,358	113,944	Jan.	3,877	2,324
Netherlands ..:	9.50	152,203	17,047	Feb.	3,642	2,148
Poland ....:	7.95	127,370	14,265	Mar.	3,990	2,597
Sweden ....:	4.70	75,300	8,434	Apr.	3,862	2,354
Lithuania ....:	2.95	47,263	5,293	May	4,146	3,895
Estonia ......:	.75	12,016	1,346	June	4,014	5,031
Finland ......:	.40	6,409	718	July	4,146	6,376
Latvia ....:	.70	11,215	1,256	Aug.	4,146	
USSR ....:	.85	13,618	1,525	Sept.:	3,633	
Argentina ....:	.70	11,215	1,256	Oct.	3,633	
United States.:3/	8.00 :3/	128,171:3/	14,355:(	Nov.	3,634)	
				(Dec.	3,634)	
Total ....:	100.00	1,602,138	179,439		46,357	

1/ Final figures with all adjustments made.
2/ Not adjusted for re-exports.
3/ Plus 0.1 percent of total to allow for adjustments in connection with
    imports through Canada.

Lard prices advanced materially during August, as indicated by Liverpool quotations, the monthly average for American refined lard standing at $13.51 per hundred pounds against $12.37 in July. Last year's comparable average, however, was $17.08. Lard imports into the United Kingdom continued at unusually low levels during July, totaling for the season to the end of that month 140,450,000 pounds against 179,700,000 pounds in 1934-35 and 279,600,000 pounds in 1933-34. Imports from the United States declined again in July to less than 6,000,000 pounds. The United States share in the total for the period October-July was 37 percent against 63 percent last season and 93 percent in the corresponding period of 1933-34.

Supplies of British and Irish fresh pork at London Central Markets during this season to July 31 were considerably higher than in any of the past several seasons. Supplies from these sources in July totaled a little over 4,000,000 pounds, which was an increase of 31 percent compared with July 1935 figures.

Denmark

A weekly slaughter of 96,000 to 101,000 hogs in Denmark is anticipated by Danish authorities for the period July-May 1936-37, according to Agricultural Commissioner H. E. Reed at Berlin. The slaughter estimate was made by the semi-official Danish Agricultural Council on the basis of the July 18 hog census, which, at 3,503,000 head, was the largest census or estimate since July 1933. On the basis of the May 1936 census, the Council had estimated weekly slaughter at about 95,000 head for the period May-February 1936-37. The weekly average for the calendar year 1935 was 83,000 head.

Most of the increase in the July 1936 estimate over those made in May and June of this year is accounted for by the larger number of pigs weighing less than 132 pounds (60 kilos). This development was to be expected from the marked increase in breeding operations in evidence for some time. Bred sow numbers, although showing a decrease of about 6 percent from the June 1936 estimates, are higher than on any other estimate or census date since April 1933. Most of the decrease from June in bred sows appeared in the gilt category.

The decline in gilts resulted from an increase in the practice of breeding for one litter and then selling as sows. It will be recalled that the Danish hog-marketing control measures apply only to hogs of bacon weight and not to pigs under 110 pounds (50 kilos) or to sows and boars. These exceptions have been found to be too liberal for exercising proper control under price conditions favorable to increasing production. The supply of light pigs for slaughter has been increased materially, under existing regulations, producers have preferred not to risk feeding pigs to bacon weights only to have them classed as excess or "non-card" hogs, which must be sold at unremunerative prices. Gilts in many instances, after producing one litter, have been marketed as sows for domestic consumption, bringing prices little less than those paid for "card" or export-bacon hogs. The sale of light pigs and of gilts as sows has prevented the low non-card prices from being as effective a limitation on production as was intended. An order effective July 1, 1936, however, now prohibits the marketing of sows under 18 months of age at the prices prescribed for sows. Such sows must be sold at the non-card prices for bacon hogs. This measure also is expected to reduce the number of young pigs, now regarded as excessive.

Germany

There has been little change during recent weeks in the limited supplies of fat available in Germany. Lard import figures for July, at 2,400,000 pounds, were more than twice as large as the June imports, but remained well below figures for all other months of the current season. German receipts of Danube Basin lard have been curtailed sharply in recent months, principally because prices in Germany have not been sufficiently high to attract the diminished supplies of the Danubian product. Of the July imports into Germany, Denmark supplied nearly 2,000,000 pounds, the United States and various European countries accounting for the small remainder.

Lard imports since May have been considerably smaller than in the corresponding 1935 period. For the current season beginning October 1935, total lard imports to July 31 were 60 percent larger than the comparable 1934-35 figures as a result of the heavier imports in the months prior to June. From October 1935 to April 1936, decreases below last year in hog marketings and slaughter tended to hold the supplies of domestic lard below the 1934-35 level. Hog marketings were heavier in May and June this year than last, but fell off again in July and August. The current season's total receipts of hogs at 14 cities as of July 31 were 19 percent below, and slaughter at 36 centers 21 percent below the corresponding 1934-35 figures.

Danube Basin

Large domestic feed crops and high hog and pork prices mark the current hog situation in the Danube Basin, according to the Belgrade office of the Foreign Agricultural Service. These conditions suggest a reversal of the material decline in hog numbers which resulted from the heavy exports of live hogs, lard, and pork in 1935 and the first half of 1936. As early as last April, hog numbers in Hungary, the Basin's leading exporting country, were down to 2,554,000 head compared with 3,176,000 head in 1935 and an average of 2,368,000 head in the period 1930-1934.

The smaller hog numbers indicate some decline in the export volume during the second half of 1936 and the first half of 1937. Of the hogs now being marketed, a relatively large proportion shows lack of finish as a result of last year's reduced feed-grain crops. This situation has brought about a decided upward movement in the prices of well-finished hogs, and a favorable hog-feed ratio. Larger feeding operations than last year are expected this fall and winter.

Lard exports from Danube countries in the first 7 months of 1936 totaled about 44,300,000 pounds against about 39,200,000 pounds in the corresponding 1935 period. Participation in this year's exports by Bulgaria and Rumania, especially the former, was considerably heavier than in 1935. Hungary, however continued as the leading shipper of Danubian lard, accounting for about 70 percent of the 1936 total compared with about 88 percent of the 1935 exports. Yugoslavian participation also has increased this year, with exports from that country about 66 percent larger than in 1935.

The relative scarcity of fat hogs in July resulted in Hungarian lard prices advancing to the point where exports to Germany, formerly the leading buyer, were no longer profitable. As a result, the July movement of Hungarian lard to Germany fell to practically nothing. During June and July the German price for Hungarian lard was set at the equivalent of about 13 cents per pound, f.o.b. Budapest. A new German price for August, equivalent to 13.7 cents, re-newed the movement of Hungarian lard. That price, however, is not entirely satisfactory to Hungary, which agreed to an August quota considerably smaller than the quota for earlier months.

Hogs and pork products: Indices of foreign supplies and demand

Country and item	Unit	1909-10 to 1913-14 average	1924-25 to 1928-29 average	Oct. - July			
				1932-33	1933-34	1934-35	1935-36
UNITED KINGDOM:							
Supplies, domestic fresh pork, London ....:	1000 pounds			46,787	65,482	56,325	64,075	69,809
Imports -							
Bacon -							
Denmark ....:	"	205,468	419,006	591,261	416,021	361,732	326,216
Irish Free State .....:	"		44,188	16,576	27,517	39,943	44,650
United States ....:	"	152,042	89,794	4,995	4,536	2,572	1,563
Canada ....,:	"	34,872	64,236	31,243	86,844	92,162	86.526
Others ....:	"	36,067	176,299	303,702	210,418	162,284	150,065
Total ....:	"	428,449	753,523	947,779	745,339	658,694	609,019
Ham, total ....:	"	79,475	106,307	82,046	71,124	64,506	62,815
Lard, total ....:	"	183,256	229,527	246,694	279,629	179,695	140,452
DENMARK:							
Exports -							
Bacon ....:	"			416,987	607,924	437,063	368,456	
CANADA:							
Slaughter -							
Hogs, inspected ....:	1000's	1,434	2,239	2,361	2,477	2,449	2,620
GERMANY:							
Production -							
Hog receipts 14 cities :	"			2,692	2,601	3,008	2,882	2,329
Hog slaughter 36 centers	"	3,708	3,354	3,534	3,920	3,871	3,039
Imports -	1000						
Bacon, total ....:	pounds	2,212	14,278	25,340	24,309	21,327	19,767
Lard, total ....:	"	167,473	185,285	183,662	103,604	44.612	71,574
UNITED STATES:							
Slaughter -							
Hogs, inspected ....:	1000's	27,789	39,898	40,589	38,668	27,268	26,365
Exports -							
Bacon -	1000						
United Kingdom ....:	pounds	108,288	55,371	2,318	2,569	1,435	825
Germany ....:	"	1,308	9,881	1,221	2,493	0	29
Cuba ....:	"	6,356	17,404	3,545	4,132	3,954	1,223
Total ....:	"	146,866	117,793	13,911	19,374	7,000	3,060
Hams, shoulders -							
United Kingdom ....:	"	117,993	121,060	54,879	50,411	42,546	34,785
Total ....:	"	137,170	144,320	63,077	58,084	50,430	37,719
Lard -							
United Kingdom ....:	"	146,075	194,326	234,050	266,573	96,508	54,797
Germany ....:	"	117,373	159,656	121,092	58,308	2,513	6,313
Cuba ....:	"	31,116	67,744	9,545	14,452	25,929	20,476
Netherlands ....:	"	30,454	34,595	32,436	20,351	10	46
Total ....:	"	396,734	613,040	481,831	459,747	135,696	86,505

Hogs and pork products: Foreign and domestic average prices per 100
pounds for the month indicated, and stocks at the end of each month

Item	1909-1913 July average	1925-1929 July average	July 1935	June 1936	July 1936
	Dollars	Dollars	Dollars	Dollars	Dollars
Prices-					
Hogs, Chicago, basis packers' & shippers' quotations	8.00	11.37	9.49	9.88	9.76
Corn, Chicago, No. 3 Yellow	1.16	1.76	1.52	1.14	1.53
Hogs, heavy, Berlin live weight	11.71	16.03	17.20	17.70	17.70
Barley, Leipzig	1.71	2.22	3.13	3.41	
Lard-					
Chicago	10.75	15.18	15.65	11.28	
Liverpool	11.86	15.80	14.46	11.83	12.37
Hamburg	12.67	16.26		11.50	12.20
Cured pork- Liverpool-					
American short cut green hams	15.80	26.01	20.65	21.95	21.97
American green bellies		21.64	13.61	Nominal	16.71
Danish Wiltshire sides	16.56	25.04	20.50	20.33	20.65
Canadian green sides	15.43	23.09	17.83	18.08	18.23
	1,000 pounds	1,000 pounds	1,000 pounds	1,000 pounds	1,000 pounds
Stocks- United States-					
Processed pork 4/		757,404	369,910	435,130	442,483
Lard in cold storage.		177,316	68,435	106,774	116,824

1/ Three weeks.
2/ No prices quoted.
3/ Two weeks.
4/ Dry salt cured and in process of cure; pickled, cured, and in process of
    cure, and frozen.

- - - - 0 - - - -

UNITED STATES DEPARTMENT OF AGRICULTURE
Bureau of Agricultural Economics
Washington

HP-83

October 27, 1936

WORLD HOG AND PORK PROSPECTS

Summary

Slaughter supplies of hogs in the United States during the marketing year which began October 1, are expected to be considerably larger than those of the last 2 years, but much smaller than average.   Because of short feed supplies, it is probable +hat there will be a decided tendency to market hogs earlier than usual this fall and winter, causing slaughter supplies from October to mid-January to be large in relation to supplies in the remainder of the 1936-37 marketing year. Some further seasonal decline in prices is now in prospect.   From December through March, however, the trend in domestic prices is expected to be generally upward.

With larger slaughter supplies of hogs in the United States in prospect for the first half of the 1936-37 marketing year, it is probable that exports of hog products will increase somewhat in this period.   In the last half of 1936-37, however, the probable smaller domestic hog slaughter is likely to result in a level of exports no greater than in the last half of 1935-36.

Latest hog census data show total hog numbers in the most important hog producing countries of Europe to be approximately 5 percent higher at the beginning of the 1936-37 hog year than at the same time a year earlier. In the United Kingdom, however, hog numbers have declined. It is probable that some modification of the British Pig Scheme will be made. possibly accompanied by an increase in pork import quotas for 1937 and the imposition of tariffs on cured pork.

The marked increase in hog production in Germany will be an outstanding feature in the coming hog marketing year in continental Europe. No pork surplus in Germany is expected to develop, however, since there is a shortage in cattle.   Germany will no doubt continue to import hogs, lard, and fatbacks, as well as beef, but only in quantities for which the supplying countries can accept payment in German goods.

Hog numbers in the Danube Basin, in contrast to those of other surplus producing countries in Central Europe, are now considerably smaller than those of a year earlier.   Exports from this area in the coming winter and spring are expected to be somewhat smaller than those of last winter and spring.   The large corn and barley crops harvested in the Basin this year, however, have given rise to a strong demand for feeder hogs, and it is anticipated that increased supplies of fat hogs and lard will be available for export in the summer and fall of 1937.

Domestic Situation

Slaughter supplies of hogs during the current marketing year (October 1, 1936 to September 30, 1937) will be considerably larger than for either of the 2 previous marketing years but will be much smaller than the average of the 5 years preceding 1934-35. Hog slaughter under Federal inspection in 1935-36 in number of head was but little different from the slaughter in 1934-35, but in total live and dressed weight it was larger because average weights were heavier.

Hogs: Inspected slaughter, average and total live weight, and average cost, 5-year average, 1934-35 and 1935-36

Year beginning Oct.	Inspected slaughter 1/	Live weight 2/		Av. price per 100 pounds
		Average	Total	
	1,000 head	Pounds	Million pounds	Dollars
Av. 1929-30 to 1933-34	45,354	230	10,429	5.71
1934-35 .....:	30,680	220	6,742	7.75
1935-36 .....:	31,022	232	7,187	9.78

1/ Bureau of Animal Industry. 2/Bureau of Agricultural Economics.

How many more hogs will be slaughtered under Federal inspection during the present marketing year than in the previous year will depend to a considerable extent upon the size of the 1936 fall pig crop . The 1936 spring pig crop for the entire country was larger than the very small spring crop of 1935 by 9,000,000 head, or 29 percent.   The June pig crop report indicated an increase of 14 percent in the number of sows to farrow in the fall of 1936.   In June, when the report was issued, prospects were favorable for at least an average corn crop in the Corn Belt States. Hog prices were at a very high level and the hog-corn price ratio was quite favorable for an expansion in hog production.   Within a few weeks after the report was issued, however, the situation was changed entirely. Corn crop prospects dwindled rapidly as severe drought spread over most of the Corn Belt.   As corn prospects declined, prices of corn increased and the hog-corn price ratio shifted from a favorable to a distinctly unfavorable level, even though hog prices also made a substantial advance during the same period. As a result of this changed situation, hog producers began to dispose of brood sows that had farrowed in the spring, as well as those intended for fall farrow, and all other hogs that could be quickly finished for marketing. This resulted in greatly increased marketings of hogs in July, August, and September.

Estimates given in the June pig crop report as to the number of hogs over 6 months old on June 1 this year compared with a year earlier, indicated that only a moderate increase in slaughter was to be expected during the 4 months June to September.   Actually, however, slaughter under Federal inspection was 51 percent larger in this period than a year earlier. This large increase in slaughter was a result of the large marketings of sows originally intended for fall farrowing, supplemented by relatively early movement of 1936 spring pigs. In view of this heavy liquidation, it seems fairly certain that the number of sows to farrow this fall will be substantially smaller than the number farrowed in 1935, although probably not so small as that in the fall of 1934.

Hog prices declined after mid-September in response to a seasonal increase in marketings, but near the end of the month and during early October they made some recovery. Because of s ort feed supplies there will be a decided tendency to market hogs earlier than usual this fall and winter, thus causing slaughter supplies from October to mid-January to be large in relation to supplies in the remainder of the 1936-37 marketing year. Some further seasonal decline in prices is in prospect. From December through March the price movement is expected to be generally upward.

The average price of hogs at Chicago declined from $10.26 per 100 pounds the second week in September to $9.38 in the fourth week, but recovered to $9.84 in the week ended October 10. Prices of butcher hogs began to decline in late August and dropped steadily for 5 weeks before the decline was checked. Prices of packing sows did not begin to decline until mid-September. The average price of hogs at Chicago for the month of September was $9.89 compared with $10.06 in August and $10.95 in September last year.

Hog slaughter under Federal inspection in September, totaling 2,403,000 head, was 7 percent larger than that in August and 65 percent larger than the unusually small slaughter of September 1935. The increase in slaughter in September over a year earlier was greater relative to the increases recorded in other recent months and reflected liquidation of both packing sows and early spring pigs.

Market prices of corn advanced sharply during the first 2 weeks of September, but declined near the end of the month to the lowest level since July. Although the average price of No. 3 Yellow corn at Chicago was lower in September than in August, the average farm price on September 15 was slightly higher than that of a month earlier. Based on farm prices on the 15th of the month, the hog-corn price ratio in the North Central States was 9.5 in both September and August, compared with 14.4 in September 1935. The ratio is expected to continue unfavorable to hog production at least until the late winter or spring of 1937.

The average weight of hogs marketed continued the decline which began in late August, and in late September they were far below those of a year earlier. The increasing proportion of light spring pigs marketed was responsible for much of the decrease in the average weight of all butcher hogs. The growing scarcity of well-finished hogs indicates a considerable decrease in average hog weights during the next several months. Average weights in the next 3 months may be as low as in late 1934 when the average for all hogs slaughtered under Federal inspection declined to about 210 pounds. The average weight of hogs at the seven leading markets in September was 232 pounds compared with 256 pounds in August and 250 pounds in September 1935.

Wholesale prices of fresh pork continued to rise in early September and in the week ended September 12 they reached the highest level since mid-August 1935. With the increase in hog marketings toward the end of September, however, prices of fresh pork declined rather sharply. Prices of cured pork were lower in September than in August and lard prices also showed some weakness. The composite wholesale price of the principal hog products at New York was $22.18 per 100 pounds in September compared with $21.94 in August and $25.79 in September a year earlier.

The United States exports of both pork and lard in August showed a decrease from those of July. Pork exports in August were about 34 percent below those of July, and 10 percent below those of the corresponding month a year earlier. The decrease was mainly in cured pork exports with the decline in shipments of hams and shoulders to the United Kingdom accounting for most of it. Exports of hams and shoulders in August, totaling 3,642,000 pounds, were 45 percent below those of July and 24 percent lower than for the same month in 1935.

Exports of lard during August were 19 percent smaller than in July but 76 percent larger than the record low level for the same month a year earlier. The last reduction in the Cuban import duty on lard and the elimination of the 1-cent per pound consumption tax on American lard, both of which were provided for in the Cuban trade agreement, became effective on September 3. The reduction of the duty and consumption tax combined amounted to $1.41 per 100 pounds.

With larger slaughter supplies of hogs in the United States in prospect for the first half of the 1936-37 marketing year, it is probable that exports of hog products will increase somewhat in this period. In the last half of 1936-37, however, the probable smaller domestic hog slaughter is likely to result in a level of exports no greater than in the last half of 1935-36.

Canada

After reaching the high point for the year of $9.57 American currency in the week ended August 13, hog prices at Toronto declined to $8.97 in the week ended September 3, and to $8.00 in the week ended October 1. The average price for the 4 weeks ended October 1 was $8.52 compared with $9.21 for the last 4 weeks in August and $9.30 a year earlier. Heavier marketings were chiefly responsible for the lower hog prices in September.

The increase in hog marketings in September over August this year was much greater than in 1935. The number of hogs graded in the 4 weeks ended October 1 was 271,000, an increase of 18 percent above the last 4 weeks of August and 45 percent above the corresponding 4 weeks of September last year. Gradings of live hogs and hog carcasses in Canada for the 1935-36 hog marketing year from October to September amounted to 3,326,000 head, an increase of 10 percent above the same period of 1934-35.

Exports of bacon from Canada to the United Kingdom in the 11 months of the hog marketing year up to August 31 1936 amounted to 122,025,000 pounds, an increase of 3 percent above the same period of 1934-35. Pork exports to the United Kingdom amounting to 896,000 pounds were almost twice as large as in the same 11-month period of last year, and lard exports, totaling to 23,660,000 pounds, were three times as large as in the same period of 1934-35. Bacon exports to the United Kingdom in August amounted to 11,535,000 pounds, a decrease of 12 percent from July, but an increase of 40 percent compared with August 1935.

Hog Numbers in European Countries

Latest hog census data show total hog numbers in the most important hog-producing countries of Europe to be approximately 5 percent higher at the beginning of the 1936-37 hog year than at the same time last year. Outstanding among the increases in hog production is the marked upturn in hog numbers in Germany. The number of hogs in Germany in early September, totaling about 25,900,000 head was 14 percent larger than a year earlier and the largest number ever reported for that country. An appreciable increase in numbers has also taken place in Denmark, and a small increase in the Netherlands, both being important surplus producing countries. In Hungary, however, hog numbers have declined. Hog numbers in the British Isles, the most important deficit area in Europe, have also been slightly reduced. The increased numbers in Denmark and Germany however, more than offset the declines which have occurred in other countries.

Germany: Number of hogs on farms, September 4, 1936 with comparisons

Sept. 1 - 4	Pigs under 8 wks.	Pigs 8 wks. to 6 mos.	Hogs 6 mos. to 1 yr. Slaugh-ter hogs	Brood sows Total	In far-row(preg-nant)	Hogs over 1 yr. Slaugh-ter hogs	Brood sows Total	In far-row(preg-nant)	Grand total 1/
	Thou-sands	Thou-sands	Thou-sands	Thou-sands	Thou-sands	Thou-sands	Thou-sands	Thou-sands	Thou-sands
1932	6,326	10,341	4,872	517	255	440	1,559	832	24,176
1933 2/	---	---	---	---	---	---	---	---	---
1934	6,348	10,594	5,559	470	229	478	1,483	768	25,047
1935	5,853	9,684	4,695	529	288	403	1,410	775	22,683
1936	6,624	11,042	5,588	576	311	373	1,582	854	25,895

Compiled from cable from Agricultural Commissioner, H. E. Reed, and original official sources.
1/ Includes boars.
2/ No September estimate available for 1933.

Denmark: Official August 29, 1936 estimate of hog numbers on farms compared with periodical estimates in 1935 and 1936

Date	Boars 4 months and over	Brood sows In farrow	Not in farrow	Total	Other hogs (new classification) 132 pounds and over	77 to 132 pounds	Under 77 pounds	Suck-ling pigs	Total
	Thou-sands	Thou-sands	Thou-sands	Thou-sands	Thou-sands	Thou-sands	Thou-sands	Thou-sands	Thou-sands
Oct. 5, 1935	21	264	141	405	534	683	792	860	3,295
Nov. 16, 1935	21	278	132	410	565	674	882	766	3,318
Dec. 28, 1935	21	278	127	405	450	723	885	732	3,216
Feb. 8, 1936	21	270	137	407	518	722	816	779	3,263
Mar. 21, 1936	22	289	140	429	558	700	826	819	3,354
May 2, 1936	23	308	132	440	562	686	852	768	3,331
June 13, 1936	24	314	141	455	559	700	826	810	3,374
July 18, 1936	23	295	154	449	540	761	843	887	3,503
Aug. 29, 1936	23	255	183	438	608	696	947	1,006	3,718

Compiled from Statistiske Efterretninger, published by the Statistical Depart-ment of Denmark, and reports from Agricultural Commissioner H. E. Reed, United States Department of Agriculture.

United Kingdom and Irish Free State

Considerable uncertainty as to the future trend of bacon-hog production in Great Britain is felt at the present time. The British Pig Scheme, designed to bring about expansion of the domestic hog and bacon industry, has failed to achieve its purpose. For a time producers expanded production in expectation of greater profits, but with contract prices averaging lower than market prices the tendency recently has been to curtail hog production. The June hog census revealed that a decline in hog numbers had occurred compared with a year earlier. Northern Ireland was the only part of Great Britain to show an increase. It is probable that some modification of the Pig Scheme will be made, possibly accompanied by an increase in pork import quotas for 1937 and the imposition of tariffs on cured pork, although the exact nature and extent of the changes to be made are as yet unknown.

Unusually high bacon prices, as reflected by Liverpool quotations, characterized the British cured-pork market during September. Danish Wiltshire sides averaged $22.45 per 100 pounds, $3.78 above the September 1935 figure and the highest September average since 1929. Canadian green sides at $19.92 per 100 pounds, although registering some decline from the average of August, were $2.57 above the September 1935 figure. American green bellies, at $17.63 per 100 pounds, made the highest monthly average since December 1930. Ham prices, in contrast to bacon prices, have declined since the first of August. Ham prices in September averaged $19.45 per 100 pounds, compared with $20.58 in August and $22.96 in September 1935.

Total imports of bacon into the United Kingdom, amounting to nearly 65,000,000 pounds, were the highest in August of any month this season. For the first 11 months of the 1935-36 season, however, total imports of bacon were about 7 percent less than those of a year earlier. Imports from Denmark during the season to August 31 amounted to about 360,000,000 pounds compared with 402,000,000 pounds in the corresponding period of 1934-35. Imports of about 97,000,000 pounds from Canada, for the season to August 31, were 2 percent below those for the corresponding period a year earlier. Imports from the Irish Free State for the first 11 months of the season, on the other hand, amounted to about 50,000,000 pounds, nearly 12 percent more than comparable 1935 imports.

Imports of ham declined during August from the relatively high level of imports for July. The total of 71,000,000 pounds for the October-August period, nevertheless, was slightly larger than imports of ham in the corresponding period of 1934-35. Ham imports from the United States during the 11 months were considerably smaller than those of a year earlier, although in August there was a substantial increase over August 1935. Ham imports from Canada, on the other hand, were maintained at a considerably higher level during 1935-36 than in any recent marketing year. Imports from the Irish Free State, although not large, exceeded all previous records.

Liverpool quotations on refined lard during September were fairly steady at the advanced level attained in July, averaging about $13.58 per 100 pounds. Lard imports into the United Kingdom from all sources amounted to less than 153,000,000 pounds for the first 11 months of the season, and

were 22 percent under those of a year ago. The amount imported during
August from the United States was the lowest for any month since last
October, and the total for the season to August 31 was 52 percent below
October-August 1935 figures. Canadian shipments of lard to the United
Kindom, however, have been running consistently higher than during previous
seasons.

Total fat supplies in Great Britain have not been reduced during the
period of smaller lard imports, margarine production having increased
sufficiently to offset the decline. A continuation of the reduced lard
imports will no doubt increase further the United Kingdom's takings of raw
materials for margarine production. This partial shift from lard to
substitute fats in the United Kingdom has not as yet reached a stage where
lard is at a permanent disadvantage. Should the reduction in lard supplies
continue for a period of years, however, it is quite likely that the British
people would become so accustomed to other fats that lard prices would have
to be reduced below those of other fats in order to move any such quantities
of lard as have been sold in the United Kingdom in previous years.

Countries Important in British Market Supplies

Denmark is entering the 1936-37 hog marketing year with an appreciable
hog surplus, and will be more than able to supply Great Britain with quota
requirements and any extra quotas which may come with a change in British
policy. The moderate increase in hog production in the Netherlands is expected to yield ample supplies for domestic market needs, with an increased
surplus for export. Uncertainty exists regarding Polish hog numbers. Hog
prices have been relatively high compared with feed prices for the last 12
months in Poland, and conditions have been favorable for increased hog
production. The great increase in Polish hog slaughter, which has occurred
during the last year, however, indicates that marketings of hogs may have
exceeded any increase in production resulting from the favorable hog-feed
price ratio. Regardless of developments in hog numbers, Poland may be
expected to export fully as much in the present marketing year as in the
last, chiefly because of her need for foreign exchange.

Continental European Importing Countries

The marked increase in hog production in Germany will be the outstanding feature in the coming hog year in continental Europe. Hog numbers, which
were about 22,700,000 on September 4, 1935, increased to nearly 25,900,000
in September this year. The number reported was larger than in September of
both 1934 and 1931, when the total number was also over 25,000,000 head.
Under ordinary conditions, this number would result in a pork surplus, although it does not provide sufficient fats to meet Germany's domestic needs.
This year no pork surplus is expected to ensue, largely because of a shortage
in cattle.

Germany will no doubt continue to import hogs, lard, and fatbacks, as
well as beef, but only in quantities for which the supplying countries can
accept payment in German goods. Such developments are in keeping with the
German trade policy, and it is becoming increasingly clear that the limiting
factor in this type of trade is the ability of the exporting country to absorb
German goods. Imports from Denmark, Poland, and Hungary have been less than

Germany permitted because of the inability of those countries to take German goods, and there is at present, no reason to expect an improvement in their takings of such goods. Present prospects are that Germany will have increased supplies of domestic lard, slightly reduced supplies of domestic butter, and reduced supplies of margarine. German margarine supplies for the coming winter appear to be a weak point in the fat situation. Recently, direct trade between Germany and the United States has been brought virtually to a standstill by exchange difficulties.

In Czechoslovakia, July census returns indicated an increase of about 6 percent in hog numbers compared with those of a year earlier. This increase, however, will not lessen Czechoslovakia's need for imported hog supplies, the latter being largely in the form of fat hogs, used mostly for lard production. It is expected that Czechoslovakia will continue to take live hogs, fatbacks, and lard from Poland and Danube Basin countries in quantities approximating those of last year.

Hog numbers in Austria have been brought approximately to the level where they can be maintained on Austrian-produced feeds, but not to the point where they can supply Austria's pork and lard requirements. Consequently, Austria may be expected to continue to import live hogs from Poland, Hungary, and Yugoslavia in numbers equal to, if not exceeding, last year's imports, provided the exporting countries can accept Austrian goods in sufficient volume to pay for the imports.

Danube Basin Exporting Countries

In the Danube Basin, large feed crops and high prices for hogs suggest a reversal of the decline in hog numbers which has been under way since the relatively short harvest of feed crops of a year ago. The large corn and barley crops harvested in the Basin this year have given rise to a strong demand for feeders. Hog numbers in Hungary, the Basin's leading exporting country, are now considerably smaller than those of a year ago, and exports in the coming winter and spring are expected to be somewhat smaller than those of last winter and spring. The present strong demand for feeders, however, gives rise to the anticipation of extensive feeding operations during the winter and increased supplies of fat hogs and lard available for export in the summer and fall of 1937.

Danubian lard exports during August totaled approximately 3,300,000 pounds compared with 2,116,000 pounds in July and 4,541,000 pounds in August 1935. About 60 percent of the exported lard originated in Hungary as against 79 percent a year earlier. Hungarian lard in August was shipped almost exclusively to Czechoslovakia. Because of less favorable prices, only small quantities were shipped to Germany. It is probable that exports to that country will continue to be small during the next few months unless

the German Livestock Monopoly consents to pay materially highe
heretofore. Prices on the Hungarian markets, at about 14 cent
were also relatively too high to make exports to England profi
slav lard exports during August, amounting to about 40 percent
from the Basin, were exclusively to Czechoslovakia at an avera
14.5 cents per pound, f.o.b. the Yugoslav frontier.

Live-hog exports from the Basin during August were esti
about 55,000 head as compared with 56,440 head in July and 56,
August 1935. Of these exports 45 percent originated in Yugosl
cause of relatively higher prices in Czechoslovakia than in Au
ments to the former were increased during August and those to
decreased. It is reported that Czechoslovak import requiremen
fall and winter months will be large. It is probable, therefo
reduced numbers available for export from the Basin will go la
Czechoslovakia and that shipments to Austria will remain below

Hogs and pork products: Indices of foreign supplies and demand

Country and item	Unit	1909-10: to : 1913-14: average:	1924-25: to : 1928-29: average:	Oct. - Aug. 1932-33	1933-34	1934-35	1935-36
United Kingdom							
Supplies, domestic	1,000						
fresh pork, London	pounds		49,475	68,385	60,081	67,679	76,941
Imports							
Bacon							
Denmark	"	225,518	461,397	644,413	459,524	402,111	359,814
Irish Free State	"		48,947	18,821	32,533	44,577	49,816
United States .	"	169,355	97,473	5,269	4,928	2,729	1,878
Canada	"	38,920	70,388	30,660	92,029	98,737	96,837
Others	"	39,755	150,552	327,975	226,849	179,848	165,554
Total bacon .	"	473,548	828,757	1,031,140	815,867	728,002	673,898
Ham, United States:							
Total	"	89,072	117,992	90,535	80,481	70,678	71,056
Lard, total	"	198,095	248,359	278,097	303,780	195,221	152,619
Denmark							
Exports, bacon			458,299	660,089	478,826	409,052	370,606
Canada							
Slaughter,							
hogs, inspected .	1000s	1,558	2,395	2,548	2,646	2,625	2,852
Germany							
Production							
Hog receipts,							
14 cities	"		2,953	2,854	3,308	3,028	2,486
Hog slaughter,							
36 centers	"	4,061	3,677	3,878	4,305	4,103	1/
Imports	1,000						
Bacon, total .. .	pounds	2,411	15,481	27,388	27,506	24,461	22,479
Lard, total .. .	"	181,568	200,678	186,768	109,159	48,005	76,493
United States							
Slaughter,							
hogs, inspected .	1000s	29,749	42,700	44,066	41,309	28,936	28,619
Exports							
Bacon	1,000						
United Kingdom	pounds	120,385	60,011	2,622	2,792	1,493	1,055
Germany	"	1,371	10,481	1,241	2,493	0	29
Cuba	"	7,421	18,955	3,876	4,602	4,165	1,389
Total bacon . .	"	163,915	129,010	15,752	21,172	7,393	3,576
Hams, shoulders . .							
United Kingdom	"	130,542	132,172	61,768	56,450	46,636	38,625
Total hams etc	"	151,831	157,357	70,608	65,034	55,206	41,361
Lard							
United Kingdom	"	157,933	210,059	255,281	287,503	97,131	57,872
Germany	"	126,440	172,290	125,438	58,404	2,513	6,406
Cuba	"	34,883	73,969	10,068	16,302	28,497	22,407
Netherlands ..	"	33,382	37,210	33,843	20,442	10	46
Total lard .	"	430,446	664,435	517,545	489,105	139,202	92,550

1/ Not available.

Hogs and pork products: Foreign and domestic average prices
for the month indicated, and stocks at the end of each

Item	1909-1913 average	1925-1929 average	Aug. 1935:	Jul
	Dollars	Dollars	Dollars	D(
Prices				
Hogs, Chicago, basis				
packers' and shippers'				
quotations	8.00	11.04	10.78	
Corn, Chicago, No. 3 Yellow	1.25	1.76	1.45	
Hogs, heavy, Berlin live				
weight	12.31	17.11	18.79	
Barley, Leipzig	1.72	2.11	3.05	
Lard				
Chicago	10.89	15.42	16.81	
Liverpool	12.10	15.58	17.08	
Hamburg	19.33	16.17	19.04	
Cured pork				
Liverpool				
American short cut				
green hams	15.70	26.49	23.29	
American green bellies		22.18	Nominal	
Danish Wiltshire sides	16.60	26.08	19.34	
Canadian green sides ..	15.67	23.28	17.24	
	1,000 pounds	1,000 pounds	1,000 pounds	]
Stocks				
United States				
Processed pork 1/		674,941	325,249	L
Lard in cold storage		158,190	53,537	]

1/ Dry salt cured and in process of cure; pickled, cured, and ir
and frozen.

Lightning Source UK Ltd.
Milton Keynes UK
UKHW010610120219
337137UK00007B/1446/P